Blackstone's Counter Fraud Professionals' Handbook

Blackstone's Counter Fraud Professionals' Handbook

Michael J. Betts

Head of Capability and Learning, Public Sector Fraud Authority, Cabinet Office, UK

Laura Eshelby

Deputy Director, Practice, Standards & Capability, Public Sector Fraud Authority, Cabinet Office, UK

David Whitehouse-Hayes

Head of Covid Business Support Enforcement Policy, Public Sector Fraud Authority, Cabinet Office, UK

OXFORD
UNIVERSITY PRESS

OXFORD
UNIVERSITY PRESS

Great Clarendon Street, Oxford, OX2 6DP,
United Kingdom

Oxford University Press is a department of the University of Oxford.
It furthers the University's objective of excellence in research, scholarship,
and education by publishing worldwide. Oxford is a registered trade mark of
Oxford University Press in the UK and in certain other countries

Published in the United States of America by Oxford University Press
198 Madison Avenue, New York, NY 10016, United States of America

British Library Cataloguing in Publication Data

Data available

Library of Congress Control Number: 2024936313

ISBN 9780198893028

DOI: 10.1093/9780191996955.001.0001

Printed and bound by
CPI Group (UK) Ltd, Croydon, CR0 4YY

FSC
www.fsc.org
MIX
Paper | Supporting
responsible forestry
FSC® C013604

Foreword

Fraud is a hidden crime and to fight it you have to find it.[1]

The inherently hidden crime of fraud is the volume crime of our times. Our data indicates that fraud is the crime that we, as individual citizens, are likely to fall victim to. As a hidden issue, it is often unseen and underestimated. Individuals and organizations can find comfort in not seeing any fraud. However, the absence of evidence is not evidence of absence. In organizations there can be significant levels of fraud hiding under the surface, unseen, underestimated but damaging the organization and what it is trying to achieve.

The mission of counter fraud experts and professionals is to find and act on this hidden crime. That action can be to get money back and bring those who have committed fraud to justice. It can also be to better understand the risks, finesse the businesses process, and improve controls to protect against it and to embed an awareness of fraud and positive ethical behaviours into the organization.

Over the fifteen years that I have worked in fighting fraud and economic crime, I have had the privilege of meeting, and working with, some incredible experts who have a passion about correcting the balance of the injustice that sits at the heart of fraud. In all of them I have seen a desire to make a difference, to push back against the dishonesty that allows some to thrive at the expense of others.

At the heart of fraud is an attack on the most vulnerable in our society. When people choose to commit fraud, for whatever reason, their impact is felt most keenly by the most vulnerable. Fraud against the public sector takes taxpayers' money away from the public services we rely on. Fraud against banks and insurance companies drives up the cost of financial products, making them more costly for people, and potentially out of reach.

Every day, thousands of people across the UK and internationally dedicate their time and energy to make a difference to fraud and economic crime. And yet, until more recently, the codification of this practice and the ability to learn it has been limited.

Good-quality training in investigation and intelligence techniques has a more established history. However, in many of the emerging disciplines—risk assessment, measurement, prevention, and the use of data and analytics—the well of knowledge beyond the wisdom of those working in it is not as overflowing as it could be. The tools and techniques that fraudsters use to attack citizens and the public sector

[1] 'The Government Counter Fraud Functional Strategy' (2024), https://assets.publishing.service.gov.uk/media/65f01d1f9812270011f61283/Cross_Government_Counter_Fraud_Functional_Strategy_2024-2027.pdf (accessed 17 May 2024).

are ever changing and the same is true of the tools and techniques that we use to protect our organizations (and ourselves). It is a fundamental truth to those who dedicate their time to acting on fraud that we need to keep ourselves aware of the changing practices and explore how we can use them to have the maximum impact.

In 2018, the UK government took the step to introduce the Government Counter Fraud Profession (GCFP). This was launched by seventeen public bodies, and it acts as the framework for public servants under which they can develop their counter fraud skills and expertise. Traditionally, countering fraud was seen as the domain of investigators and auditors. The more mature learning environments set up around investigation are as a direct result of the historic focus on reactive investigative work.

However, fraud experts know that we cannot investigate our way out of the challenge of fraud. It takes a broader range of skills and disciplines to take effective action—to protect our organizations and be efficient in acting. The GCFP created the Counter Fraud Framework to show the range of disciplines that those fighting fraud have to call upon.

Those disciplines include the more proactive disciplines of risk assessment and prevention. They also include the traditional disciplines of intelligence and investigations as, while our focus should be on prevention, we will also never be able to completely design out the risk of fraud from our processes and services.

This book draws on the standards and guidance developed by the GCFP and its Counter Fraud Framework. It sets out the latest techniques that counter fraud practitioners can use to measure, detect, prevent, and understand fraud risk. It also provides insights into who commits fraud, the relevant legislation, and an understanding of the disciplines needed for a truly proactive counter fraud approach—moving beyond the reactive investigation-only approach and setting out approaches into how to plan preventive and deterrent activity to minimize the harm and loss caused by fraud. The book provides insight into who may commit fraud, bribery, and corruption, as well as the motivators that inform prevention and deterrence models for fraud.

While we challenge ourselves to do more to find and combat fraud, we must remember that we are not alone in this effort. In 2018 I set up the International Public Sector Fraud Forum (IPSFF), which brings together experts from Australia, Canada, New Zealand, the US, and the UK. This has helped me and those I work with meet and learn from even more brilliant experts making an impact in this space.

That Forum has gone from strength to strength and has released a number of best practice guides for fraud experts across the world. These include topics such as managing fraud in the public sector, managing fraud in emergencies, understanding the total impact of fraud, and thinking about the use of artificial intelligence in fighting fraud. In its first guide, the Forum set principles for how fraud against the public sector should be approached. These set the tone for those, like me, who focus on better understanding and reducing fraud against the government and our public institutions.

Five principles from IPSFF Guide to Managing Fraud in Public Bodies are:

(1) There is always going to be fraud.
(2) Finding fraud is a good thing.
(3) There is no one solution.
(4) Fraud and corruption are ever changing.
(5) Prevention is the most effective way to address fraud and corruption.

All of those who dedicate some of their career in this area want to have an impact—to make a difference to the levels of fraud and the inherent fairness and justice in our society. As well as making an impact now, we can also play a role in helping all of those who take up the mantle in the future to go further and faster. Our success, and our failures, can be built on to increase our collective impact in the future—stopping more fraud, saving more taxpayers' money, and better protecting our public services and communities.

That is why books like this and the wider effort to build capability in countering fraud are so important. The effort of codifying our approaches and sharing practice widely will help us to strive together, now and in the future to uncover the hidden crime and reduce the damage that it does.

I would like to thank Laura, Mike, and David for their extensive efforts in drawing together the excellent content for this book and for allowing me to contribute both through this foreword and with content for the chapter on risk assessment. I hope that all who read this book draw significant value from it, and that it helps them and those they work with to have a bigger impact in this important area.

Mark Cheeseman OBE
Chief Executive, Public Sector Fraud Authority
February 2024

Mark Cheeseman OBE is a leading expert in the field of fraud risk assessment and the authors are grateful for his significant contribution to the chapter on fraud risk assessment. He is the Chief Executive of the Public Sector Fraud Authority and a fraud and financial crime expert, specializing in risk assessment and measurement. He led the development of the UK government's Counter Fraud Function and the Government Counter Fraud Profession as well as the creation of organizational standards and the use of data sharing and analytics, transforming the way that central government deals with fraud—leading to an increase of detected and prevented fraud of over 250 per cent and £100 million in audited benefits from counter fraud activity. He also helped set up and currently acts as an adviser to the Australian government's Commonwealth Fraud Prevention Centre and supported the New Zealand government in creating their Counter Fraud Centre. He led the creation of the International Public Sector Fraud Forum, a group of leading experts on fraud management who produce international guidance on leading practice.

Acknowledgements

The authors are grateful to the following people for providing their support of this publication:

Manni Conroy for her support in coordinating the development of the book.

PSFA for allowing the use of materials to inform the publication, and their support to allow us the time to bring this together in this book.

Cross Sector Advisory Group for all their expertise and insight in the development of the products and standards for the GCF Profession that inform this publication.

GCFP members and Oversight Board for their support and insight that led to the development of the Profession structures, and the standards for professionals they contributed to.

Contents

Figures

Tables

Abbreviations

ACFE	Association of Certified Fraud Examiners
ACPO	Association of Chief Police Officers
AG	Attorney General
AGO	Attorney General's Office
AI	artificial intelligence
ANPR	automatic number plate recognition
AO	authorizing officer
BBL	Bounce Back Loan
BP	business partner
CAA	Civil Aviation Authority
CCJ	county court judgment
CCTV	closed-circuit television
CEMA 1979	Customs and Excise Management Act 1979
CEO	chief executive officer
CFA 2017	Criminal Finance Act 2017
CFCD	Counter Fraud & Compliance Directorate
CFF	Counter Fraud Framework
CFF	Counter Fraud Function
CFPC	Commonwealth Fraud Prevention Centre
CHIS	covert human intelligence sources
CIA	Central Intelligence Agency
CID	Criminal Investigation Department
CIPD	Chartered Institute of Personnel and Development
CJSNI	Criminal Justice System Northern Ireland
COLP	City of London Police
COPFS	Crown Office and Procurator Fiscal Service
CPIA 1996	Criminal Procedure and Investigations Act 1996
CPR	Civil Procedure Rules
CPS	Crown Prosecution Service
CRCA 2005	Commissioners for Revenue and Customs Act 2005
CS	Civil Service
DoJ	Department of Justice
DPA	Deferred Prosecution Agreement
DPA 2018	Data Protection Act 2018
DPP	Director of Public Prosecutions
DSA	data sharing agreement
DWP	Department for Work and Pensions

E&W	England and Wales
EU	European Union
FCA	Financial Conduct Authority
FOP	future overpayments prevented
FRA	fraud risk assessment
GCFP	Government Counter Fraud Profession
HMG	His Majesties Government
HMICFRS	HM Inspectorate of Constabulary and Fire & Rescue Services
HMRC	His Majesties Revenue & Customs
HMT	His Majesty's Treasury
HO	Home Office
HR	human resources
ICIJ	International Consortium of Investigative Journalists
ICO	Information Commissioner's Office
IFIA	initial fraud impact assessment
Interpol	International Criminal Police Organization
IPSFF	International Public Sector Fraud Forum
ISP	internet service provider
JIC	Joint Intelligence Committee
JIT	joint investigation team
KDL	key decision log
MoJ	Ministry of Justice
MoU	memorandum of understanding
NAO	National Audit Office
NCIS	National Criminal Intelligence Service
NECC	National Economic Crime Centre
NFI	National Fraud Initiative
NHS	National Health Service
NHSCFA	National Health Service Counter Fraud Authority
NICtS	Northern Ireland Court Service
NIO	Northern Ireland Office
NPCC	National Police Chiefs' Council
OECD	Organisation for Economic Co-operation and Development
OFSI	Office of Financial Sanctions Implementation
OSINT	internet open source intelligence
PAC	Public Accounts Committee
PACE 1984	Police and Criminal Evidence Act 1984
PAYE	Pay As You Earn
PBNI	Probation Board for Northern Ireland
POCA 2002	Proceeds of Crime Act 2002
PPS	Public Prosecution Service
PSFA	Public Sector Fraud Authority
PSNI	Police Service of Northern Ireland
RIPA 2000	Regulation of Investigatory Powers Act 2000

RTI	real-time information
RUSI	Royal United Studies Institute
SAFO	specified anti-fraud organization
SAR	suspicious activity report
SFO	Serious Fraud Office
SIA	Secret Intelligence Service
SIO	senior investigating officer
SIS	Secret Intelligence Service
SPA	service prosecuting authority
SRO	senior responsible owner
T&CG	tasking and coordinating group
TI	Transparency International
TIE	transparency, incentivization, and environment
TMA 1970	Taxes Management Act 1970
ToR	terms of reference
UC	Universal Credit
UK	United Kingdom
UKBA 2010	UK Bribery Act 2010
UKFIU	UK Financial Investigation Unit
UNODC	UN Office on Drugs and Crime
US[A]	United States [of America]
UWO	Unexplained Wealth Order
VAT	value-added tax
YJA	Youth Justice Agency

1

Fraud: The Evolving Threat

Blackstone's Counter Fraud Professionals' Handbook. Michael J. Betts, Laura Eshelby, and David Whitehouse-Hayes, Oxford University Press.

DOI: 10.1093/9780191996955.003.0001

1.1 Introduction

In this chapter, we explore the evolving threat of fraud, its drivers, and enablers. We examine the methods used to commit fraud including the use of technology and the impact of new payment systems. We examine a range of fraud typologies and highlight the lessons to be learned for the counter fraud practitioner following the Covid-19 pandemic.

Dissecting fraud offending is key to unlocking its secrets and bringing offenders to justice; those countering fraud should know the enemy; how it operates, and the attack routes being used to target victims, whether they are individuals, organizations, or the state. This chapter also explores the impact and scale of fraud-related offending.

It introduces the Counter Fraud Framework (CFF) which is designed to provide a series of tactical options for the counter fraud practitioner.

KEY POINTS—DISSECTING FRAUD

To be an effective and competent counter fraud practitioner, it is important to be able to:

(1) understand the range of fraud typologies;
(2) recognize fraud indicators and how they link to offending;
(3) understand the profile of the fraudster;
(4) identify key fraud enablers;
(5) know methods to contain and stop fraud offending.

1.2 Background

Fraud is now the most prolific crime in the UK, whose growth has been fuelled by a diverse range of enablers including faster payment systems, the use of the internet and professional enablers, namely corrupt accountants, lawyers, and company formation agents. This is linked to a desire for an aspirational lifestyle, promoted by the media, social influencers, and the advertising industry, which drives citizens' unrealistic expectations of wealth and riches.

KEY POINTS—LIFESTYLE DRIVERS

- Digital advertising spending worldwide 2022 $567.49 billion;[1]
- Facebook: April 2024 there were 3065 million active users per month;[2]
- Tik Tok: April 2024 there were 1582 million users per month.[3]

Fraud is not new, it has been a feature of society throughout history, the growth was to some extent limited by the fraudsters ability to reach potential victims; to move and conceal the proceeds of crime; this sadly is no longer a 'control' on the growth of fraud.

1.3 Defining Fraud

Fraud as defined by the Fraud Act 2006 (with applicability in England, Wales and Northern Ireland) is an offence, with clear and concise points to be proven in any prosecution; it has three variables described in ss. 2–4 namely:

(1) A person is guilty of fraud if he is in breach of any of the sections listed in subs. (2) (which provide for different ways of committing the offence).[4]
(2) The sections are—

(a) s. 2 (fraud by false representation),
(b) s. 3 (fraud by failing to disclose information),
(c) s. 4 (fraud by abuse of position).

Under s. 2 of the Fraud Act 2006 there are three key points for the counter fraud practitioner to consider: the false representation, the financial gain or loss, and the dishonesty.

KEY POINTS—FRAUD OFFENCES IN SCOTLAND

In Scotland, fraud is dealt with under common law.

The common law offence is committed when someone achieves a result under a false pretence/representation. Proving an intention to commit the offence is an essential element of the offence.

There are also a range of statutory offences with applicability to fraud in Scotland these include:

- Companies Act 2006;
- Computer Misuse Act 1990;

[1] cycles, T. text provides general information S. assumes no liability for the information given being complete or correct D. to varying update and Text, S.C.D.M. up to Date D.T.R. in the (n.d.). Topic: Advertising worldwide. Statista, www.statista.com/topics/990/global-advertising-market/#dossier-chapter2 (accessed 24 July 2023).

[2] S.J. Dixon, 'Most Popular Social Networks Worldwide as of January 2024, Ranked by Number of Monthly Active Users' (2024), Statista, www.statista.com/statistics/272014/global-social-networks-ranked-by-number-of-users/ (accessed 24 May 2024).

[3] Ibid.

[4] Fraud Act 2006, www.legislation.gov.uk/ukpga/2006/35/contents (accessed 24 July 2023).

- Forgery and Counterfeiting Act 1982;
- Insolvency Act 1986.

An important aspect of the Fraud Act 2006 is this is an offence of false representation, not deception; deception does not need to occur as the offence is focused on the offender's intent.

Section 2 of the Fraud Act describes a two-way transaction: the fraudster's communication with the victim and the movement of tokens of value ('money') from the victim (organization or individual) to the fraudster, causing a gain or loss (or its potential) as shown in Figure 1.1.

The fraudster has a range of communication routes to attack potential victims, as illustrated in Figure 1.2. It is important for the counter fraud practitioner to

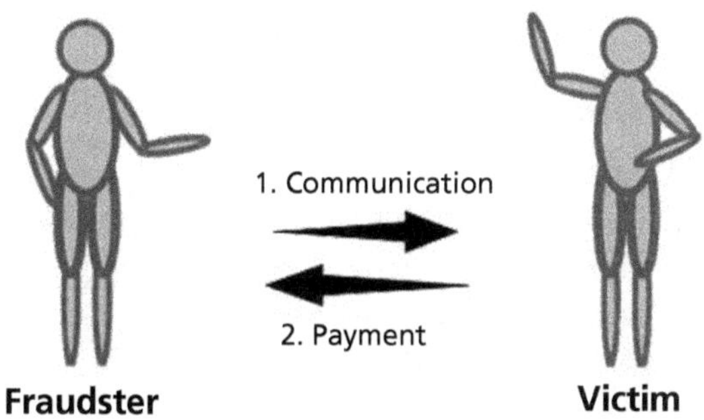

Figure 1.1 Fraud as a two-way transaction

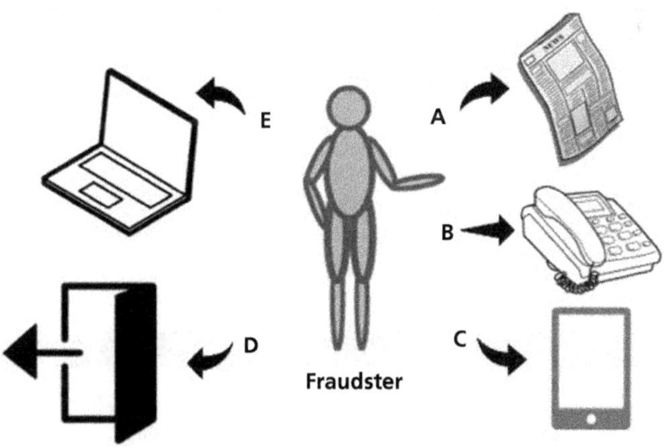

A	In Writing	B	Mobile Device	C	Landline
D	In Person	E	Digital Platform		

Figure 1.2 Communication routes used by the fraudster

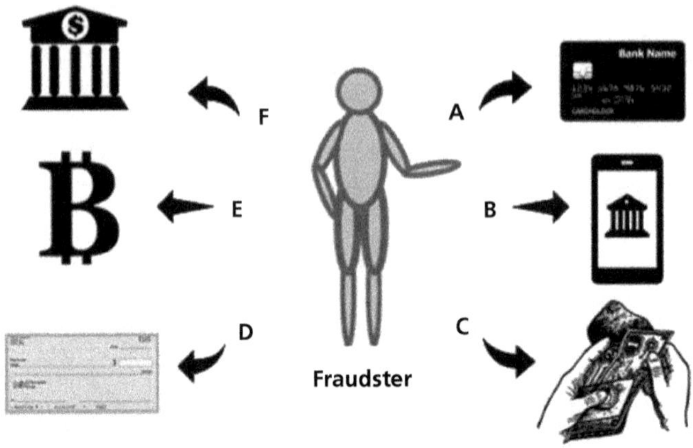

A	Plastic Card	B	Digital Banking	C	Cash
D	Cheque	E	Digital currency	F	Hawala

Figure 1.3 Methods to move tokens of value

understand these routes, as they are fundamental to effective fraud prevention, detection, and investigation.

Similarly understanding the way tokens of value (money) can be transferred is critical for the counter fraud practitioner to understand. Again, fraud prevention, detection, investigation, and the recovery of the proceeds of crime require an understanding of the various financial services available that can be exploited by the fraudster (see Figure 1.3).

1.4 **Understanding Money**

Money can be a complex concept, however in essence it is a medium of exchange and a method of storing wealth, which is underpinned by confidence that the relevant medium will maintain or increase its value. Over the course of history, medium of exchanges have varied from stones, coins, notes, and more recently digital currency. It is money which funds everyday expenses, assets, and for some flamboyant lifestyles.

KEY POINTS—GLOBAL WEALTH

According to the Credit Suisse 2022 Global Wealth Report 2022[5] the following global wealth figures were reported:

- Total global wealth was estimated to be US$463.6 trillion.

[5] Credit Suisse, *Global Wealth Report* (2022), www.credit-suisse.com/about-us/en/reports-research/global-wealth-report.html (accessed 24 July 2023).

- There are around 62.5 million millionaires worldwide.
- The average wealth per adult was estimated to be US$87,489.

1.5 Frauds Threat, Impact, and Scale

The Royal United Services Institute (RUSI) report 'The Silent Threat—The Impact of Fraud on UK National Security'[6] makes the case for fraud to be classified as a national security concern.

The significance of the loss due to fraud from the UK government cannot be underestimated. It is often those most in need who suffer from the callous actions of the fraudster. The services so required by society are at jeopardy when funds are stolen which are there to provide safety, health, and welfare.

In March 2023, the Public Accounts Committee (PAC) echoed the concern of the serious impact of fraud and the lack of response. The PAC reported that the UK risked being seen as a 'haven for fraudsters' where fraud is 'everyone's problem but no one's priority'.[7]

Dame Meg Hillier MP, the Chair of the Public Accounts Committee, said:

> Becoming a victim of fraud can cause lasting psychological damage. It can mean losing a lifetime's savings, your whole retirement plan, or even your current business and livelihood.[8]

The impact on the individual victim can be harrowing, Tom Winsor, the then Chief Inspector of Constabulary, stated in a BBC *Newsnight* interview in 2022 that:

> When an elderly person has lost his or her savings and hangs himself in the garage or throws himself off a cliff, that's a murder. It's just a murder in slow motion.[9]

KEY POINTS—THE SCALE OF FRAUD

Fraud offending in England and Wales (2022)

- fraud against businesses and individuals accounted for 41 per cent of all crimes committed;

[6] H. Wood, T. Keatinge, K. Ditcham, and A. Janjeva, 'The Silent Threat—The Impact of Fraud on UK National Security' (2021), https://static.rusi.org/the_silent_threat_web_version.pdf (accessed 23 July 2023).

[7] https://committees.parliament.uk/committee/127/public-accounts-committee/news/194542/pac-uk-risks-being-seen-as-haven-for-fraudsters-where-fraud-is-everyones-problem-but-no-ones-priority/ (accessed 23 July 2023).

[8] https://committees.parliament.uk/committee/127/public-accounts-committee/news/194542/pac-uk-risks-being-seen-as-haven-for-fraudsters-where-fraud-is-everyones-problem-but-no-ones-priority/ (accessed 24 July 2023).

[9] https://twitter.com/BBCNewsnight/status/1501981214927818756, https://twitter.com/BBCNewsnight/status/1501981214927818756 (accessed 24 July 2023).

- 3.8 million incidents of actual or attempted fraud;
- approximately 7 per cent of adults experienced fraud;
- UK Home Office estimates that the cost of fraud to individuals is £4.7 billion a year.

Fraud offending Scotland[10]

- 2021–22: Scottish government reported that fraud had increased by 86 per cent since 2012–13;
- 2021–22: 16,536 fraud-related offences were recorded;
- cybercrime-enabled fraud was estimated to account for 48 per cent of the offences reported.

Further Reading

- PAC Report Forty-Third Report—Progress combatting fraud, https://committees.parliament.uk/publications/34609/documents/190751/default/ (accessed 24 July 2023);
- Royal United Services Institute for Defence and Security Studies, 'The Silent Threat—The Impact of Fraud on UK National Security', https://rusi.org/explore-our-research/publications/occasional-papers/silent-threat-impact-fraud-uk-national-security (accessed 24 July 2023);
- KPMG Fraud Barometer 2022, https://assets.kpmg.com/content/dam/kpmg/uk/pdf/2022/02/fraud-barometer-2022.pdf (accessed 24 July 2023);
- Credit Suisse Global Wealth Report, www.credit-suisse.com/about-us/en/reports-research/global-wealth-report.html (accessed 24 July 2023).

1.6 The Scale of Fraud

Measuring the scale and threat of fraud presents several challenges: often a financial figure is presented when quantifying the fraud loss, but this is often based on the best estimate available. The 2023 Crowe, Peters & Peters and University of Portsmouth report entitled 'The Annual Fraud Indicator' estimated the loss to fraud in the UK to be £219 billion[11] per year; globally the figure is stated to be £4.37 trillion.[12] The Public Sector Fraud Authority (PSFA) estimated the financial loss to fraud and error across government in 2020–21

[10] 'Crimes of Dishonesty' (June 2022), www.gov.scot/publications/recorded-crime-scotland-2021-2022/pages/7/ (accessed 24 July 2023).

[11] 'Annual Fraud Indicator' (2023), www.crowe.com/uk/insights/annual-fraud-indicator (accessed 24 July 2023).

[12] *ACFE Report to the Nations: 2022 Global Fraud Study*, https://legacy.acfe.com/report-to-the-nations/2022/?_ga=2.161839996.1112429651.1690183179-474221888.1688109120 (accessed 24 July 2023).

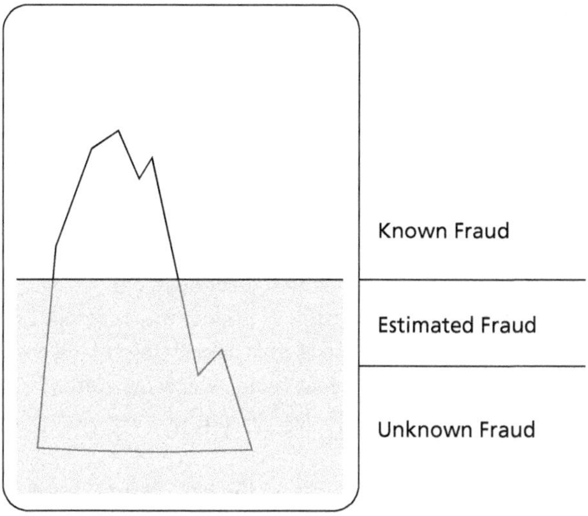

Figure 1.4 The fraud iceberg

to be between £33.2 and £58.8 billion.[13] The World Economic Forum estimates that corruption costs the world economy 5 per cent of GDP each year, which is equivalent to US$3.6 trillion.

The total cost to society in England and Wales of fraud against individuals was estimated to be at least £6.8 billion (2019–20).[14]

1.6.1 **The Fraud Iceberg**

The Fraud Iceberg is used to visualize the scale of fraud (see Figure 1.4). The tip of the iceberg is what is detected, but, as with any iceberg, it is what is beneath the surface that reveals the true scale. Below the surface we have our estimations of fraud and dropping deeper below the surface, we have our unknown region. A key message is fraud is a hidden crime and to counter it you need to find it first.

1.7 **Literature and Mythology**

Fraud is not a new phenomenon, Greek mythology from 900/800 bc presents us with one of the first representations of fraud. 'Apate' the so-called goddess of fraud has a persona of deceit, fraud, and guile; she is described as particularly cunning and

[13] NAO (2023), 'Tackling Fraud and Corruption against Government' (NAO, press release, 30 March 2023), www.nao.org.uk/press-releases/tackling-fraud-and-corruption-against-government/ (accessed 24 July 2023).

[14] Home Office, 'Fraud Strategy: Stopping Scams and Protecting the Public (Accessible)' (2023), www.gov.uk/government/publications/fraud-strategy/fraud-strategy-stopping-scams-and-protecting-the-public#foreword (accessed 24 July 2023).

cruel, features which are similar to the modern-day fraudster when preying on the vulnerable. She was one of the evil spirits released from the mythical Pandora's box, a large jar described as containing all the evils of the world.

1.7.1 Dante's Inferno

Dante Alighieri was born in 1265, a famous Italian writer, often referred to as the 'supreme' poet. He wrote extensively, one of his most renowned works being the *Divine Comedy*, a text which is still widely studied today. Part 1 of the *Divine Comedy* is called 'Inferno' which follows the journey of Dante who is guided by a poet, Virgil, through hell. This journey is described as nine descending circles, each with its own hellish features, the eighth circle being fraud, which interestingly is sandwiched between violence and treachery. The descriptions of those occupying each circle provides the first fraudster personas.

To enter the fraud circle Dante travels on the back of a winged beast, called the Geryon. This beast is described as the image of fraud, having an honest face, a beautifully coloured wyvern and the paws of a lion; however, it has a poisonous sting in its scorpion-like tail. Lying within the fraud circle there are descriptions of ten ditches each containing a different type of fraudster including corrupt politicians with their sticky fingers, hypocrites, and the falsifiers who are referred to as a disease on society.

1.8 Infamous Fraudsters

Over the centuries there have been many fraudsters, some known, some not, particularly those that have successfully avoided conviction. Often the fraudulent scheme is designed to maximize the financial remuneration of those taking part; desire for financial gain is often the motive for fraudulent activity.

1.8.1 Hegestratos

One of the first reported cases was an attempted fraud by a Greek merchant, Hegestratos and his business partner in 360 bc. They devised a scheme to sail a ship from Syracuse to Athens loaded with corn. The cargo was purchased through a cash advance which was to be paid with interest once the cargo was delivered. When the boat sailed it had no cargo and the ship was insured against loss. After a few days, the pair tried to sink the ship, they were disturbed in the act, and Hegestratos fled overboard where he promptly drowned.

1.8.2 The South Sea Bubble

The South Sea Bubble occurred early in the eighteenth century and is synonymous with the development of fraudulent schemes known today as Ponzi frauds. In 1711

South Sea Company was formed and went on to underwrite the English national debt, for a return of 5 per cent, it was also granted a monopoly in trade in South America. Shares in the company rose steadily, but the growth in the commercial opportunities did not keep pace with the value of the shares.

In January 1720, the directors of the company are alleged to have circulated false claims regarding the potential for growth and stocks rose rapidly. Several of those associated with the South Sea Company sold their shares which in turn led to panic selling by others. The rise was simply unsustainable and the bubble burst in September 1720. Many investors lost their fortunes, including Jonathan Swift the author of *Gulliver's Travels* who lost a considerable amount of money. It is reported that 462 members of the House of Lords participated in the crash. In January 1721, the formal investigation report found corruption and deceit at the heart of the South Sea Bubble, and subsequently several members were expelled from Parliament including the Chancellor of the Exchequer John Aislabie. The South Sea directors were taken into custody and their estates forfeited.

1.8.3 **George Hudson Railway Mania**

In the ninetieth century, 'railway mania' became a feature of Victorian Britain. With the onset of industrialization there was a massive expansion of the railways. George Hudson was one of the most powerful men in the railway industry. He was the chair of the Eastern Counties Railway and the York and North Midland Railway; he was also the representative for Sunderland in the House of Commons and the Mayor of York. He presided over the expansion of a number of lines, the financing of which was seen as attractive to investors who were promised significant returns on their investments (of up to £2,000 per mile). These returns were unrealistic and in 1849 Hudson was shown to have been involved in fraudulent activity. He had been partly responsible for paying dividends from the capital of the company to keep it afloat. He was eventually arrested for debt and served time in prison; he lost his parliamentary seat. One of the investors who lost much of her inheritance was Charlotte Bronte.

1.8.4 **Carlo Ponzi**

The twentieth century had a rich history of economic crime and is blighted by the activities of notorious fraudsters. Carlo Ponzi was one such fraudster—indeed his name is given to a particular type of fraud, the Ponzi scheme. Carlo Ponzi often referred to as Charles was born in Italy in 1882. He left Italy and arrived in America in 1903, where he began a life of crime. In 1907, he moved to Montreal in Canada and became a bank teller. He used his access to customer information to steal and in 1908 was convicted of forgery and sentenced to three years' imprisonment. When he was released, he returned to America, sought a job, and was employed as a clerk in an export firm. He identified a scheme involving postal reply to coupons. These coupons were issued by the US International Postal Congress and could be redeemed for postage stamps in participating countries. Ponzi calculated that due to differences in the international exchange rates he could make money by purchasing the coupons in Europe, then having them sent to the US where he would replace them with stamps. In November 1919, he set up the Securities Exchange Company to facilitate his scheme. Ponzi is described in the introduction to his autobiography *The Rise of Mr Ponzi* as:

> A dapper con man with a winning smile and the gift of the gap.[15]

He claimed investors could make a 50 per cent profit in 45 days or 100 per cent profit in 90 days. The scheme ran for about a year before running into trouble, when the authorities became suspicious, and articles appeared in the newspapers questioning the validity of the scheme. As a result, investors started to lose confidence and demanded the return of their investments. The scheme had attracted so many investors that Ponzi had not been able to sustain the return on the coupons scheme and had been paying the investors out of capital, a fraud which is still common today. When the scheme collapsed, the losses to investors was an estimated US$20 million. On 1 November 1920, following an investigation by the authorities, Ponzi was charged with eighty-six counts of fraud-related offences; he pleaded guilty to one charge of fraud, and was jailed for five years. In his autobiography Ponzi describes the moment in the investigation when his fraud had been discovered:

> My house of cards had collapsed! My bubble had busted! I had lost! Lost everything! Millions of dollars.[16]

1.8.5 **Bernie Madoff**

In the twenty-first century, fraud continues to produce fraudsters on an almost industrial scale. Infamous fraudsters include: Bernie Madoff sentenced to 150 years for his Ponzi fraud valued at an estimated US$65 billion; Jeffrey Skilling the chief executive officer (CEO) of Enron who was indicted on charges of insider trading which reportedly wiped US$78 billion off the US stock market was sentenced to twenty-four years' imprisonment; Bernard Ebbers the CEO of WorldCom who was convicted of fraud in 2005 and sentenced to twenty-five years' imprisonment.

1.9 **The Growth of Fraud**

The growth of fraud is undoubtedly connected to developments in technology, diversity in payment systems, and medium of exchanges (tokens of value) including both physical and digital currencies. The growth of fraud can be seen in the recorded crime figures in England and Wales and the Crime Survey for England and Wales (Figure 1.5).

---

[15] Charles Ponzi, *The Rise of Mr Ponzi* (Naples, FL: Inkwell Publishers, 2001).

[16] Ibid.

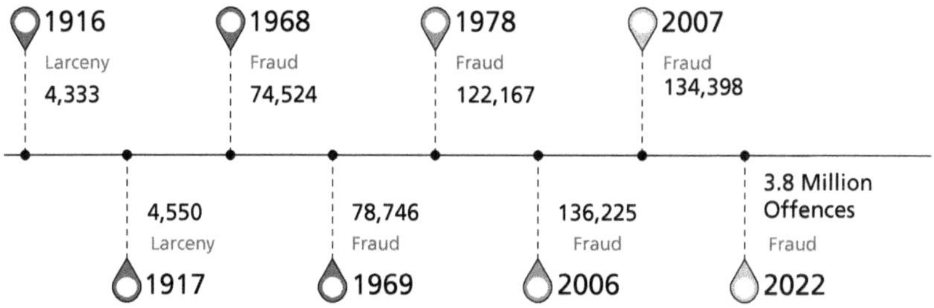

Figure 1.5 Exponential growth in fraud

The key enablers for the fraudster are access to the means to commit fraud; the internet providers the fraudster with both the knowledge and the highway to a range of victims. Communication devices, including telephones, also provide a similar gateway to many victims. The ability to move the proceeds of crime at speed, across platforms, and jurisdictions has never been greater. Added to this are the professional enablers, those that facilitate fraud; linked offenders in this category are the accountants, lawyers, and company formation agents.

KEY POINTS—TECHNOLOGICAL DEVELOPMENTS

The development of technology and payment systems:

- 1984—Martin Cooper a Motorola engineer developed the first hand-held phone;
- 1990—Tim Berners-Lee a computer scientist invented the World Wide Web;
- 1997—Nationwide was the 'first UK provider' to launch an internet banking service;
- 2009—Bitcoin introduced.

1.10 **Trends in Fraud Offending**

Fraud offending is diverse in nature and fraudsters target multiple sectors and individuals. The UK'S Action Fraud reported in its Annual Assessment of Fraud Crime Trends 2020/21 that:[17]

- 80 per cent of fraud is cyber enabled;
- social media and encrypted messaging services as enablers are increasing throughout all aspects of fraud;
- victims reported £2.35 billion in losses.

[17] https://data.actionfraud.police.uk/cms/wp-content/uploads/2021/07/2020-21-Annual-Assessment-Fraud-Crime-Trends.pdf (accessed 24 July 2023).

The top three frauds reported were:

- cheque, plastic card, and bank account—336,707 reports;
- online shopping and auctions fraud—103,254 reports;
- application fraud (excluding mortgages)—91,593 reports.

According to various reports 70 per cent of fraud impacting on UK victims has an international component;[18] and 36per cent of fraud incidents lead to no financial loss (but were attempted fraud).[19]

KEY POINTS—HOME OFFICE FRAUD STRATEGY 2023

The Strategy[20] cites the advances in technology that provide fraudsters more access to victims and data as a driver for the increase in fraud offending:

- More and more data is held online, large-scale data breaches enable fraudsters to access and use stolen personal information to commit their frauds.
- Availability of bulk communications, such as text messaging services, allow fraudsters to target thousands of people at once: number 'spoofing' allows fraudsters to impersonate a legitimate UK number or business and trick people into answering calls they might otherwise ignore.
- The emergence of new artificial intelligence large language models such as ChatGPT and clever machine learning tools allows fraudsters to target and tailor their scams to be more effective.

The Police Foundation's report 'Understanding the Characteristics of Serious Fraud Offending in the United Kingdom' (2023), reviewed several cases in England and Wales and sought to improve the understanding of the most serious fraud offences perpetrated in the UK.[21] It confirms that the evidence on fraud offending is limited as this cohort of 'offenders' remain hidden. The report identifies two categories of fraud:

(1) commercial frauds that primarily involved the use of sales and marketing strategies to sell misrepresented products or services;
(2) predatory frauds that commonly involved the impersonation of a legitimate individual or organization.

---

[18] Police Foundation, 'Serious Fraud Offending in the UK' (2023), www.police-foundation.org.uk/2023/05/serious-fraud-offending-in-the-uk/ (accessed 24 July 2023).

[19] Office for National Statistics, 'Crime in England and Wales' (2023), www.ons.gov.uk/peoplepopulationandcommunity/crimeandjustice/bulletins/crimeinenglandandwales/yearendingseptember2022 (accessed 24 July 2023).

[20] Home Office, 'Fraud Strategy: Stopping Scams and Protecting the Public (Accessible)' (2023) www.gov.uk/government/publications/fraud-strategy/fraud-strategy-stopping-scams-and-protecting-the-public#executive-summary (accessed 24 July 2023).

[21] www.police-foundation.org.uk/publication/understanding-the-characteristics-of-serious-fraud-offending-in-the-uk/ (accessed 24 July 2023).

Case Study—iSpoof

On 19 May 2023, Tejay Fletcher was jailed for thirteen years and four months after pleading guilty to offences that included the making or supplying articles for use in fraud, encouraging or assisting the commission of an offence, possessing criminal property and transferring criminal property; this followed what the Metropolitan Police called their 'biggest' fraud investigation.

Fletcher was the leading administrator of the iSpoof website, which enabled fraudsters to conceal their identity when calling a victim and the phone number purported to be from a range of institutions; these included a range of banks and HMRC. iSpoof was marketed on a channel on the encrypted messaging app Telegram.

It was reported that as many as twenty people every minute were being targeted by criminals using iSpoof.[22] The website had 59,000 users and the average loss of those who reported being targeted to Action Fraud was £10,000. The overall fraud loss in the UK is estimated to exceed £43 million.

Fletcher benefited by approximately £2 million in the cryptocurrency and bought a Lamborghini and two Range Rovers.

1.11 Fraudster Personas and Profiles

Fraudster personas, profiles, and types are useful in helping understand those who are typically involved in fraudulent activities, though the counter fraud practitioner should be aware the exception makes the rule—and care should be taken with the use of such personas. With regard to categorization of the fraudster, those involved in internal fraud are often described as 'occupational fraudsters' or 'insiders'. Those who commit fraud on an organization are the external fraudsters. A significant focus has been on the internal fraudster, where great attention, interest, and research has been on the discovery of why so-called good people go 'bad' in the workplace. There is not as much research on why external fraudsters commit that crime type; the link to criminology and why people in general turn to crime may offer an understanding of non-occupational fraud.

[22] *Sky News*, 'Tejay Fletcher Jailed for Running Multimillion-Pound Criminal Website iSpoof' (19 May 2023), https://news.sky.com/story/tejay-fletcher-jailed-for-running-multimillion-pound-criminal-website-ispoof-12883414 (accessed 24 July 2023).

1.12 **Root Causes of Crime**

The *Oxford English Dictionary* defines crime as:

> an act or omission which constitutes an offence and is punishable by law.

Interestingly what is a crime today may not be a crime tomorrow and what is not a crime today may be in the future. The criminalization of activity changes with the times and is dependent on the social, political, and societal attitudes to the activity of citizens and politicians.

The root causes of crime are subject to extensive research and are in the main attributable to four key factors: opportunity, motivation, environmental, and psychological. It is the combination of these factors that may lead to numerous types of crime being committed whether it be a crime of violence, assault, or theft.

KEY POINTS—REASONS FOR CRIME

Causation factors for crime include:

- poverty/deprivation/marginalization;
- guardian/parental neglect;
- alcohol and drug abuse;
- peer pressure/culture;
- unemployment/lack of opportunity;
- lack of education;
- social inequality;
- subcultures with shared experience;
- lack of mental well-being.

A prison survey conducted by the Scottish Prison Service in 2019 provided insight into offender behaviour and the factors that contributed to offending:[23]

(1) mental health 27%;
(2) alcohol abuse 24%;
(3) substance abuse 24%;
(4) financial difficulties 15%;
(5) unemployment 16%;
(6) family relationships 16%;
(7) lack of support in the community 14%.

It is against this backdrop that researchers, academics, and practitioners have attempted to understand the motivations and rationalization for those that engage

[23] *17th Prisoner Survey 2019*, https://www.sps.gov.uk/sites/default/files/2024-02/17thPrisonSurvey_2019_Research.pdf (accessed 26 April 2024).

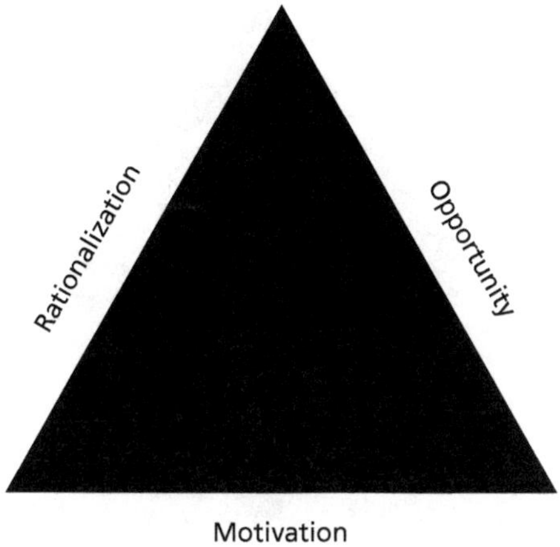

Figure 1.6 Cressey fraud triangle

in fraudulent activity. Of particular interest has been the internal fraudster who in general does not 'fit' the profile of those engaged in general criminality.

1.13 Theories Relating to Internal Fraud

There are many studies and theories that focus on the factors that are present to motivate the occupational fraudster to commit internal fraud. These theories include those of Edwin Sutherland (1940), who described fraud as 'a white-collar crime committed by a person of respectability and high social status in the course of his occupation'.[24] He believed that the learning process to commit 'white-collar crime' involved two factors:

(1) the techniques to commit crime;
(2) the attitudes, drives, rationalizations, and motives of the criminal mind.

Academic research on why people commit fraud has offered a number of theories of which one of the best known is Cressey's fraud triangle. This states that people commit fraud when three factors are present: opportunity, motivation, and rationalization (Figure 1.6).

Hermanson and Wolfson (2004)[25] developed this theory further by creating a fraud diamond (Figure 1.7), through the inclusion of a fourth component 'capability' which includes factors such as position, intelligence, professional skills, and ego.

---

[24] Edwin H. Sutherland, 'White-Collar Criminality', *American Sociological Review* (1940) 5(1): 1–12, www.jstor.org/stable/2083937 (accessed 17 December 2020).

[25] David T. Wolfe and Dana R. Hermanson, 'The Fraud Diamond: Considering the Four Elements of Fraud', *CPA Journal* (2004) 74(12): 38–42.

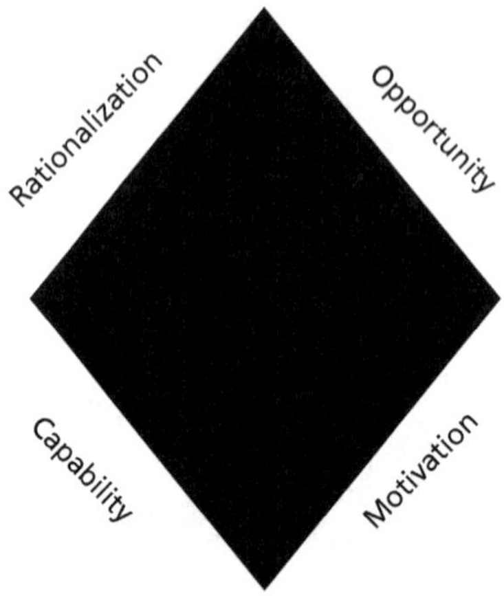

Figure 1.7 Fraud diamond (Wolfe and Hermanson, 2004)

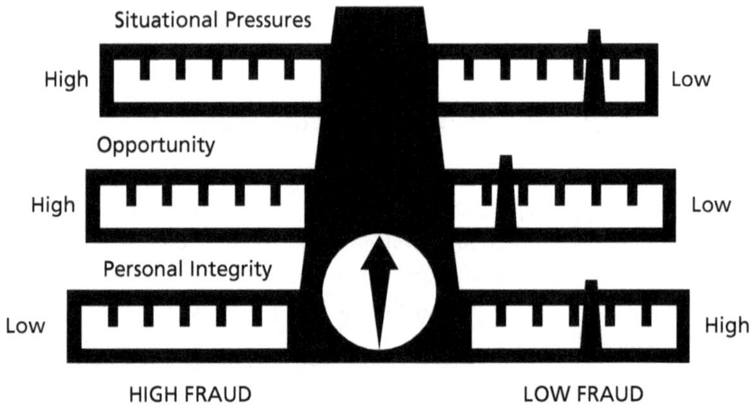

Figure 1.8 Albrecht fraud scale

In 1984, Steve Albrecht and colleagues devised the Fraud Scale (see Figure 1.8). The development of the scale was based on an analysis of a range of frauds and looked at the predominant factors. The scale has virtual sliders to indicate the likelihood of the conditions present for fraud to occur. The scale mirrors elements of the fraud triangle with pressure and opportunity, but replaces rationalization with personal integrity.

Sridhar Ramamoorti believes that a multilevel behavioural analysis is needed to understand a subject as complex as fraud because it can spread from a bad apple (a single person) to a bushel (group or team) and a crop (the entire organization) (see Figure 1.9).

Bad Apple (Person) | Bad Bushel (Group or Team) | Bad Crop (Organization)

Figure 1.9 Ramamoorti ABC theory

1.13.1 **Fraudster Personas**

The Commonwealth Fraud Prevention Centre has undertaken a significant amount of research to develop a range of fraudster personas. These are useful to aid understanding of the methods deployed by fraudsters. They can help in fraud prevention, detection, and investigation as each has differing modi operandi.[26]

KEY POINTS—COMMONWEALTH FRAUD PREVENTION PERSONAS

The Commonwealth Fraud Prevention Centre has identified eight differing fraud personas that can assist the counter fraud practitioner:[27]

(1) **Reckless**—acts without care, responsibility, or regard to the consequences of their actions by disregarding requirements, procedures, warnings, or directions to gain personal benefits.
(2) **Deceiver**—makes others believe something that is not true to dishonestly gain personal benefits.
(3) **Impersonator**—pretends they are another person or entity to dishonestly gain personal benefits.
(4) **Fabricator**—invents or produces something that is false to dishonestly gain personal benefits.
(5) **Coercer**—influences, manipulates, or bribes another person to act in a desired way to dishonestly gain personal benefits.
(6) **Exploiter**—uses something for a wrongful purpose to dishonestly gain personal benefits.
(7) **Concealer**—hides their actions from being seen or known about to dishonestly gain personal benefits.
(8) **Organized**—are groups which use a combination of methods in planned, coordinated, and sophisticated ways to dishonestly gain benefits.

[26] 'a particular way or method of doing something'.
[27] Commonwealth Fraud Prevention Centre, 'The Impersonator' (2020), www.counterfraud.gov.au/i-want-discover-different-types-fraudsters/impersonator (accessed 24 July 2023).

Table 1.1 The internal fraudster profile

Typical age of fraudster	36–40 (20%)
Gender male	73%
Gender female	27%
Behavioural red flags	Living beyond means 39%
Criminal background	No previous convictions 87%
Control weakness	Lack of internal controls 29%
Discovery method	Tip off (whistle-blower) 42%

Source: Data from *ACFE Report to the Nations* (2022)

1.14 Insider Fraud Profile

Recent reports from KPMG, PWC, and the Association of Certified Fraud Examiners (ACFE) have explored the profile of the internal fraudster. The results of their research may assist in informing where the fraud risks are higher, detecting fraud, and may inform the prevention activities (see Table 1.1).

Further Reading

- *ACFE Report to the Nations 2022*, https://legacy.acfe.com/report-to-the-nations/2022/ (accessed 24 July 2023);
- KPMG Fraud Barometer 2021, https://assets.kpmg.com/content/dam/kpmg/uk/pdf/2022/02/fraud-barometer-2022.pdf (accessed 24 July 2023);
- PwC's Global Economic Crime and Fraud Survey 2022, www.pwc.com/gx/en/services/forensics/economic-crime-survey.html (accessed 24 July 2023);
- Crowe, 'The Financial Cost of Fraud Report 2021', www.crowe.com/uk/insights/financial-cost-fraud-data-2021 (accessed 24 July 2023);
- Scottish Prison Service 17th Prisoner Survey 2019, www.sps.gov.uk/Corporate/Publications/Publication-7196.aspx (accessed 24 July 2023);
- Commonwealth Fraud Prevention Centre (Fraud Personas), www.counterfraud.gov.au/discover-different-types-fraudsters (accessed 24 July 2023).

1.15 Understanding Fraud Typologies

Fraud typologies are a useful way of understanding the offender's typical dynamics of how the fraud is committed, detection opportunities, the most effective prevention techniques, to inform any investigation, and for its reporting. A range of

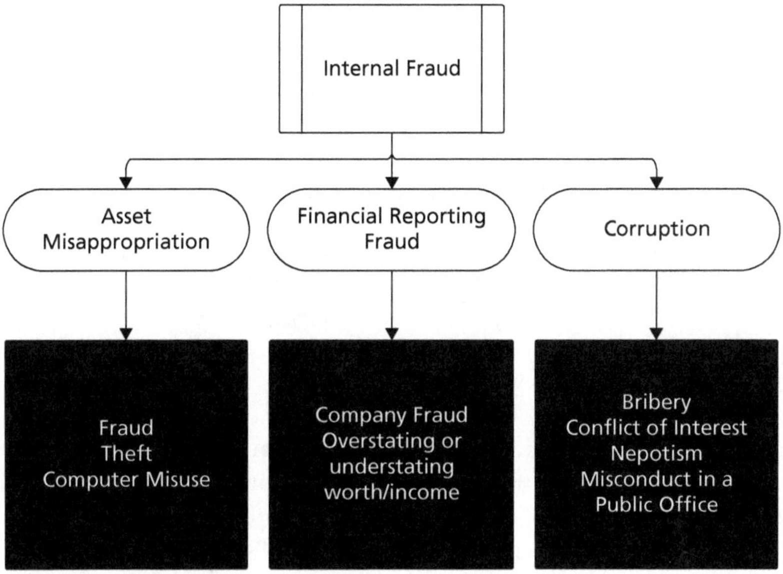

Figure 1.10 Internal fraud typologies

methods are used to develop categories of fraud which group together typologies that share similarities.

Collins Dictionary defines a typology as:

> A typology is a system for dividing things into different types, especially in science and the social sciences.[28]

Typologies are in essence 'types' of fraud and can be grouped together for ease of reference and analysis. The Home Office have published guidance on the recording of fraud offences as part of documentation on the counting rules for recorded crime. This document details the unique codes attributable to sixty-three specific fraud types and descriptions of each typology.

1.16 Internal Fraud Typologies

Typically, internal fraud types (also known as occupational fraud), is often grouped into three subcategories: corruption, asset misappropriation, and financial reporting fraud (Figure 1.10).

Understanding internal fraud typologies provide the counter fraud practitioner with the insight to inform the required counter fraud activity. The nature of the fraud will correspond with the threat type, its prevention, detection, and importantly the

[28] www.collinsdictionary.com/dictionary/english/typology#:~:text=A%20typology%20is%20a%20sys tem,%5Bformal%5D (accessed 24 July 2023).

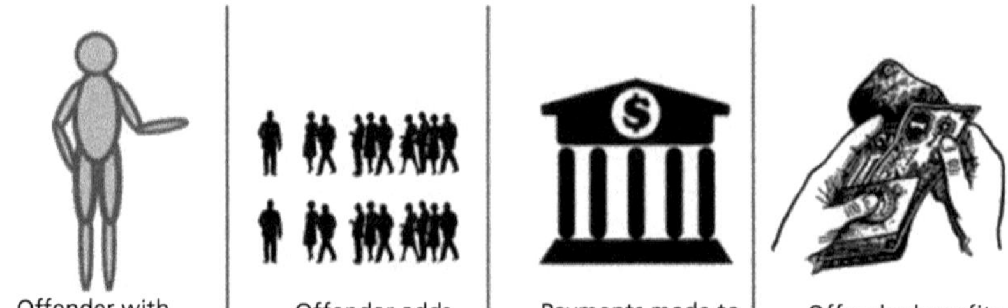

Figure 1.11 Payroll fraud

investigative process. In internal fraud cases the victim will normally be the organization, the relevant material to be gathered and examined will include material held by the organization.

If we take an example of payroll fraud where the offender creates fictitious employees onto the organization's payroll and direct payments to their own accounts we can dissect this typology to the benefit of the counter fraud practitioner (Figure 1.11).

Knowing the typology type informs the counter fraud activity in the following ways:

(1) Fraud risk assessment—we understand the risk of staff members with access to the payroll, the risk can be assessed, and suitable controls implemented.
(2) Detection—we can use data analytics to identify third-party payments that are being made to an account linked to the employee.
(3) Investigation—we know that both the personnel and financial records will have been manipulated in these schemes and this knowledge can aid the development of the working hypothesis.

1.17 External Fraud Typologies

External fraud typologies include fraud where the organization, state, or those operating within financial services are the victim; the offender is not an insider but outside the organization (Figure 1.12).

An example of external fraud is mandate fraud; this type of fraud occurs when a fraudster researches an organization, communicates with that organization, and directs payments to be made to an account in their control (Figure 1.13).

Again, knowing the typology type informs the counter fraud activity in the following ways:

(1) Fraud risk assessment—we understand the risk of requests to change the payment details and how this may benefit a fraudster.

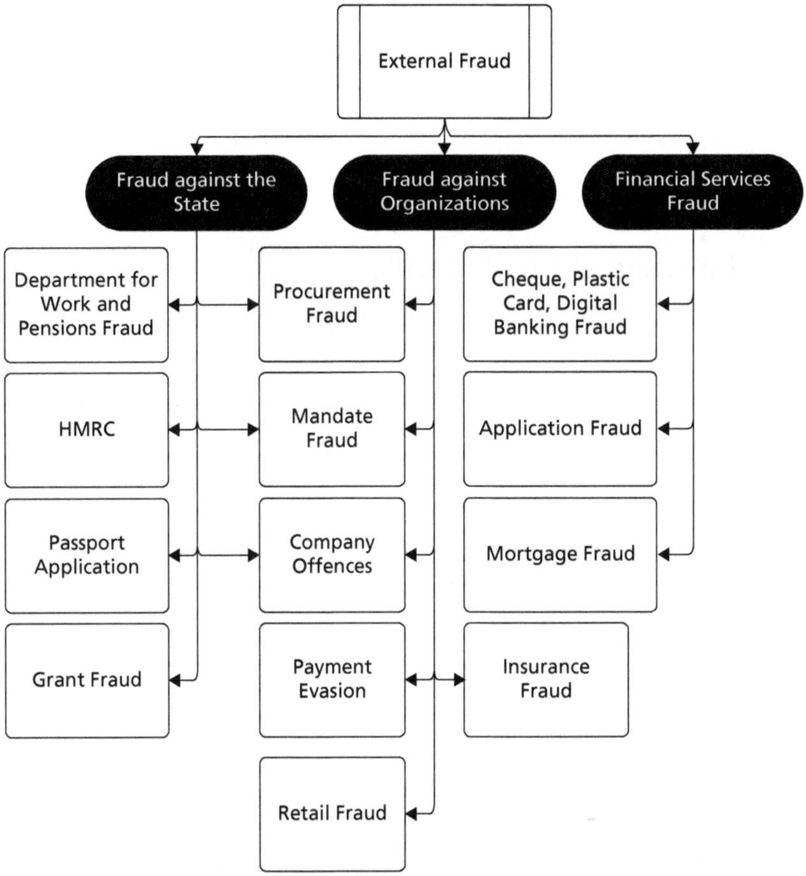

Figure 1.12 External fraud typologies

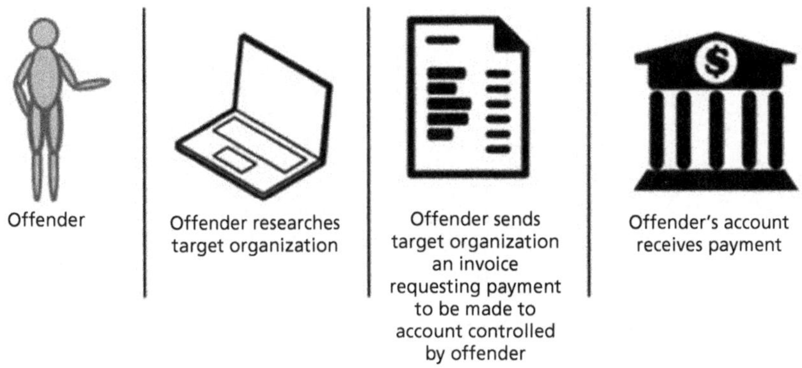

Figure 1.13 Mandate fraud

(2) Detection—we can use data analytics or employee awareness to identify requests to change the payment details that are being requested by a fraudster.
(3) Investigation—we know that a fraudster will need to communicate the request to change payments and that the funds will be directed to an account under the control of the fraudster.

1.18 **Individual Victim Frauds**

Individual fraud typologies are those impacting on individuals where the citizen will be the victim (see Figure 1.14).

Further Reading

- Home Office Counting Rules for recording fraud, https://assets.publishing.service.gov.uk/government/uploads/system/uploads/attachment_data/file/1155666/nfib-fraud-april-2023.pdf (accessed 24 July 2023).

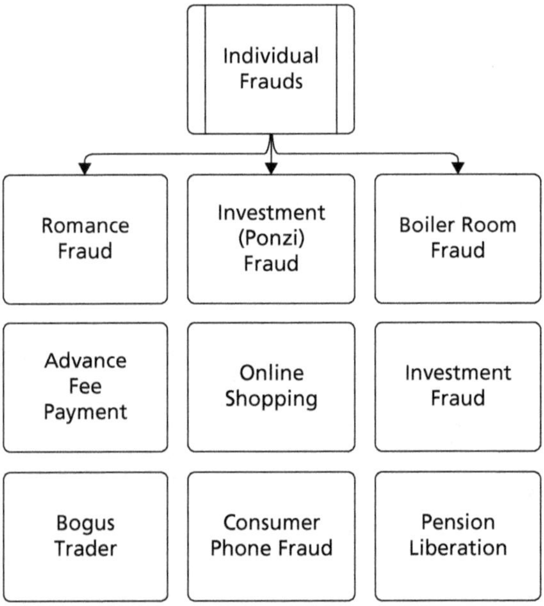

Figure 1.14 Individual fraud types

1.19 **Pandemic Fraud Lessons Learned**

During the Covid-19 pandemic, much was learned about the nature of fraud and the fraudster, and the controls required to prevent fraud. The scale of reported and suspected fraud was significant, and much research has been undertaken to identify how to target hardened schemes and economic support provided by the state in future events.

Procurement fraud posed a particular issue during the pandemic and a number of organizations did post event research to identify the lessons learned. The National Audit Office (NAO) investigation into government procurement[29] during the Covid-19 pandemic stated that:

- Widespread use of direct awards to procure goods, services and works may increase the chances that some procurement risks materialise if not correctly mitigated;
- Procurement processes established by the cross-government PPE team enabled PPE to be purchased quickly, but some procurements were carried out before all key controls were put in place;
- Inadequate documentation in a number of cases on how the risks of procuring suppliers without competition had been mitigated;
- Some contracts were awarded retrospectively after some work had already been carried out;
- Not always a clear audit trail to support key procurement decisions.

Another NAO report entitled *NAO Initial Learning from the Governments Response to the Covid 19 Pandemic*[30] brings together government learning across six themes:

- risk management;
- transparency and public trust;
- data and evidence;
- coordination and delivery models;
- supporting and protecting people;
- financial and workforce pressures.

The report recommended that should the widespread need to procure goods with extreme urgency happen again, the associated risks to public money and propriety are managed effectively by:

(1) Awarding bodies should publish basic information on contracts in a reasonable time, in line with guidance to publish within ninety days of award.

[29] NAO, *Investigation into Government Procurement during the Covid-19 Pandemic* (2020), www.nao.org.uk/reports/government-procurement-during-the-covid-19-pandemic/ (accessed 24 July 2023).

[30] NAO, *Initial Learning from the Governments Response to the Covid 19 Pandemic* (2021), www.nao.org.uk/insights/initial-learning-from-the-governments-response-to-the-covid-19-pandemic/ (accessed 24 July 2023).

(2) Cabinet Office should continue to monitor the use of regulation 32(2)(c) (under these regulations public bodies are permitted to procure goods, services, and works with extreme urgency, including the use of direct awards to suppliers without any competition (e.g. Covid)).
(3) Awarding bodies should provide clear documentation for establishing and using procedures that may result in unequal treatment of suppliers.
(4) When procuring directly from suppliers, awarding bodies need to provide clear documentation on how they have considered and managed potential conflicts of interest or bias in the procurement process.
(5) Before awarding contracts, awarding bodies should document due diligence checks carried out on suppliers and associated parties.
(6) Steps to manage actual and perceived conflicts of interest should be properly documented.
(7) Cabinet Office should review whether requirements for disclosure and management of relevant interests are sufficient in cases where public officeholders hold cross-government responsibilities for awarding contracts or procurement.

KEY POINTS—LESSONS LEARNED FROM FIGHTING FRAUD IN A PANDEMIC COMMONWEALTH PREVENTION CENTRE

Mark Cheeseman CEO of the PSFA identified five key lessons learned to combat fraud during a pandemic:[31]

- a structure for fraud risk assessment which should take place against a common standard;
- understanding the environment and acting with common purpose;
- having the conversation and having it with integrity;
- instigate post-event reviews and getting money back;
- breaking out of our silos and sharing.

Case Study—Covid-19-related Fraud Rais Kayani[32]

In July 2023 Rais Kayani, was sentenced to sixteen months' imprisonment, suspended for eighteen months at Southwark Crown Court in London, having pleaded guilty to one count of entering into a money laundering arrangement.

During the Covid-19 crisis the British government had made emergency funds available to companies in need of urgent help via the Small Business Grant Fund which was

[31] Mark Cheeseman, 'Lessons Learnt from Fighting Fraud during the Covid-19 Pandemic' (2020), www.counterfraud.gov.au/news/general-news/mark-cheeseman-lessons-learnt-fighting-fraud-during-covid-19-pandemic-16-october-2020 (accessed 24 July 2023).

[32] Crown Prosecution Service, 'Covid-19 Fraudster Sentenced for Laundering Nearly £200k from Taxpayers' (July 2023), www.cps.gov.uk/cps/news/covid-19-fraudster-sentenced-laundering-nearly-ps200k-taxpayers (accessed 24 July 2023).

administered by local authorities. An investigation revealed that multiple false applications were made for the Small Business Grant Fund at St Helen's, Thurrock, and Rochdale local authorities. The three councils were defrauded resulting in a loss of £195,000.

Kayani was the beneficiary of a series of false applications to local authorities in various parts of the country from where his business operated. Having dishonestly benefited from the fraudulent applications for the Small Business Grant Fund, he transferred the proceeds overseas.

Checklist—Debarment Databases

There are some useful databases to help identify whether companies or individuals are subject to debarment:

- Procurement—World Bank Listing of Ineligible Firms and Individuals, www.worldbank.org/en/projects-operations/procurement/debarred-firms (accessed 24 July 2023);
- US Department of Labour Office of Federal Contract Compliance Programs Debarred Companies, www.dol.gov/agencies/ofccp/debarred-list (accessed 24 July 2023);
- Companies House—Search for disqualified company directors, www.gov.uk/search-the-register-of-disqualified-company-directors (accessed 24 July 2023).

Further Reading

- NAO, *Investigation into Government Procurement during the Covid-19 Pandemic* (2020), www.nao.org.uk/reports/government-procurement-during-the-covid-19-pandemic/ (accessed 24 July 2023);
- NAO Good Practice Guidance Fraud and Error, www.nao.org.uk/wp-content/uploads/2021/03/010381-001-Fraud-and-Error-Accessible.pdf (accessed 24 July 2023);
- NAO, *Initial Learning from the Governments Response to the Covid 19 Pandemic* (2021), www.nao.org.uk/insights/initial-learning-from-the-governments-response-to-the-covid-19-pandemic/ (accessed 24 July 2023).

1.20 **Counter Fraud Framework**

The CFF is useful for assisting in the mapping of the response to fraud referrals. To counter fraud effectively and reduce the level of harm and loss, every effort must be made at all stages to stop future frauds.

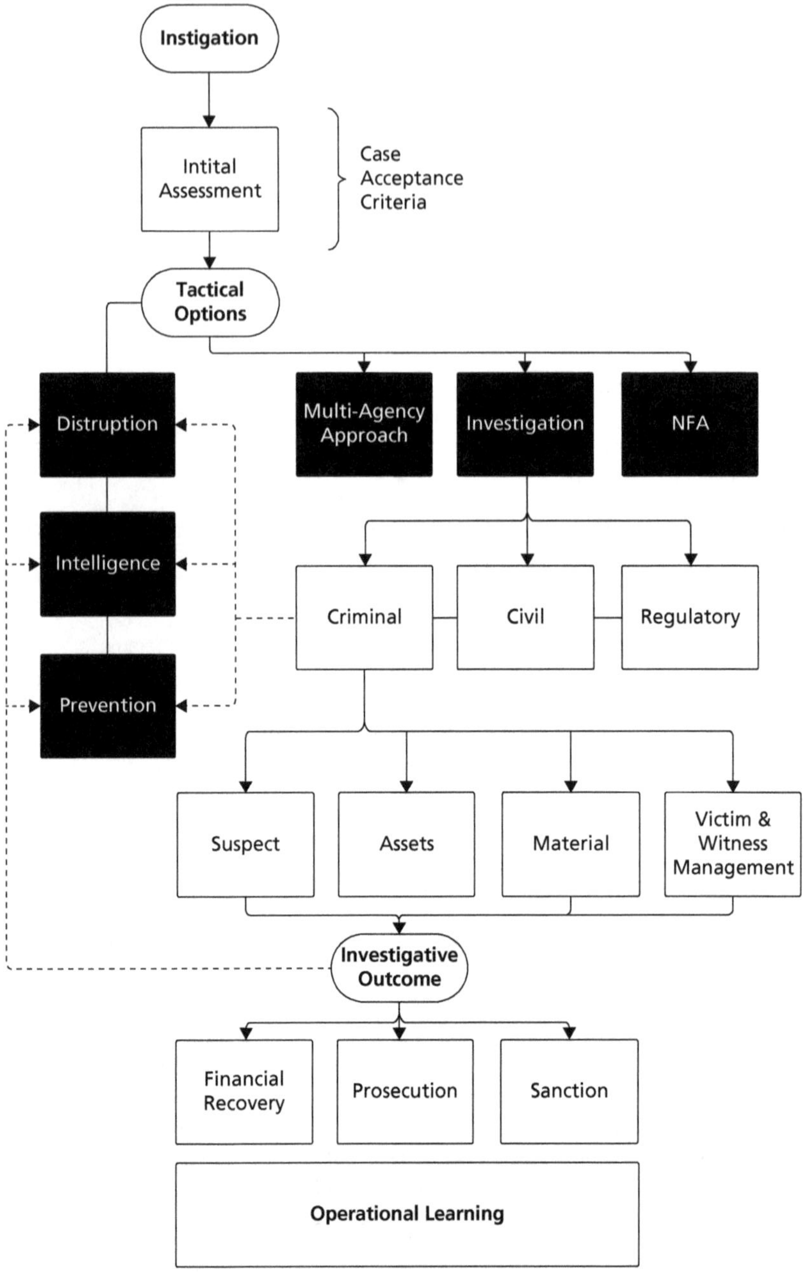

Figure 1.15 Counter Fraud Framework

Effective fraud prevention is the responsibility of all counter fraud practitioners and should be at the forefront of the counter fraud mindset. Traditionally roles have been specific whether they be investigators, intelligence, or risk assessment; while core skills and roles continue to be important, each role should complement the other.

The CFF offers a range of tactical options following a fraud referral; the options continue to be available through the lifecycle of that referral as shown in Figure 1.15.

We explore the CFF in detail in the investigation chapter.

2

Countering Fraud Organizations and Frameworks

Blackstone's Counter Fraud Professionals' Handbook. Michael J. Betts, Laura Eshelby, and David Whitehouse-Hayes, Oxford University Press.

DOI: 10.1093/9780191996955.003.0002

2.1 Introduction

In this chapter, we will explore the fraud landscape, the ecosystem of organizations involved in responding to fraud in the UK and beyond, and the structures they have introduced. This will include an introduction to the recently launched Public Sector Fraud Authority (PSFA).

We will reference the Government Counter Fraud Profession (GCFP) and associated standards for practitioners, including leadership, management, and strategy, with a focus on their practical application. The Fraud Management Model is described which was developed from domestic and international best practices, and we consider how to deter fraud.

2.2 UK Public Sector Counter Fraud Organizations

For a fraud practitioner new to the field or more experienced, there are a wealth of organizations both national and international with a responsibility for countering fraud. In this section, we will explore the roles and responsibilities of a range of the national public sector organizations, information, and resources available to draw from these (as illustrated in Figure 2.1).

Figure 2.1 National public sector organizations with a counter fraud role

2.2.1 City of London Police (CoLP)

Law enforcement bodies can offer insights into current threats and provide access to resources to aid fraud management. City of London Police (CoLP) is the national lead police force for fraud with oversight in England and Wales. They investigate some of the most complex cases of fraud, set the national policing strategy, and coordinate the operational response. They also host the national reporting centre for fraud and cybercrime, on behalf of policing.[1] CoLP resources include information relating to building capability, via the City of London Police Economic Crime Academy,[2] and the learning programmes they deliver.

Following the Attorney General review of fraud, published in 2006, a national fraud reporting centre, Action Fraud, and the National Fraud Intelligence Bureau (NFIB) were established, hosted by the CoLP. The national approach aimed to introduce central reporting, dissemination, and information on fraud.

KEY POINTS—COLP NATIONAL LEAD FOR FRAUD

The CoLP acts as the national lead for fraud and has the following areas of responsibility:

- investigate (on behalf of UK policing) fraud that impacts the UK and causes the greatest harm;
- accept inquiries and provide guidance as an authority on fraud crime;
- receive requests for assistance or guidance from and offer help to UK regional police forces, business, industry, the NFIB, and the National Crime Agency (NCA);
- liaise and develop usually beneficiary and cooperative relationships, with foreign law enforcement and services involved in fighting crime;
- implement a centre of excellence to educate and upskill individuals across sectors, enabling them to identify and combat fraud.

2.2.2 National Crime Agency (NCA)

The NCA is a national law enforcement agency and counters organized crime; human, weapons, and drug trafficking; cybercrime; and economic crime that goes across regional and international borders. The NCA can be tasked to investigate any crime.

The NCA targets the highest threats to the UK in three ways:

(1) conducting its own operations;
(2) providing support and expertise to other operations;

[1] Police Scotland have their own fraud reporting processes.
[2] See https://academy.cityoflondon.police.uk/ (accessed 17 July 2023).

(3) providing leadership to wider law enforcement to use resources effectively.

The NCA mission is to 'lead the UK's fight to cut serious and organised crime, protecting the public by targeting and pursuing those criminals who pose the greatest risk to the UK'.

Within the NCA they have developed the National Economic Crime Centre (NECC) to bring together law enforcement and justice agencies, government departments, regulatory bodies, and the private sector with shared objectives of driving down serious organized economic crime, protecting the public, and safeguarding the prosperity and reputation of the UK as a financial centre. The NECC launched in 2018, with representatives from Serious Fraud Office (SFO), NCA, Financial Conduct Authority, COLP, His Majesties Revenue & Customs (HMRC), Crown Prosecution Service, and Home Office (HO).

KEY POINTS—NCA

The NCA lead the UK's response locally, regionally, and nationally to reduce the impact of serious and organized crime on the UK and communities. The NCA's focus is on:

- building the best possible intelligence picture of all serious and organized crime threats;
- pursuing the most serious and dangerous offenders;
- developing and delivering specialist capabilities on behalf of law enforcement and other partners.

2.2.3 The National Cyber Security Centre (NCSC)

The National Cyber Security Centre (NCSC) launched in 2016 and brought together experts from Communications–Electronics Security Group (CESG)[3] (information assurance arm of Government Communications Headquarters), the centre for cyber assessment, and the Centre for Protection of National Instructure. The NCSC provides a single point of contact for small and medium-sized enterprises, larger organizations, government agencies, the public, and government departments. They also work with other law enforcement, defence, the UK's intelligence and security agencies, and international partners.

[3] CESG (originally Communications–Electronics Security Group) is the branch of GCHQ (Government Communications Headquarters) which works to secure the communications and information systems of the government and critical parts of UK national infrastructure.

Checklist—NCSC areas of focus

The NCSC's areas of focus are:

- defending digital infrastructure;
- understanding the environmental implications of future technologies;
- supporting organizations working on environmental solutions with their cyber security challenges;
- encourage knowledge, sharing, and engagement on sustainability across the UK cyber security industry;
- become an exemplar in running our organization sustainably.

2.2.4 Serious Fraud Office (SFO)

The SFO is a specialist prosecuting authority tackling the top level of serious or complex fraud, bribery, and corruption, with a remit covering England, Wales, and Northern Ireland. The SFO investigates a small number of large economic crime cases. The director may investigate any suspected offence which based on reasonable grounds appears to involve serious or complex fraud, bribery, or corruption.

Checklist—SFO investigation considerations

In considering whether to authorize an investigation, the director will consider the actual or intended harm that may be caused to:

- the public, or
- the reputation and integrity of the UK as an international financial centre, or
- the economy and prosperity of the UK and whether the complexity and nature of the suspected offence warrants the application of the SFO's specialist skills, powers, and capabilities to investigate and prosecute.

The SFO also pursues criminals for the financial benefit they have made from their crimes, and assists overseas jurisdictions with their investigations into serious and complex fraud, bribery, and corruption cases. Since 30 September 2017, the SFO have had the power to investigate and prosecute the new offence of corporate failure to prevent the facilitation of overseas tax evasion.

The SFO are unusual in the UK in that they both investigate and prosecute their cases. They were set up this way to allow lawyers and investigators to work together from the beginning on what are complex cases.

The SFO[4] was created and given its powers under the Criminal Justice Act 1987 and was established in 1988. The SFO is superintended by the Attorney General in accordance with a protocol which sets out the relationship between the Attorney and the Law Officers' Departments.

2.2.5 National Protective Security Authority (NPSA)

The recently launched National Protective Security Authority (NPSA),[5] the UK government's National Technical Authority for physical and personnel protective security, provides support and resources aimed at reducing the vulnerability of the national infrastructure. This is more targeted at national security threats, counter-terrorism, but as fraud and associated economic crime can have close links to such activity, it is useful to access and utilize these resources to strengthen any fraud management response.

2.2.6 The UK National Audit Office (NAO)

The UK National Audit Office (NAO) provide insight and information[6] to support organizations to understand and find more fraud. Their most recent publications focused on fraud risk, fraud, and corruption as well as scheme-specific studies, on which they regularly offer their views and guidance. For practitioners and fraud leaders, their unique insights and deep understanding of issues and recommendations to improve a fraud response form a helpful group of resources to draw upon.

2.2.7 Public Sector Fraud Authority (PSFA)

The PSFA was developed out of the foundation of the Centre of Expertise (COEX) for the Government Fraud Function. The COEX introduced in 2018 the International Public Sector Fraud Forum (IPSFF), working with Australia, Canada, New Zealand, the UK, and the US collectively known as the Five Eyes countries to develop leading practices on tackling fraud. The IPSFF have successfully developed and published a variety of guidance, from risk management, managing fraud in an emergency to most recently fraud in international aid. Representatives include members of the Australian Attorney General's Office, Inspectors General from the USA, tax fraud leads from Canada, and members of the SFO in New Zealand. The best practice

[4] Serious Fraud Office, 'About Us' (2023), www.sfo.gov.uk/about-us/ (accessed 17 July 2023).

[5] National Protective Security Authority (NPSA), www.npsa.gov.uk/ (accessed 17 July 2023).

[6] National Audit Office (NAO), 'Fraud and Error Archives' (2023), www.nao.org.uk/topics/fraud-error/ (accessed 17 July 2023).

guides[7] cover a range of topics, including: managing fraud in emergencies, procurement risk, and fraud and international aid. There is also best practice guidance on building capability and fraud awareness, helpful to anyone establishing or refreshing their organization's approach to fraud.

The PSFA is also the home of the GCFP, whose aim is to build capability across the public sector and beyond. The Profession provides access to a range of practice guidance and standards for professionals, including those available under open government licence including for risk assessment, investigation, and bribery and corruption. The standards include process, products, and competencies required for each discipline to effectively counter fraud.[8] Alongside this the Profession offers access to ongoing development support, and guidance on how to access training resources.

In the Spring Statement of March 2022, the Chancellor announced the creation of the PSFA[9] bringing together experts from across sectors in an integrated way with Cabinet Office and His Majesty's Treasury (HM Treasury). The PSFA puts a greater focus on performance and outcomes, as well as building deeper and broader expert-led services to support government departments and public bodies to reduce the impact of fraud. It will also become the centre of the Counter Fraud Function (CFF).

KEY POINTS—PSFA'S MISSION

The PSFA's mission is to:

- Modernize the fraud and error response by widening access and use of leading practices, tools, and technology—better protecting taxpayers' money.
- Build expert-led services that collaborate with experts in departments and public bodies to better fight fraud and error through risk, prevention, data, and enforcement techniques.
- Develop capability in the public sector to find, prevent, and respond to fraud and error—both organizationally and individually.
- Put performance at the heart of the public sector fraud conversation—focusing on investments and outcomes.
- PSFA will aim to be seen as a beacon of fraud and error expertise and a destination for those wanting to be effective in fighting public sector fraud.

The PSFA was launched with a view to building service and function areas over the following years. These include data analytics, intelligence and enforcement services, and functions focused on performance, policy, practice standards, and capability.

[7] www.gov.uk/government/publications/international-public-sector-fraud-forum-guidanc (accessed 17 July 2023).

[8] GOV.UK, 'Government Counter Fraud Function and Profession' (n.d.), www.gov.uk/government/groups/counter-fraud-standards-and-profession (accessed 17 July 2023).

[9] GOV.UK, 'PSFA' (n.d.), www.gov.uk/government/organisations/public-sector-fraud-authority (accessed 17 July 2023).

The PSFA leads on the publication of fraud and error losses annually for the public sector. This insight is unique, with the UK being the only jurisdiction that openly reports losses to this level of transparency. The reporting is found in the Annual Fraud Landscape Report,[10] and details the success of the response to fraud and trends/patterns for detected, prevented, and recovered fraud over time. It is interesting for all fraud leads and practitioners to consider how they encourage transparency in their organizations and sectors, as this scrutiny enables a greater acceptance of the fraud problem.

Further reading

- GCFP Standards, www.gov.uk/government/groups/counter-fraud-standards-and-profession (accessed 17 July 2023);
- NAO, www.nao.org.uk/ (accessed 17 July 2023);
- NPSA, www.npsa.gov.uk/ (accessed 17 July 2023);
- SFO, www.sfo.gov.uk/ (accessed 17 July 2023).

2.3 International Counter Fraud Organizations

There are several international organizations with a role in countering fraud, a selection of which are illustrated in Figure 2.2.

2.3.1 Commonwealth Fraud Prevention Centre (CFPC)

Australia has established the Commonwealth Fraud Prevention Centre (CFPC), which is operated out of the Attorney General's Office.

KEY POINTS—CFPC'S AIMS

The CFPC has three key aims:

(1) **Equip**—equip Australian government entities with guidance and tools to strengthen the foundation of leading counter fraud capability.
(2) **Enable**—enable Australian government entities to respond to emerging issues, connect, collaborate, and share data and information.
(3) **Empower**—empower Australian government entities to create positive change, embed leading practice capability, measure the fraud problem, and measure the return of investment and impact of their counter fraud activities.

[10] GOV.UK, 'Cross-Government Fraud Landscape Annual Report 2022' (21 March 2023), www.gov.uk/government/publications/cross-government-fraud-landscape-annual-report-2022 (accessed 17 July 2023).

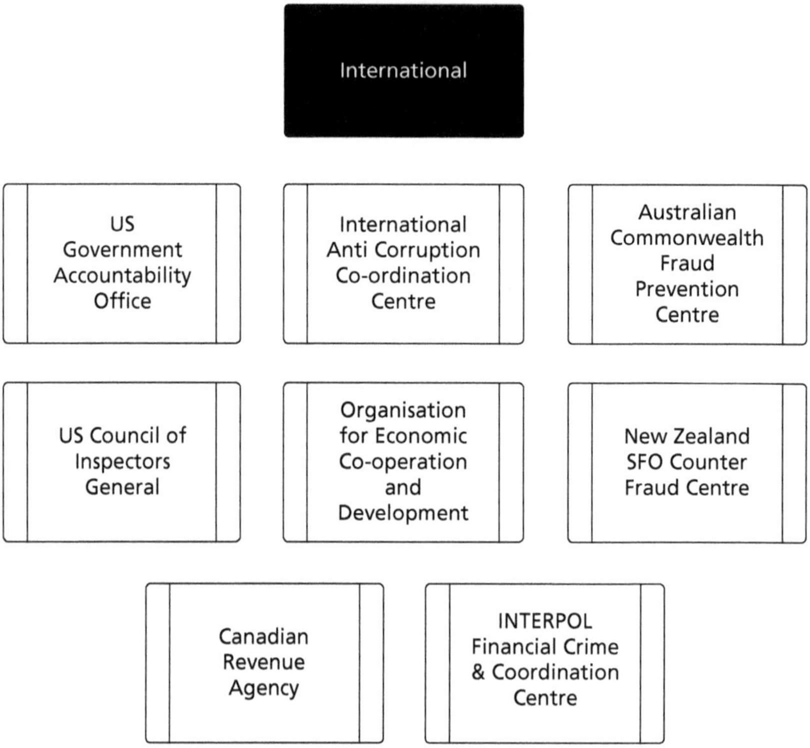

Figure 2.2 International counter fraud organizations

The CFPC has a range of tools and guidance aimed at supporting organizations in the public sector to understand and tackle fraud. This includes toolkits on understanding fraud risk, exploring the fraud problem, and setting out common counter measures used in response to detect fraud. They also provide detailed information on how to develop control strategies. Although developed in an international context, the CFPC works closely with the PSFA, and the toolkits and guidance have good portability to be used in the UK context. One guidance toolkit for fraud management to reference would be 'Fundamentals for Fraud Control' a great reference point if you are early on your journey to consider how to manage fraud.[11]

[11] Commonwealth Fraud Prevention Centre, 'Find Where to Start' (2021), www.counterfraud.gov.au/find-where-to-start#fundamentals-for-sound-fraud-control (accessed 17 July 2023).

2.3.2 US Council of the Inspectors General of Integrity and Efficiency (CIGIE)

Over in the USA, the Council of the Inspectors General of Integrity and Efficiency (CIGIE)[12] operate as an independent body established within the executive branch to address integrity, economy, and effectiveness issues that apply across individual government agencies. They support the establishment and oversee the Offices of Inspectors General. They have available a wealth of information and resources, including guidance and training materials, again which have a good alignment with the UK approach and can support strategic thinking and planning in fraud management.

2.3.3 US Government Accountability Office (GAO)

Also in the USA, they have a dedicated team of professionals focused on understanding and managing fraud, the Government Accountability Office (GAO).[13] The GAO offers a range of resources to understand what fraud is and how to respond, including a detailed Conceptual Fraud Model they have designed, by fraud type. This is available for free, and covers the several types of fraud, risks, the mechanisms used by individuals to perpetrate fraud and, finally, the impact. This was modelled on real fraud activity, historical in nature including those that led to criminal outcomes; an insightful resource to help inform a fraud leader's own understanding of types of frauds, methods deployed, and to help build an understanding of risk.

2.3.4 New Zealand Counter Fraud Centre

Housed in the SFO of New Zealand is the recently established Counter Fraud Centre. The centre leads on prevention efforts and sits alongside the traditionally investigation-focused SFO. The role of the new centre is to bring the public sector together and establish a shared narrative on counter fraud to strengthen the overall response. To date they have developed best practice guidance and are in the process of establishing national strategy on financial crime and corruption.[14]

2.3.5 Canada Revenue Agency

The Canadian government operates a decentralized model to manage fraud against the public sector. Most of its resource sits within the Canadian Revenue Authority and Service Canada, the equivalents of the UK's Department for Work and Pensions and HMRC departments in the UK. The Royal Canadian Mounted Police are the lead law enforcement unit that deals with fraud.

---

[12] IGNET, Council of the Inspectors General on Integrity and Efficiency (CIGIE), www.ignet.gov/ (accessed 17 July 2023).

[13] GAO, Antifraud Resources, https://gaoinnovations.gov/antifraud_resource/whatisfraud (accessed 17 July 2023).

[14] Serious Fraud Office, NZ, 'What We Do' (n.d.), https://sfo.govt.nz/counterfraud/what-we-do/ (accessed 17 July 2023).

2.3.6 Organisation for Economic Co-operation and Development (OECD)

The Organisation for Economic Co-operation and Development (OECD) is an international organization that leads on policy development with a focus on prosperity, equality, opportunity, and well-being. This includes a focus on anti-corruption and brings together evidence on a global scale and provides tools, guidance, and assistance to practitioners in this field, and access to consistent practice and standards.[15]

The OECD published support for those working in the protection of European Union funds. These five steps have wider utility in a range of sectors for effective fraud response:

(1) Develop cooperation mechanisms at a national level for detecting and tackling fraud.
(2) Maintain risk registers and integrate risk-based control activities.
(3) Use data-driven analysis to inform detection and action.
(4) Improve governance by establishing counter fraud policies.
(5) Regularly monitor and evaluate to improve your fraud risk management approach.

2.3.7 International Anti-Corruption Coordination Centre (IACCC)

The International Anti-Corruption Coordination Centre (IACCC) brings together specialist law enforcement officers from multiple agencies around the world to tackle allegations of grand corruption.[16] Acts that fall into this category include:

- bribery of public officials;
- embezzlement;
- abuse of function;
- the laundering of the proceeds of crime.

KEY POINTS—IACCC'S OBJECTIVES

The objectives of the IACCC are:

- inform—which organizations and initiatives can help;
- assist—with practical actions and advice;
- collect—information to form a single picture of grand corruption;
- coordinate—an effective global law enforcement response;
- collaborate—by creating a constructive, cooperative, and agreed approach.

---

[15] www.oecd.org/gov/ethics/fraud-corruption-esif.htm (accessed 17 July 2023).

[16] NCA, International Anti-Corruption Coordination Centre, www.nationalcrimeagency.gov.uk/what-we-do/crime-threats/bribery-corruption-and-sanctions-evasion/international-anti-corruption-centre (accessed 17 July 2023).

During the 2016 Anti-Corruption Summit, the UK committed to establishing and hosting the IACCC. The IACCC was officially launched in July 2017 and is hosted by the NCA in London. Law enforcement that are participants can draw upon the cooperation and support of the IACCC. In the UK, this includes the NCA.

2.3.8 Interpol's Financial Crime and Anti-Corruption Centre (IFCACC)

In 2022 the Interpol's Financial Crime and Anti-Corruption Centre (IFCACC)[17] was introduced to expand and streamline their existing initiatives in tackling financial crimes, illicit money flows, and asset recovery.

IFCACC will adopt a multi-agency approach, and work closely with stakeholders to strengthen efforts against financial crime and corruption. Noted stakeholders include the Financial Action Task Force (FATF), the FATF-Style Regional Bodies, the Egmont Group of Financial Intelligence Units, law enforcement agencies, police organizations, and the financial sector.

IFCACC offers a range of services, focused on the key areas outlined below. This includes investigative, operational, analytical, and capacity-building support.

KEY POINTS—IFCACC'S OPERATIONS

- Fraud and payment crime—IFCACC will support member countries in their transnational investigations, and will share significant modus operandi with relevant stakeholders.
- Anti-money laundering and asset recovery—IFCACC will bring a multidisciplinary response to target global illicit financial flows. The focus is on several types of money laundering schemes and the use of virtual assets as well as identification of criminal assets and forfeiture.
- Anti-corruption—efforts against corruption will span various crime types, including doping in sport, the corruption of public officials, and grand corruption (involving senior political figures). IFCACC will strengthen member countries' ability to combat grand corruption both nationally and internationally.

2.3.9 International Public Sector Fraud Forum (IPSFF)

The IPSFF[18] was introduced by the centre of His Majesties Government (HMG) fraud function (now the PSFA) in 2018. It was established to bring together the Five Eyes countries to develop leading practices on tackling fraud, with a focus on public sector loss. Representatives include members of the Australian Attorney General's

[17] Interpol, 'Our Role in Fighting Financial Crime' (2017), www.interpol.int/en/Crimes/Financial-crime/Our-role-in-fighting-financial-crime (accessed 17 July 2023).

[18] GOV.UK, 'International Public Sector Fraud Forum Guidance' (n.d.), www.gov.uk/government/publications/international-public-sector-fraud-forum-guidance (accessed 17 July 2023).

Office, Inspectors General from the USA, tax fraud leads from Canada, and members of the SFO in New Zealand.

The IPSFF have successfully developed and published a variety of guidance, from risk management, managing fraud in an emergency situation to most recently fraud in international aid, all available on www.gov.uk.

In the published guidance on managing fraud for public bodies,[19] the IPSFF set out five helpful principles that we can draw upon when developing an effective fraud response. Developed for the public sector, the guidance helpfully has wider applicability to other sectors.

KEY POINTS—MANAGING FRAUD—IPSFF 2019

- **There is always going to be fraud.** It is a fact that some individuals will look to make gain where there is opportunity, and organizations need robust processes in place to prevent, detect, and respond to fraud and corruption.
- **Finding fraud is a good thing.** If you do not find fraud you cannot fight it. This requires a change in perspective, so the identification of fraud is viewed as a positive and proactive achievement.
- **There is no one solution.** Addressing fraud needs a holistic response incorporating detection, prevention, and redress, underpinned by a strong understanding of risk. It also requires cooperation between organizations under a spirit of collaboration.
- **Fraud and corruption are ever changing.** Fraud and counter fraud practices evolve very quickly, and organizations must be agile and change their approach to deal with this evolution.
- **Prevention is the most effective way to address fraud and corruption.** Preventing fraud through effective counter fraud practices reduces the loss and reputational damage (although this can be difficult to measure). It also requires fewer resources than an approach focused on detection and recovery.

2.4 Other Sectors—Services and Tools

In the private sector domestically, there are a wealth of industry and membership bodies who provide a range of free and paid-for services to assist in the management of fraud. Note the approach of the UK government is to not outsource accountability of fraud management, however, we would advocate working across sectors, and utilizing any and all resources available to maximize your response.

[19] International Public Sector Fraud Forum, 'A Guide to Managing Fraud for Public Bodies' (2019), https://assets.publishing.service.gov.uk/government/uploads/system/uploads/attachment_data/file/1115931/GuideToManagingFraudForPublicBodies.pdf (accessed 17 July 2023).

Further resources

- www.cifas.org.uk/ Offer resources and paid-for services, and publish annual data/insights via www.fraudscape.co.uk/ (accessed 17 July 2023);
- www.cipfa.org/ Offer resources and paid-for services, including capability and training with a focus on fraud risk (accessed 17 July 2023);
- www.acfe.com/ ACFE membership organization offers resources, paid-for training and services and case studies to help in the understanding of fraud (accessed 17 July 2023);
- www.int-comp.org/ International Compliance Association, offering paid-for qualifications, training, courses, and membership (accessed 17 July 2023);
- www.fraudadvisorypanel.org/ Fraud membership advisory group, including paid-for events and resources (accessed 17 July 2023);
- www.cimaglobal.com/ Offers resources, case studies, training, and paid-for services for range of disciplines including fraud (accessed 17 July 2023);
- www.gov.uk/government/organisations/public-sector-fraud-authority PSFA, government-led authority in Cabinet Office, integrated with HM Treasury, offers services and functions to those working in fraud across the public sector (accessed 17 July 2023);
- www.gov.uk/government/groups/counter-fraud-standards-and-profession GCFP, issues under open government licence practice, standards, and guidance for fraud practitioners (accessed 17 July 2023).

2.5 Counter Fraud Frameworks

2.5.1 The Fraud Management Model

To effectively respond to fraud, *a multi-disciplinary approach* must be taken.[20]

This is not a novel concept or approach, but it is increasingly being adopted by practitioners and leaders, tasked with tackling fraud across sectors and organizations.

To enable the organizations to understand and respond effectively to fraud, a model incorporating understanding fraud risk, influencing the fraud risk appetite, and setting an effective counter fraud strategy are all key, which in turn will allow a response to be set that effectively targets and minimizes the risk and threats an organization faces from fraud.[21] The remit and threats to different organizations may vary, so this may also include counter bribery and corruption, anti-money laundering, and wider business ethics activity.

[20] McKinsey & Company, 'Four Key Capabilities to Strengthen a Fraud Management System' (8 November 2022), www.mckinsey.com/capabilities/risk-and-resilience/our-insights/four-key-capabilities-to-strengthen-a-fraud-management-system (accessed 17 July 2023) (emphasis added).

[21] GCFP Leadership, Management and Strategy standards for available via gcfp@cabinetoffice.gov.uk.

Case Study 1—The importance of effective fraud management: 'Senior Civil Servant Stole £1.7m from Ministry of Justice'

The offender, aged 37, masterminded a 'sophisticated' fraud by setting up payments to a fake company for two years. He, a Grade 7 civil servant, used the cash to buy an Audi SQ5, an Audi A3, and a five-bedroom manor house with 1.1 acres in Hampshire.

At his sentencing, prosecutor Gregor McKinley told Southwark crown court: 'This was a sophisticated fraud ... and would have resulted in further loss to the taxpayer if it had not been discovered'.

Police discovered the offender had transferred almost £1.4 million of MoJ funds to himself and £400,000 was in the fake firm's account.

He pleaded guilty to fraud and transferring criminal property. Judge Joanna Korner QC told him: 'You conceived of this plan to make yourself richer ... It was both sophisticated and greedy'. It was noted in court how the offender had used his knowledge of the organization's controls to circumvent them.[22]

The multidisciplinary approach may also incorporate the exploration and use of data and analytics to inform the identification and understanding of risks, which in turn will help to influence the overall strategy and response.

Fraud is an issue that all organizations may face regardless of size, industry, or country. It is often high-profile frauds in large multinational organizations that are reported in the media, and smaller organizations may feel they are unlikely to be a target of fraudsters. However, small businesses (classified as those with fewer than 100 employees) suffer fraud more frequently than large organizations and are hit by higher average losses. When small companies are hit by large fraud losses, they are less likely to be able to absorb the damage than a larger company and may even go out of business as a result.[23]

Case Study 2—The importance of effective fraud management: corporate fraud

WorldCom

WorldCom filed for bankruptcy protection in June 2002. It was at the time the biggest corporate fraud in history, a result of treating operating expenses as capital expenditure. WorldCom (now renamed MCI Communications Corporation) admitted in March 2004 that the total amount by which it had misled investors over the previous

[22] R. Burford, 'Senior Civil Servant Stole £1.7m from Ministry of Justice', *Evening Standard* (7 January 2020), www.standard.co.uk/news/crime/senior-civil-servant-stole-ps1-7m-from-ministry-of-justice-a4328096.html (accessed 17 July 2023).

[23] CIMA, 'Fraud Risk Management: A Guide to Good Practice' (2008), www.cimaglobal.com/Documents/ImportedDocuments/cid_techguide_fraud_risk_management_feb09.pdf.pdf (accessed 17 July 2023).

ten years was almost US$75 billion (£42 billion) and reduced its stated pretax profits for 2001 and 2002 by that amount. WorldCom stock began falling in late 1999 as businesses slashed spending on telecom services and equipment.

A series of debt downgrades raised borrowing costs for the company, struggling with about US$32 billion in debt. WorldCom used accounting tricks to conceal a deteriorating financial condition and to inflate profits. Former WorldCom chief executive Bernie Ebbers resigned in April 2002 amid questions about US$366 million in personal loans from the company and a federal probe of its accounting practices. Ebbers was subsequently charged with conspiracy to commit securities fraud and filing misleading data with the Securities and Exchange Commission (SEC) and was sentenced to twenty-five years in prison. Scott Sullivan, former chief financial officer, pleaded guilty to three criminal charges and was sentenced to five years in prison.

Losses to WorldCom shareholders were close to US$180 billion and the fraud also resulted in the loss of 17,000 jobs. The SEC said that WorldCom had committed 'accounting improprieties of unprecedented magnitude'—proof, it said, of the need for reform in the regulation of corporate accounting.[24]

In practice, a counter fraud lead may be operating in an organization with varying levels of resources dedicated full-time to counter fraud. The fraud lead has the overall responsibility and accountability for the fraud management is a key consideration upfront, as any lack of clarity may be problematic when an organization is faced with a large-scale or continued fraud problem. The size of an organization may influence key decisions including who will be responsible for signing off the fraud strategy, fraud response, and associated action plans.

Although fraud is prevalent across organizations of all sizes and in all sectors and locations, research shows that certain business models will involve greater levels of fraud risk than others.[25]

2.6 Government Counter Fraud Professional Leadership

The Government Counter Fraud Professional Leadership, Management and Strategy (LMS) standards, states that functional leads[26] are responsible for ensuring the right skills and capabilities exist in an organization to appropriately respond to the fraud risk faced. They may determine that the requirement for counter fraud services is best acquired by being outsourced; in this case the accountability for counter fraud would remain with the organization.

[24] Ibid.

[25] Ibid.

[26] The functional lead is the term given to the senior civil servant or equivalent in an arm's-length body/wider public sector, aka the fraud lead, responsible for the counter fraud response.

Ideally the functional lead role should not be outsourced. However, an organization may decide that this route provides the most appropriate response. If the role is outsourced, the contractor should meet all the government counter fraud LMS skill and capability standards and competencies.[27] In a large and complex organization there is likely to be more than one functional lead and responsibilities may be divided.

As the case studies above illustrate, it is important to those leading a fraud function that they maintain a close relationship with the audit function within their organization, as well as also proactively seeking their own unit and outcomes are regularly and independently audited. Fraud leads should work with their internal and external audit functions to agree the scope and set an appropriate timescale between each audit. If a technical review is included, fraud leads should ensure that the reviewer has appropriate counter fraud capability. Functional leads may want to mentor or provide advice to smaller and less mature CFFs.

The GCFP LMS standard sets out the Government Fraud Management Model. The model details how to effectively lead and manage a CFF. It describes three cycles that should form a continuous process, namely:

(1) fraud risk management;
(2) strategy management;
(3) operational management.

The model sets out six core pillars that functional leads should ensure the organization has met or has in place, as described below.

Pillar 1—The counter fraud function is acknowledged and supported by the board and has an agreed level of investment

This sets the tone from the top, through board-level buy-in and support for the CFF that permeates through all management levels and is crucial to effective fraud management, the development of a counter fraud and ethical culture and longer-term investment in resources.

Checklist—Pillar 1 counter fraud function

It is essential to have:

- Senior level buy-in and overt support for the CFF that is regularly reinforced by an accountable individual at board level.
- An approved counter fraud strategy, which has been developed in partnership with key stakeholders and signed off by the accountable individual at board level, which will assist in determining appropriate investment.

[27] For details of standards and further insight, see www.gov.uk/government/groups/counter-fraud-standards-and-profession#gcfp (accessed 17 July 2023).

- Agreed outcome-based metrics regularly reported to the accountable individual and senior stakeholders, as appropriate to track progress against the strategy and annual action plan.
- Regular meetings with the board and accountable individual to review and redefine the organization's risk appetite and counter fraud maturity.
- Agreed commitment from senior management to high standards of business ethics and integrity. Ensure messaging is relevant and communicated internally and externally and permeates through all levels.
- An agreed level of investment commensurate to the level of risk and spend within the organization.

Pillar 2—Counter fraud functional standards—met or in progress

Functional Standards for fraud and error were developed by the centre of the Government Fraud Function, now operated by the PSFA, in collaboration with experts across government. They have been shared with experts in counter fraud from across government, industry, and academia. They were originally agreed in 2018, and republished in 2021, and are summarized below.[28] The standards were produced with public sector bodies in mind but would be equally applicable and have wider utility across sectors to manage fraud effectively.

Checklist—Government Standard 013: counter fraud

The Government Standard 013 describes counter fraud organizational basics, which include these key considerations:

- have an accountable individual at board level who is responsible for counter fraud, bribery, and corruption;
- have a counter fraud, bribery, and corruption strategy that is submitted to the centre;
- have a fraud, bribery, and corruption risk assessment that is submitted to the centre;
- have a policy and response plan for dealing with potential instances of fraud, bribery, and corruption;

[28] HM Government, 'Government Functional Standard: GovS 013: Counter Fraud' (version 2, August 2021), www.gov.uk/government/publications/government-functional-standard-govs-013-counter-fraud (accessed 17 July 2023). The eleven CFF standards build on what is currently in GOV.UK, 'Managing Public Money' (4 May 2023), www.gov.uk/government/publications/managing-public-money (accessed 17 July 2023).

- have an annual action plan that summarizes key actions to improve capability, activity, and resilience in that year;
- have outcome-based metrics summarizing what outcomes they are seeking to achieve that year. For organizations with 'significant investment' in counter fraud, bribery, and corruption or 'significant estimated' fraud loss, include metrics with a financial impact;
- have well-established and documented reporting routes for staff, contractors, and members of the public to report suspicions of fraud, bribery, and corruption and a mechanism for recording these referrals and allegations;
- report identified loss from fraud, bribery, corruption and error, and associated recoveries, to the centre in line with the agreed government definitions;
- have agreed access to trained investigators that meet the agreed public sector skill standard;
- undertake activity to try to detect fraud in high-risk areas where little or nothing is known of fraud, bribery, and corruption levels, including loss measurement activity where suitable;
- ensure all staff have access to and undertake fraud awareness, bribery, and corruption training as appropriate to their role;
- have policies and registers for gifts, hospitality, and conflicts of interest.

The functional standards set out an expectation that all organizations will have an accountable individual at board level who is responsible for counter fraud. These form the organizational level of the LMS standards. They aim to improve consistency across counter fraud in government and provide an entry point to organizational activity on counter fraud in one place.

Organizations must implement or meet all the requirements detailed in the checklist but should not limit activity to those, but should additionally implement or undertake further areas of activity to make an impact on their organization's fraud challenges to reduce both economic and reputational harm. These standards pinpoint the fundamentals of what is expected in a counter fraud response, they are intentionally set at an accessible level.

Pillar 3—Functional lead understands the organization and how it operates

Counter fraud leads who understand the organization and how it operates will be better placed to implement initiatives that impact on the fraud challenges the organization faces.

Checklist—Organizational initiatives to impact fraud

Counter fraud leads should ensure the following:

- Have a continued understanding of the bigger picture to identify future issues which may affect the needs of the organization and the counter fraud response.
- Influence and promote the position of the counter fraud agenda within the organization and wider government priorities so that fraud risk management is seen as supportive of organizational objectives.
- Liaise with stakeholders, brief ministers and policy officials, where applicable, so that progress is made and achieved against the counter fraud strategy and annual action plan; and actively seek and become involved and influential within the organization's business ethics and integrity agenda.

Pillar 4—Functional lead understands the legislative framework and the function has the powers they need

It is essential to have a continued understanding of the legislative, policy, and governance framework that the organization operates within and the powers available to the CFF. It is also essential to ensure guidance is available to counter fraud staff so that legislation is adhered to and not overreached. It is vital that the function lead can work and influence to shape legislative reform as appropriate, to challenge the status quo, and to strive for enhanced access to powers needed. This may be done in isolation or by working with wider stakeholders in the public/private sector to join existing reform programmes or push for variation to existing legal schedules/gateways.

Pillar 5—All staff receive appropriate fraud awareness training

Employees cannot always be expected to understand what fraud is, how to report it, and what impact it can have on an organization without it being defined and explained. It is essential to provide all employees with information on why people commit fraud, how to identify fraud (red flags), and how to report fraud. Additionally, employees should receive reassurance that any report made in good faith will not result in retaliation and that the organization operates a zero-tolerance policy in respect of retaliation of any kind. It is also important to repeat training regularly to reinforce the counter fraud messaging. It is essential to ensure that all employees have access to policies and documents promoting the organization's response to fraud with details of reporting lines and accountabilities.

Pillar 6—Counter fraud culture developed

A counter fraud culture should be developed throughout the organization and continually reinforced.

Checklist—Pillar 6—Counter fraud culture development

The following are elements required to develop a counter fraud culture:

- Mechanisms to remind all staff that everyone has a part to play in the management of fraud risk, especially during times of change and uncertainty. The use of a responsibilities matrix reinforces this message on a day-by-day basis.
- Clear and appropriate vetting policies and processes to screen all new entrants including contractors, subcontractors, and consultants; have a clear policy on any future monitoring for those persons with access to systems and data.
- Champion the Civil Service Code of Conduct and ensure it is available to all staff, contractors, subcontractors, and consultants. Reinforcing the Code of Conduct sets the tone for the organization's overall control environment and integrity.
- Champion and embed the counter fraud profession's Code of Ethics[29] to ensure the highest standards of professionalism and conduct.
- Encourage policy leads to consider fraud risks as part of the policy development or change process (i.e. use of impact assessments and consulting CFFs when designing new programmes, procedures, systems, and products to ensure that these contain essential controls).
- A fair, consistent, and proportional response to fraud incidents. Inconsistent outcomes, unfair treatment of individuals, and disproportionate sanctions can undermine the development of a counter fraud culture and deter people from raising concerns.
- Ensure the organization is part of the 'Internal Fraud in Government' programme (or equivalent schemes in industry/other sectors). This promotes a zero-tolerance approach to internal fraud across the civil service and helps to develop a strong counter fraud culture and uphold the Civil Service Core Values.[30]

When used together, the Six Pillar approach is an effective model for fraud management. We started our deep dive into this area, noting that the model by the

[29] GOV.UK, 'Counter-Fraud Standards and Profession' (n.d.), www.gov.uk/government/groups/counter-fraud-standards-and-profession (accessed 17 July 2023).

[30] Public sector organizations can see information via internalfraud@caboinetoffice.gov.uk; for private sector organizations, information can be found via www.cifas.org.uk. Cifas, Enhanced Internal Fraud Database, www.cifas.org.uk/fraud-prevention-community/member-benefits/data/ifd (accessed 17 July 2023).

GCFP included fraud risk management, strategy management, and operational management.

2.7 National and International Best Practice

2.7.1 National Best Practice

We have already started to explore the model as set out by the GCFP in s. 2.1 for fraud management. The GCFP is housed in the PSFA. The PSFA was launched in August 2022[31] with a view to building service and function areas over the following years. These include data analytics, intelligence, and enforcement services, with functions focused on performance and practice standards and capability.

2.8 The Essence of Fraud Deterrence

In this section, we will consider the essence of fraud deterrence. We often hear and read about academics and the like stating the value of deterrence. But what does this really mean, and why is it important?

2.8.1 Defining Fraud Deterrence

In the recently published GCFP standards for Practitioners in Prevention, the GCFP states that:

> the aim of deterrence controls are to neutralise the fraudster's intent. The individual should work with behavioural scientists and communications teams to successfully embed deterrence controls and messaging throughout the organisation.

KEY POINTS—DETERRENCE

Deterrence can be characterized in many cases as:

> 'I would commit this fraud. I could do it, and have no moral objection, but I have no intent because I fear x'

or

> 'I could commit fraud, but the complexity/cost to undertake is too high in comparison to the return on my investment, which makes this fraud unappealing'.[32]

---

[31] More information can be found about the PSFA in s. 2.7 and at www.gov.uk/government/organisations/public-sector-fraud-authority (accessed 17 July 2023).

[32] GOV.UK, 'Fraud Prevention Standard for Counter Fraud Professionals' (17 July 2023), www.gov.uk/government/publications/government-counter-fraud-profession-standards-and-guidance/fraud-prevention-standard-for-counter-fraud-professionals-html (accessed 30 March 2023).

From this description, it is clear that to deter a fraudster, or a group of fraudsters, specific and proactive steps must be taken. If we were to look to the dictionary to clarify the essence and meaning of deterrence we learn, it is to 'discourage (someone) from doing something by instilling doubt or fear of the consequences'.[33]

As well as steps being proactive, sanctions must be widely publicized, unavoidable, and severe enough to put off perpetrators from committing further or future fraud.

2.9 How to Deter People from Committing Fraud

In the UK, the College of Policing considered how to deter offenders more generally,[34] and concluded that the key way to achieve this was to increase the likelihood of a perpetrator being caught, as well as reducing the opportunity for crime to be committed.

In the public sector, one tool that aids prevention and deterrence of fraud is the evaluation of controls and amendments put in place to reduce the opportunities.

Further guidance from the GCFP sets out that the fraud practitioner should embed deterrence controls throughout business processes to deter fraudulent intent. This may include, but is not limited to:

- clear consequences of non-compliance;
- statements communicating that fraud is an offence;
- statements communicating that the organization will actively detect fraud and act;
- statements communicating that the organization will consider applying sanctions, including criminal prosecutions, where appropriate;
- statements to influence emotions appealing to morals and ethics (i.e. how fraud impacts victims).

The statements will be most effective when coming from the executive level of the business and cascaded all the way down through the organization. It is important that the tone from the top of the organization clearly sets out the consequences of non-compliance, and communication to clearly set out via the fraud response plan, action that will be taken to detect and respond to fraud.

A clearly documented and available to all staff policy on *sanctions and redress* is also a key tool in the organization's armour to deter individuals from committing fraud. The range of sanctions should include administrative, recourse to civil redress, as well as being clear that criminal action will be taken for the most egregious of cases. A policy setting out when and how sanctions will be applied should be transparent, and regularly updated with input from the counter fraud team(s) working alongside the legal function, to ensure it is current and considering any

[33] *Oxford Dictionary* (2023), https://languages.oup.com/google-dictionary-en/ (accessed 17 July 2023).

[34] College of Policing, 'What Stops People Offending?' (1 July 2021), www.college.police.uk/research/what-works-policing-reduce-crime/what-stops-people-offending (accessed 17 July 2023).

opportunities to amend and improve the robustness of the sanctions and penalties available.

Alongside a clear policy, it is equally important to then consider the communication and amplification of any action taken against those that commit fraud. This is a further deterrent tool, which will dissuade others from committing offences, when they are aware that the organization in question does act when fraud is detected. As recognized in the Fraud Advisory Panel guidance 'Fraud Communications', raising the profile of action taken will keep the issue of fraud in people's minds, making them also more likely to spot it and report it.[35]

2.10 The Government Counter Fraud Profession (GCFP)

The GCFP is a structure for counter fraud professionals across central government and beyond in the UK and is believed to be the first of its kind across the world.[36]

It brings the counter fraud community together under a common set of standards and structures, with the overall aim of developing that community as they focus on protecting public services and fighting economic crime.

The GCFP was established formally in 2018, the coming together of then eighteen public sector organizations to develop a structure that allowed individuals working in counter fraud to be able to self-assess against a common set of criteria, codified in professional standards. At the time of writing, membership was approximately 7,000 strong, across fifty-nine organizations, across central/local government and some policing units.

As part of this evolving community, members will gain recognition and credibility for their specialist skill set, and will have access to the standards, guidance, and products to help members develop their own career—not just with a focus on investigation, but now with a move towards new areas of counter fraud, including measurement, risk, culture, and prevention.

By ensuring that organizations across government know how to effectively prevent and tackle fraud, the GCFP puts HM Government in a much stronger position to deal with the challenges presented by fraud, bribery, and corruption; and enhances the UK's reputation as a global leader in this field.

2.10.1 GCFP 2023–2025 Strategy

The GCFP released a new strategy, which was published in 2023. This sets out five core areas of focus, with an overall emphasis on developing skills, competencies, and

[35] www.fraudadvisorypanel.org/wp-content/uploads/2020/01/Counter-Fraud-Communications.pdf (accessed 18 July 2023).

[36] GOV.UK, 'GCFP Strategy 2023–2025' (2 March 2023), www.gov.uk/government/publications/government-counter-fraud-profession-strategy-2023-2025 (accessed 18 July 2023).

career pathways in counter fraud, so beyond investigation only. This includes a focus on risk, prevention, measurement, and culture. The strategy outlines the key objectives against each core area of focus and includes the ambition to broaden training for members, including bespoke leadership training (counter fraud leader's programmes), and the development of fraud risk assessment and fraud loss measurement training too. Alongside this, the strategy sets out the ambition to focus on future talent management and supporting career development for those working in counter fraud.

2.10.2 **Routes to Membership**

Public sector counter fraud professionals have a number of routes to becoming a member of the GCFP. These include the following areas: investigation, intelligence, counter fraud, leadership management and strategy, with membership levels available at foundation and practitioner level, and entry/established for leadership.

Checklist—GCFP routes to membership

There are three routes currently into the GCFP:

- Route 1—an enhanced collective membership route for individuals in organizations who meet the required criteria. This route enables members to be recognized in investigation and intelligence disciplines in foundation and practitioner.
- Route 2—The second route is for senior civil servants across government who upon successful completion of the counter fraud leadership programme can gain individual membership to the profession at entry and established levels.
- Route 3—The third route open is for those successfully completing the counter fraud investigation apprenticeship, gaining practitioner level membership on successful completion.

The routes are set out in the Figure 2.3. The GCF Profession membership is currently available for central/local government organizations and policing units. The aim is to open up more routes including more disciplines (e.g. counter fraud, bribery and corruption) and to reach more sectors beyond 2025, following the short-term position which is to focus on development of training and guidance in risk and measurement and a new apprenticeship for counter fraud with a focus on prevention, risk assessment, and measurement.

2.11 **Understanding the (GCFP) Counter Fraud Standards**

The GCFP develops practice guidance and standards for professionals, which are released under open government licence for use across sectors.

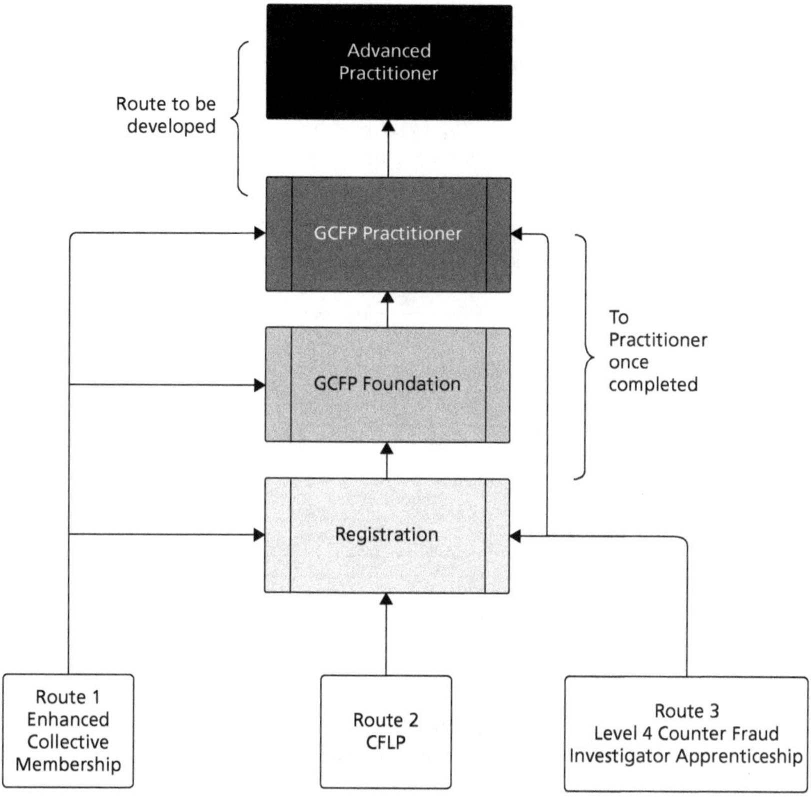

Figure 2.3 Entry routes into the GCFP

The GCFP standards and guidance are designed to present a consistent approach to countering fraud and economic crime and raise the capability of individuals and, through this, increase the quality of organizations' counter fraud work.

The GCFP standards include guidance on products, processes for practitioners in a range of disciplines as set out in the framework (see s. 2.6) and set out the knowledge, skills, and competencies required to achieve recognition at particular levels, and gain membership for that discipline. These can be utilized by practitioners to self-evaluate their current competence, and target learning to focus on specific areas as needed. The process and product aspects of the guidance help steer practitioners on the best practice approaches for that discipline, helping to ensure a consistent approach that is most effective for the organization in tackling fraud.

The standards for practitioners are shared under open government licence on www.gov.uk to allow private sector organizations and academics to develop learning and development products and tools to bring wider consistency to counter fraud practice across sectors.

The GCFP standards cover several disciplines and are set out in Figure 2.4.

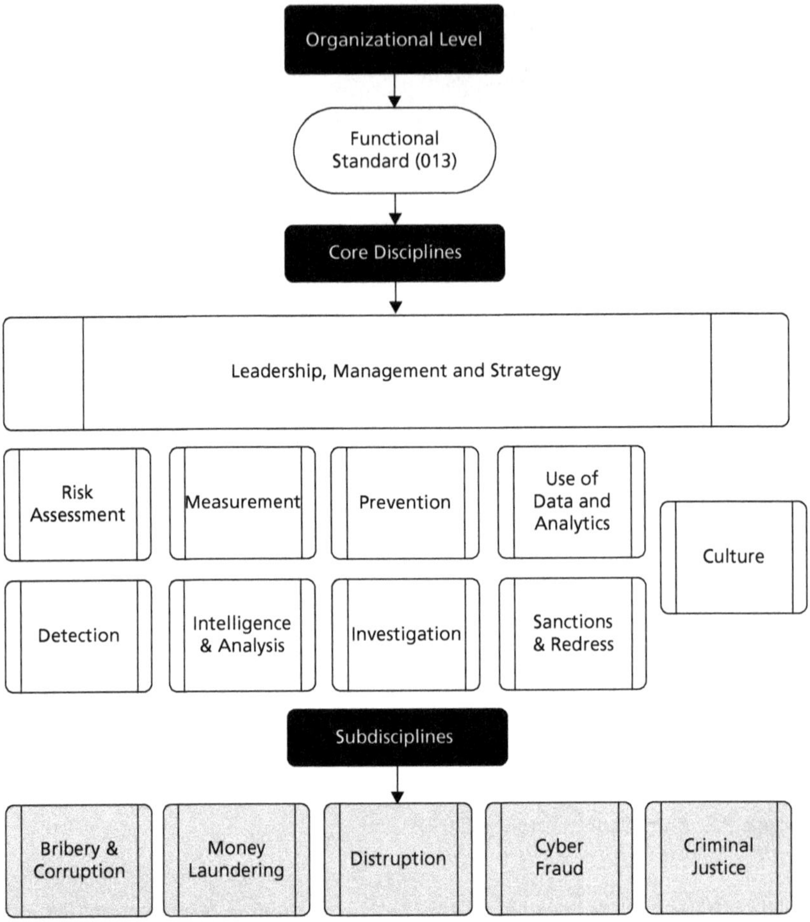

Figure 2.4 GCFP Framework

The standards are not intended to cover every eventuality or every specific issue that may arise and should be adapted to the organization's resources and fraud risk profile.

3

Legislative Frameworks

Blackstone's Counter Fraud Professionals' Handbook. Michael J. Betts, Laura Eshelby, and David Whitehouse-Hayes, Oxford University Press.
DOI: 10.1093/9780191996955.003.0003

3.1 Introduction

It is important that counter fraud practitioners understand relevant legislation that allows them to gather evidence, share or access data, and that they understand their obligations onwards in relation to disclosure. There are equally important frameworks safeguarding how we operate in both civil and criminal contexts. For the purpose of this chapter, we will focus on criminal legislation and procedures.

The importance of understanding the legislative framework relevant to fraud investigation cannot be underestimated. Without an awareness of legislation, practitioners put themselves at risk of acting without a lawful basis and open themselves and their organization up to legal challenge, including judicial review. This can be costly, time-consuming, and reputationally damaging for individuals and organizations alike.

KEY POINTS—ESSENTIAL FRAUD-RELATED LEGISLATION

In England and Wales, the essential legislation relating to the investigation of fraud-related offending includes:

- Fraud Act 2006, www.legislation.gov.uk/ukpga/2006/35/contents (accessed 25 July 2023);
- Proceeds of Crime Act 2002 (POCA 2002), www.legislation.gov.uk/ukpga/2002/29/contents (accessed 25 July 2023);
- Computer Misuse Act 1990 (CMA 1990), www.legislation.gov.uk/ukpga/1990/18/contents (accessed 25 July 2023);
- Bribery Act 2010, www.legislation.gov.uk/ukpga/2010/23/contents (accessed 25 July 2023);
- Criminal Procedure and Investigations Act 1996 (CPIA), see www.legislation.gov.uk/ukpga/1996/25/contents (accessed 25 July 2023);
- Public Interest Disclosure Act 1998 (PIDA 1998), www.legislation.gov.uk/ukpga/1998/23/contents (accessed 25 July 2023).

3.2 The Role of Managers and Senior Investigating Officers (SIOs)

Alongside the counter fraud practitioner, it is equally important that managers or SIOs give direction as to what they believe is the most appropriate course of action to take and advise others.

Checklist—Essential Knowledge for Managers and Leaders

It is essential that managers and leaders should understand the following:

- legal definitions of offences likely to be encountered;
- points that must be proven;
- potential defences available from statute and case law;
- powers that support and regulate the investigation process;
- relevant rules of evidence.

Without this required level of knowledge, managers and leaders may take action that is unlawful or gather material in such a way as to make it unlikely that it will be admissible as evidence in court.

Maintaining a current knowledge of the relevant legislation will support and assist managers and leaders to deploy the full range of investigative techniques and ensure that investigations are able to withstand the high level of scrutiny applied to them by the criminal justice system and tribunals.

3.3 Fraud-Related Legislation

The main legislation covering fraud-related offending in England, Wales, and Northern Ireland is the Fraud Act 2006.

3.3.1 The Fraud Act 2006

The Fraud Act provides for a general offence of fraud with three ways of committing it, which are by false representation, by failing to disclose information, and by abuse of position. It also incorporates offences of obtaining services dishonestly and of possessing, making, and supplying articles for use in frauds. It also contains an offence of fraudulent trading applicable to non-corporate traders. The maximum sentence for offences against ss. 2–4 is ten years.

KEY POINTS—THE REPEAL OF THEFT ACT 1968 OFFENCES

The Fraud Act 2006 (the Act), which came into force on 15 January 2007, applies in England, Wales, and Northern Ireland, and repealed:

- the deception offences in ss. 15, 15A, 16, and 20(2) of the Theft Act 1968 (c. 60);
- ss. 15, 15A, 16, and 19(2) of the Theft Act (Northern Ireland) 1969 (c. 16 (NI));
- ss. 1 and 2 of the Theft Act 1978 (c. 31);
- articles 3 and 4 of the Theft (Northern Ireland) Order 1978 (SI 1978/1407 (NI 23)).

Each section of the Fraud Act 2006 (the Act)[1] either details the specific offences or states the relevant definitions, they are as set out below.

3.3.1.1 **Fraud (s. 1)**

A person is guilty of fraud if they are in breach of any of the sections listed in subs. (2) which provide for different ways of committing the offence.

The sections are:

(1) s. 2 (fraud by false representation);
(2) s. 3 (fraud by failing to disclose information);
(3) s. 4 (fraud by abuse of position).

3.3.1.2 **Fraud by false representation (s. 2)**

A person is in breach of this section if they:

- make a false representation;
- knowing that the representation was or might be untrue or misleading;
- acted dishonestly;
- intend to make a gain for himself or another, to cause loss to another, or to expose another to risk of loss.

There are three key elements of the offence as detailed in Figure 3.1.

KEY POINTS—TEST FOR DISHONESTY

Court of Appeal in *R* v. *Barton and Booth* (2020)

- A change to the test for dishonesty followed a case brought by the Crown Prosecution Service (CPS) about a dishonest care homeowner who defrauded wealthy residents of more than £4 million clarified the definition of dishonesty in criminal law.
- The Court of Appeal heard appeals against the convictions of David Barton and Rosemary Booth for their sustained frauds against older people.
- The Court's ruling means that juries must consider the facts in a case, including the defendant's knowledge or belief in the facts, before deciding whether the defendant's behaviour is dishonest by the standards of ordinary reasonable people.[2]

[1] Contains public sector information licensed under the Open Government Licence v3.0 www.nationalarchives.gov.uk/doc/open-government-licence/version/3/ (accessed 25 July 2023).

[2] CPS, 'Update: CPS Case Redefines the Legal Test for "Dishonesty" in Criminal Law' (23 June 2020), www.cps.gov.uk/cps/news/update-cps-case-redefines-legal-test-dishonesty-criminal-law (accessed 26 July 2023).

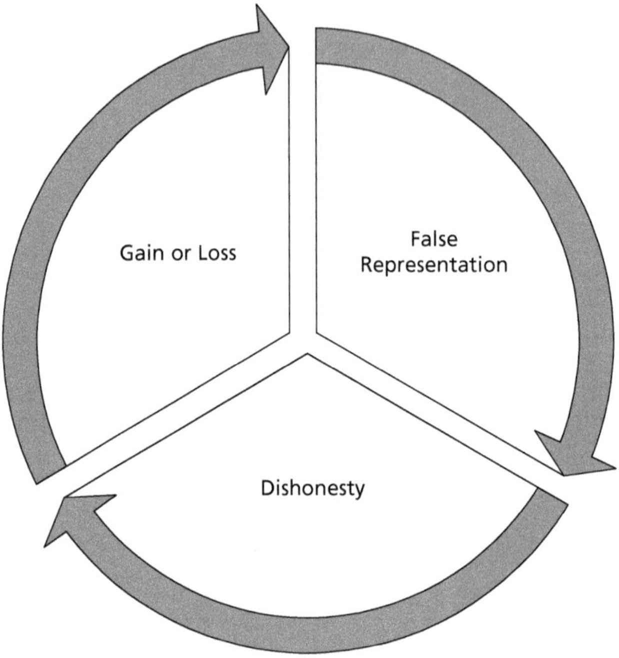

Figure 3.1 Fraud Act 2006, s. 2 key elements

3.3.1.3 Fraud by failing to disclose information (s. 3)

A person is in breach of this section if they:

- failed to disclose information to another person;
- when they are under a legal duty to disclose that information;
- dishonestly intending, by that failure, to make a gain or cause a loss.

The key elements of this offence are shown in Figure 3.2.

The term 'legal duty' has a wide interpretation and includes where there is a fiduciary relationship between two or more parties.

Whereas the s. 2 offence of fraud by false representation is often an active offence (the act of false representation), this offence is often where the offender fails to disclose something they should.

3.3.1.4 Fraud by abuse of position (s. 4)

A person is in breach of this section if they:

- occupy a position in which he was expected to safeguard, or not to act against, the financial interests of another person;
- abuse that position;
- dishonestly;

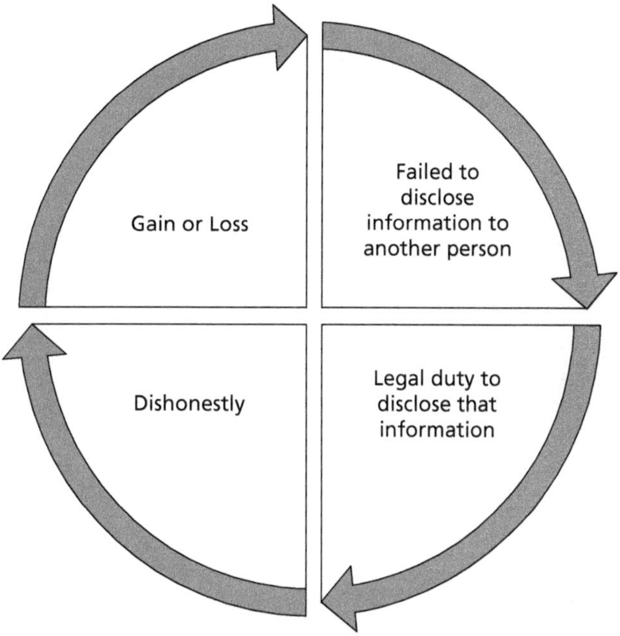

Figure 3.2 Fraud Act 2006, s. 3 key elements

- intending by that abuse to make a gain/cause a loss.

The abuse may consist of an omission rather than an act, the key elements of this offence are shown in Figure 3.3.

3.3.1.5 **Defining gain and loss (s. 5)**

Section 5 of the Act defines the meaning of 'gain' and 'loss' for the purposes of ss. 2–4. Under these definitions, 'gain' and 'loss' are limited to gain and loss in money or other property; this includes any such gain or loss whether temporary or permanent.

3.3.1.6 **Possession etc. of articles for use in frauds (s. 6)**

Section 6 of the Act makes it an offence for a person to possess or have under his control any article for use in the course of or in connection with any fraud. For the Fraud Act offence, the articles at the place of abode, or any other location under the control of the offender.

3.3.1.7 **Making or supplying articles for use in frauds (s. 7)**

Section 7 of the Act makes it an offence to make, adapt, supply, or offer to supply any article knowing that it is designed or adapted for use in the course of or in connection with fraud, or intending it to be used to commit or facilitate fraud.

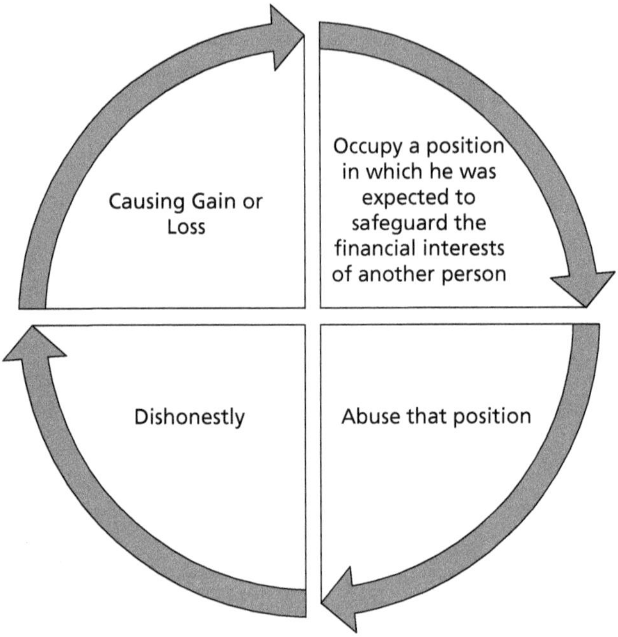

Figure 3.3 Fraud Act 2006, s. 4 key elements

3.3.1.8 **Article (s. 8)**

Section 8 extends the meaning of 'article' for the purposes of ss. 6 and 7 and certain other connected provisions so as to include any program or data held in electronic form.

3.3.1.9 **Participating in fraudulent business carried on by sole traders etc. (s. 9)**

Section 9 of the Act makes it an offence for a person knowingly to be a party to the carrying on of fraudulent business where the business is not carried on by a company or (broadly speaking) a corporate body and includes sole traders, partnerships, trusts, and companies registered overseas. This offence mirrors the existing offence that applies in the case of fraudulent businesses carried on by companies and certain other corporate bodies.

3.3.1.10 Participating in fraudulent business carried on by company etc.: penalty (s. 10)

(repealed)

3.3.1.11 **Obtaining services dishonestly (s. 11)**

Section 11 of the Act makes it an offence for any person, by any dishonest act, to obtain services for which payment is required, with intent to avoid payment. The person must know that the services are made available on the basis that they are chargeable, or that they might be. It is not possible to commit the offence by omission alone and it can be committed only where the dishonest act was done with the intent not to pay for the services as expected. This new offence contains no deception element.

3.3.1.12 **Liability of company officers for offences by company (s. 12)**

This section provides that if persons who have a specified corporate role are party to the commission of an offence under the Act by their body corporate, they will be liable to be charged for the offence as well as the corporation. This offence applies to directors, managers, secretaries, and other similar officers of companies and other bodies corporate.

3.3.1.13 **Evidence (s. 13)**

Under this section there are protections for a person from incriminating themselves or their spouse or civil partner for offences under the Act and related offences, while still being obliged to cooperate with certain civil proceedings relating to property.[3]

3.3.2 **Fraud Act 2006: Summary**

The Fraud Act was based on the recommendations in the Law Commission's report on fraud in 2002 and a Home Office consultation in May 2004 entitled 'Fraud Law Reform', which proposed reform on the basis that the deception-based offences in the Theft Acts 1968–78 which were deemed too specific, overlapped, and were outdated.

The objectives of the Act were to clarify and modernize the law, and to make fraud law more straightforward for juries and practitioners. The offences contained in the Act were intended to provide a modern and flexible law of fraud capable of combating the increasing sophistication of fraudulent activity and the rapid technological advances made by fraudsters.

In summary the Fraud Act repealed many aspects of the Theft Act 1968, which is all documented throughout the Act clearly for practical purposes.

In a post-legislative assessment of the Act, in 2012,[4] opinions were sought from a range of practitioners and stakeholders involved in the prosecution of fraud cases, including the City of London Police (COLP), the Serious Fraud Office (SFO), the Attorney General's Office (AGO), and the Department for Work and Pensions (DWP).

There was agreement that the Act had simplified the law relating to fraud and had provided a suite of offences that are straightforward to apply and can be understood by practitioners. The general nature of the offences allows prosecutors to use them

[3] See Fraud Act 2006, ss. 14–16, which set out minor amendments, commencement, and short title for further information and research for readers of this book

[4] https://assets.publishing.service.gov.uk/government/uploads/system/uploads/attachment_data/file/1081362/fraud-memo-2022-print.pdf (accessed 25 July 2023).

in a diverse range of cases. It also allowed them to respond quickly to emerging fraudulent behaviours rather than waiting for the creation of a new offence.

KEY POINTS—2002 MINISTRY OF JUSTICE FRAUD ACT 2006 MEMORANDUM

In 2022 the Ministry of Justice (MoJ) published a memorandum[5] on the Fraud Act 2006 to assess whether the Fraud Act 2006 remained an effective tool for tackling fraud that is able to cope with rapidly developing technology.

The memorandum concluded:

> The nature of fraud cases makes them difficult to prove. The Fraud Act 2006 was enacted to give law enforcement the tools they needed to tackle it effectively. The responses obtained in the review show that fifteen years on, the Fraud Act 2006 continues to deliver on its objectives and is still regarded as an incredibly useful piece of legislation.
>
> The offences are wide enough to cover most fraudulent offending, including those which are digitally enabled, and flexible enough to adapt to developing technology. Practitioners are satisfied that the core offences are fit for purpose and meet their needs and do not require amendment. Respondents overwhelming felt that the common law offence of conspiracy to defraud continues to be useful and should remain. Its ability to address the complexity and scale of multi-handed frauds is not otherwise capable of being caught under the Act is invaluable and it should simply be left alone.[6]

3.4 Proceeds of Crime Act 2002 (POCA 2002)

The POCA 2002[7] is an Act of the Parliament of the UK which provides for the confiscation or civil recovery of the proceeds from crime and contains the principal money laundering legislation in the UK. It was originally introduced to support the aims of the Asset Recovery Agency, and subsequently has been utilized by law enforcement and crime fighting agencies across the UK including the National Crime Agency, SFO, and policing financial crime units. When bodies are being considered for addition to the schedule, there is a public consultation.[8]

---

[5] MoJ, 'Post-Legislative Assessment of the Fraud Act 2006: Memorandum to the House of Lords Select Committee on the Fraud Act 2006 and Digital Fraud' (2022), https://assets.publishing.service.gov.uk/government/uploads/system/uploads/attachment_data/file/1081360/fraud-memo-2022.pdf (accessed 25 July 2023).

[6] MoJ, 'Post-Legislative Assessment of the Fraud Act 2006'.

[7] POCA 2002, www.legislation.gov.uk/ukpga/2002/29/introduction (accessed 25 July 2023).

[8] Home Office, 'Changes to Bodies Granted Investigatory and Other Powers under the Proceeds of Crime Act 2002', www.gov.uk/government/consultations/proceeds-of-crime-act-2002-accredited-financial-investigations-powers/changes-to-bodies-granted-investigatory-and-other-powers-under-the-proceeds-of-crime-act-2002 (accessed 25 July 2023).

The POCA sets out the legislative scheme for the recovery of criminal assets with criminal confiscation being the most commonly used power.[9] Confiscation occurs after a conviction has taken place.

Other means of recovering the proceeds of crime which do not require a conviction are provided for in the Act, namely civil recovery, cash seizure, and taxation powers. The aim of the asset recovery schemes in POCA is to deny criminals the use of their assets, recover the proceeds of crime, and disrupt and deter criminality.

The Act also provides for a number of investigative powers, such as search and seizure powers, and powers to apply for production orders, disclosure orders, and allows for the 'restraint' or 'freezing' of assets to prevent dissipation of assets prior to a confiscation order being made.

3.4.1 **POCA 2002 Money Laundering (Part 7)**

Part 7 of POCA 2002 provides for various money laundering offences. A person commits an offence if he/she:

- conceals, disguises, converts, or transfers criminal property or removes it from England and Wales or Scotland or Northern Ireland;
- enters into or becomes concerned in an arrangement which he or she knows, or suspects facilitates the acquisition, retention, use or control of criminal property;
- acquires, uses, or has possession of criminal property.

Checklist—POCA 2002 Money Laundering Offences

Specific criminal offences detailed in Part 7 POCA 2002:

- POCA 2002, s. 327 (concealing etc.), www.legislation.gov.uk/ukpga/2002/29/section/327 (accessed 6 September 2023);
- POCA 2002, s. 328 (arrangements), www.legislation.gov.uk/ukpga/2002/29/section/328 (accessed 6 September 2023);
- POCA 2002, s. 329 (acquisition, use, and possession), www.legislation.gov.uk/ukpga/2002/29/section/329 (accessed 25 July 2023);
- POCA 2002, s. 330 (failure to disclose regulated sector), www.legislation.gov.uk/ukpga/2002/29/section/330 (accessed 25 July 2023);
- POCA 2002, s. 331 (failure to disclose nominated officers in the regulated sector), www.legislation.gov.uk/ukpga/2002/29/section/331 (accessed 25 July 2023);

[9] https://assets.publishing.service.gov.uk/government/uploads/system/uploads/attachment_data/file/317904/Fact_Sheet_-_Overview_of_POCA__2_.pdf (accessed 25 July 2023).

- POCA 2002, s. 332 (failure to disclose other nominated officers), www.legislation.gov.uk/ukpga/2002/29/section/332 (accessed 25 July 2023);
- POCA 2002, s.333 (tipping off) www.legislation.gov.uk/ukpga/2002/29/section/333 (accessed 25 July 2023);
- POCA 2002, s. 333A (tipping off: regulated sector), www.legislation.gov.uk/ukpga/2002/29/section/333A (accessed 25 July 2023).

3.4.2 Reporting Suspicious Activity

Part 7 of POCA 2002 requires financial institutions and businesses in the regulated sector to report to the UK Financial Intelligence Unit, which is part of the National Crime Agency, any suspicions about criminal property or money laundering. Even if a person is not in the regulated sector, they must report any suspicions if they come across any suspicious activity through their trade, business, or profession.

3.4.3 POCA 2002 Part 8: Investigations

Part 8 of POCA sets out confiscation, civil recovery, detained cash, money laundering, and exploitation proceeds investigations. It also provides for the investigative powers to conduct these investigations, including the powers to obtain production orders, search warrants, disclosure orders,[10] customer information orders, and account monitoring orders. Only an appropriate officer may make applications for these investigative tools to a court. Applications for orders in civil recovery and exploitation proceeds investigations must be made to the High Court. All other applications may be made to the Crown Court. Powers of entry are provided under search warrants and in limited circumstances.

3.5 Computer Misuse Act (CMA) 1980

The CMA 1980[11] is concerned with the unauthorized access to IT systems and data that an individual would not be allowed to access. The offences covered under the act range from unauthorized access to computer material through to unauthorized access with the intention of committing serious harm to individuals, the economy, the environment, and human welfare. The maximum sentences for each of the offence reflects the gravity of the offending, as shown in Figure 3.4.

[10] Disclosure orders require an application by a 'relevant authority', which can have a variety of meanings (s. 357(7)).

[11] www.legislation.gov.uk/ukpga/1990/18/contents (accessed 25 July 2023).

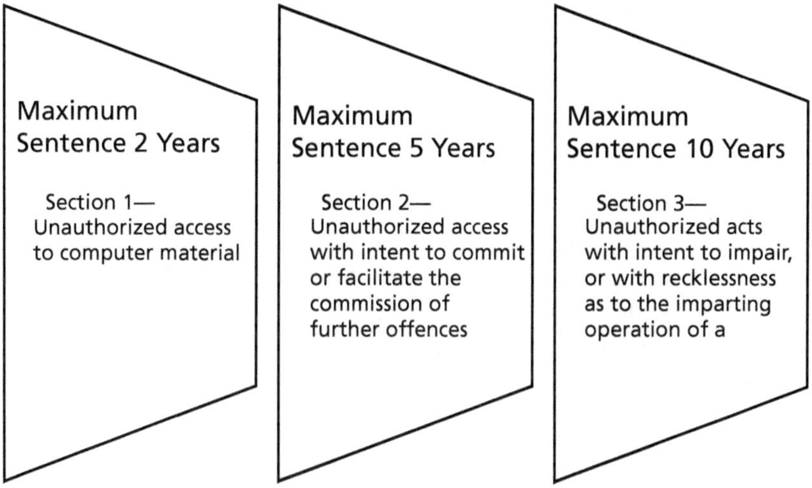

Figure 3.4 CMA 1980 maximum sentences (ss. 1–3)

We explore these sections in more detail below.

3.5.1 Unauthorized Access to Computer Material (s. 1)

The offence is made out, once a defendant has caused a computer, which would include his own computer, to perform a function with intent to secure unauthorized access or enable unauthorized access to be secured. The access to the program or data which the accused intends to secure must be 'unauthorized' access.

There are two elements to consider:

(1) there must be knowledge that the intended access was unauthorized;
(2) there must have been an intention to secure access to any program or data held in a computer.

When dealing with cases involving employees careful consideration should be given to the employee's contract of employment, together with any surrounding information (e.g. oral advice given or office practices), in order to determine whether the employer had clearly defined the limits of the employee's authority. Such cases normally depend on whether the evidence available demonstrates sufficiently that the conduct complained of was unauthorized.

The maximum penalty on indictment is two years' imprisonment.

3.5.2 Unauthorized Access with Intent to Commit or Facilitate the Commission of Further Offences (s. 2)

The offence under s. 2 is committing the unauthorized access offence under s. 1 with intent to commit or facilitate the commission of a further offence capable of carrying a prison sentence of five years or more. It is not necessary to prove that the intended further offence has actually been committed.[12]

The maximum penalty on indictment is five years' imprisonment.

3.5.3 **Unauthorized Acts with Intent to Impair, or with Recklessness as to the Imparting Operation of a Computer etc. (s. 3)**

The effect of s. 3 is that a person commits an offence if he performs any unauthorized act in relation to a computer, knowing it to be unauthorized, if he intends by doing the act to do one of the things set out in s. 3(2), or if he is reckless as to whether by doing the act he will do one of the things set out in s. 3(2).

Examples of this are deliberate or reckless impairment of a computer's operation, preventing or hindering access to computer material by a legitimate user, or impairing the operation or reliability of computer-held material. The offender must know that the act was unauthorized.

The maximum sentence on indictment is ten years' imprisonment.

3.5.4 **Unauthorized Acts Causing, or Creating Risk of Serious Damage (s. 3ZA)**

Section 41(2) of the Serious Crime Act 2015 inserted s. 3ZA, with effect from 3 May 2015. The maximum sentence on indictment is fourteen years, unless the offence caused or created a significant risk of serious damage to human welfare or national security, as defined in s. 3(a)–(b), in which case a person guilty of the offence is liable to imprisonment for life.

Section 3ZA is designed to cater for computer misuse, where the impact is to cause damage to, for example, critical national infrastructure[13] and where the maximum penalty of ten years available under s. 3 may be inadequate.

3.5.5 **Making, Supplying, or Obtaining Articles for Use in an Offence under s. 1, 3, or 3ZA (s. 3(A))**

The maximum sentence on indictment is two years' imprisonment. The rationale behind the creation of this offence is the market in electronic malware or 'hacker tools', which can be used for breaking into or compromising computer systems.

[12] It is notable that a person found not guilty of a s. 2 or 3 offence by a jury can be convicted of a s. 1 offence (Criminal Law Act 1967, s. 6(3)).

[13] When considering, the definition of 'critical national infrastructure' (in line with European Directive (2013/40/EU)) it could be understood to be an asset, system, or part thereof located in member states, which is essential for the maintenance of vital societal functions, health, safety, security, economic or social well-being of people, such as power plants, transport networks, or government networks, and the disruption or destruction of which would have a significant impact in a member state as a result of the failure to maintain those functions.

Section 3A (2) of the CMA covers the supplying or offering to supply an article 'likely' to be used to commit, or assist in the commission of an offence, contrary s. 1 or 3.

3.5.6 **CMA 1980 Summary**

In a modern fraud response, it is important that practitioners and managers alike have a full understanding of the CMA1980, and how it can be applied in cases to seek complementary and alternative sanctions when offences occur. The legislation is substantial and detailed in nature, which is necessary given the complexity of investigating and prosecuting for such offences.

3.6 **Criminal Procedure and Investigations Act 1996 (CPIA 1996)**

The statutory framework for criminal investigations and disclosure is contained in the CPIA 1996.[14] CPIA aims to ensure that criminal investigations are conducted in a fair, objective, and thorough manner, and requires prosecutors to disclose to the defence material which has not previously been disclosed to the accused and which might reasonably be considered capable of undermining the case for the prosecution against the accused or of assisting the case for the accused.

The CPIA therefore requires a timely dialogue between the prosecution, defence, and the court to enable the prosecution to properly identify such material.

Part 2 of the CPIA 1996 makes provision for the publication of a Code of Practice which sets out how to record, retain and reveal to the prosecutor material obtained in a criminal investigation, the most recent version being published in September 2020.

In May 2014, the Magistrates' Court Disclosure Review recommended a streamlined procedure in summary cases that are expected to end in a guilty plea, so that a schedule of unused material need not be served in such cases. To this end, it recommended amendments to the code, some of which are incorporated in the revised code.

KEY POINTS—CIVIL PROCEDURE RULES 1998

The Civil Procedure Rules provide guidance and obligations for those in the pursuit of civil remedy and undertaking investigations:

- s. 31.2 defines disclosure as, 'A party discloses a document by stating that the document exists or has existed'. The obligation is on parties to adhere to this throughout proceedings.

[14] CPIA 1996, www.legislation.gov.uk/ukpga/1996/25/contents (accessed 25 July 2023).

For criminal procedures, there is extensive guidance issued by the CPS, as well as the Attorney General's Department, detailing the approach to disclosure during the criminal process.

Further Reading

- CPIA 1996—the Act that details the provisions of criminal procedure, roles, responsibilities, and obligations relating to the disclosure of material. See www.legislation.gov.uk/ukpga/1996/25/contents (accessed 6 September 2023).
- CPS, 'Disclosure—A Guide to "Reasonable Lines of Enquiry" and Communications Evidence' (24 July 2018). This sets out guidance as to the approach that ought to be adopted by prosecutors, in accordance with their duties under the CPIA 1996, and the relevant Codes issued under and in pursuance to that Act. See www.cps.gov.uk/legal-guidance/disclosure-guide-reasonable-lines-enquiry-and-communications-evidence#:~:text=In%20conducting%20an%20investigation%2C%20the,depend%20on%20the%20particular%20circumstances (accessed 25 July 2023).
- CPS, 'Disclosure, National Standards' (25 May 2018). This document contains a statement of the national standards for the completion of the MG6 schedules and the Streamlined Disclosure Certificate. See www.cps.gov.uk/legal-guidance/disclosure-national-standards (accessed 25 July 2023).
- CPIA 1996 (s. 23(1)) Code of Practice, www.gov.uk/government/publications/criminal-procedure-and-investigations-act-1996-section-231-code-of-practice (accessed 6 September 2023).

3.6.1 CPIA 1996: Summary

Following the correct procedures and adhering to investigation guidance lines is essential, so as to not undermine your aims and undermine the course of justice. Disclosure is particularly critical for investigations, and above we have set out information in relation to a criminal context. Every unused item should be considered to see if it may support the defence or undermine the prosecution case. Failure to do so can lead to case collapse, reputational damage, and financial consequences for those involved who may seek redress.

3.7 Public Interest Disclosure Act 1998 (PIDA 1998)

The PIDA 1998 was introduced to 'protect individuals who make certain disclosures of information in the public interest; to allow such individuals to bring action in respect of victimization; and for connected purposes'.[15] For the purposes of the Act,

[15] PIDA 1998, www.legislation.gov.uk/ukpga/1998/23/introduction.Accessed (25 July 2023).

protected disclosures are defined as 'a qualifying disclosure (as defined by section 43B) which is made by a worker in accordance with any of sections 43C to 43H'.

Section 43(B) sets out that a 'qualifying disclosure' means any disclosure of information which, in the reasonable belief of the worker making the disclosure, tends to show one or more of the following—

(a) that a criminal offence has been committed, is being committed or is likely to be committed;
(b) that a person has failed, is failing or is likely to fail to comply with any legal obligation to which he is subject;
(c) that a miscarriage of justice has occurred, is occurring or is likely to occur;
(d) that the health or safety of any individual has been, is being or is likely to be endangered;
(e) that the environment has been, is being or is likely to be damaged, or
(f) that information tending to show any matter falling within any one of the preceding paragraphs has been, is being or is likely to be deliberately concealed.

Section 43C–H sets out disclosures may be made to these qualifying groups:

- employer or other responsible person;
- legal adviser;
- Minister of the Crown;
- prescribed person (prescribed by order by Secretary of State);
- in other cases (as set out in s. 43G);
- in circumstances of exceptionally serious failure.

The PIDA 1998 protects any whistle-blowing worker who discloses their concerns in the public interest. This protects whistle-blowers from detrimental treatment by their employer (amending the Employment Rights Act 1996) as a result of making a public interest disclosure.

The Act protects most workers in the public, private, and voluntary sectors. The Act does 'not' apply to genuinely self-employed professionals (other than in the NHS), voluntary workers (including charity trustees and charity volunteers), police officers, or the intelligence services.

The Act protects workers in a number of ways, for example:

- if an employee is dismissed because he has made a protected disclosure that will be treated as unfair dismissal;
- in any event workers are given a new right not to be subjected to any 'detriment' by their employers on the ground that they have made a protected disclosure, and may present a complaint to an employment tribunal if they suffer detriment as a result of making a protected disclosure.

Through the introduction of protection for workers who blow the whistle on wrongdoing within or concerning an organization, the legislation aims to increase the accountability of organizations in the public, private, and voluntary sectors. Charities (as part of the voluntary sector) are within the jurisdiction of the Act.

The Act makes special provision for disclosures to 'prescribed persons'. The Charity Commission is the regulatory body to whom workers can make appropriate disclosures on matters relating to 'the proper administration of charities and funds given, or held, for charitable purposes'.

KEY POINTS—PIDA QUALIFICATION

For a disclosure to be protected by the Act's provisions it must relate to matters that 'qualify' for protection under the Act. Qualifying disclosures are disclosures which the worker believes tends to show that one or more of the following matters is either happening now, took place in the past, or is likely to happen in the future:

- a criminal offence;
- the breach of a legal obligation;
- a miscarriage of justice;
- a danger to the health and safety of any individual;
- damage to the environment; or
- deliberate concealment of information tending to show any of the above five matters.

The key learning here is to understand your obligations and responsibilities as an individual, manager and also part of your wider organization in relation to PIDA. And remember: if a worker experiences any form of reprisal or mistreatment from their employer after raising a concern, they may have the right to compensation at an employment tribunal.

Further Reading

- On PIDA 1998, see Charity Commission for England and Wales, 'The Public Interest Disclosure Act' (15 April 2020), www.gov.uk/government/publications/guidance-for-auditors-and-independent-examiners-of-charities/the-public-interest-disclosure-act--2 (accessed 25 July 2023);
- HM Guidance, 'Report Serious Wrongdoing at a Charity as a Worker or Volunteer' (11 October 2018), www.gov.uk/guidance/report-serious-wrongdoing-at-a-charity-as-a-worker-or-volunteer (accessed 6 September 2023).

3.8 Data Sharing, Legislation, and Regulatory Routes

When considering data sharing it is equally important to consider the practical implications and preparing to do so, alongside ensuring the correct application of relevant legislation and regulations that apply.

As part of the investigation process, information and intelligence may be required to be shared between two or more parties. Under normal circumstances, access to this information may be restricted and denied, but by the creation of a data sharing agreement prescribed parties may agree to share such information for the purpose of a criminal investigation, and sharing it is in the public interest.

To ensure that such data is protected, each party will need to be satisfied about the provenance of the data, how it will be controlled, managed, and how it will be protectively stored especially in relation to sensitive data. Compliance with legislation is important and each party will need to be able to evidence this along with their level of security vetting and clearance.

There is no formal definition of data sharing within the legislation, although the scope of this code is defined by s. 121 of the Data Protection Act 2018 (DPA 2018) as:

> the disclosure of personal data by transmission, dissemination or otherwise making it available.

This means giving personal data to a third party, by whatever means, and includes when you give a third-party access to personal data on or via your IT systems.

Further Reading

- Information Commissioner's Office (ICO), 'Data Sharing: A Code of Practice', https://ico.org.uk/for-organisations/uk-gdpr-guidance-and-resources/data-sharing/data-sharing-a-code-of-practice/ (accessed 25 July 2023);
- ICO, 'UK GDPR Guidance and Resources', https://ico.org.uk/for-organisations/uk-gdpr-guidance-and-resources/ (accessed 25 July 2023);
- Digital Economy Act 2017 (DEA 2017), www.legislation.gov.uk/ukpga/2017/30/contents/enacted (accessed 6 September 2023).

3.8.1 ICO Code and Regulation

This is a statutory code of practice prepared under s. 121 of the DPA 2018. The code contains practical guidance on how to share data fairly and lawfully, and how to meet your accountability obligations. It does not impose any additional barriers to data sharing but will help you comply with your legal obligations under the GDPR and the DPA.

It also contains some optional good practice recommendations, which do not have the status of legal requirements but aim to help you adopt an effective approach to data protection compliance.

In accordance with s. 127 of the DPA, the Commissioner must take the code into account when considering whether you have complied with your data protection obligations in relation to data sharing. In particular, the Commissioner will take the code into account when considering questions of fairness, lawfulness, transparency, and accountability under the GDPR or the DPA. The code can also be used in evidence in court proceedings, and the courts must take its provisions into account wherever relevant

If you do not comply with the guidance in this code, you may find it more difficult to demonstrate that your data sharing is fair, lawful, accountable, and complies with the GDPR or the DPA. For serious breaches of the data protection principles, the ICO may issue fines up to €20 million or 4 per cent of an organization's annual worldwide turnover, whichever is higher.

The government has devised a framework for the sharing of personal data, for defined purposes across the public sector, under the DEA 2017. Data sharing under the DEA powers has to comply with the data protection legislation and with codes of practice that are consistent with this code

3.9 Digital Economy Act 2017 (DEA 2017)

The DEA 2017 provides the legal gateway for specific areas of the public sector to share personal data, and aims to:

- ensure clarity and consistency in how the public sector shares personal data;
- improve public services through the better use of data;
- ensure data privacy.

Part 5 of the DEA focuses on digital government, providing gateways that allow specified public authorities to share data with each other. Some of these gateways enable the sharing of personal data, while others allow the sharing of non-identifying data. Part 5 of the DEA:

- states that all processing of information under the DEA powers must comply with data protection legislation;
- prohibits the disclosure of information where it would contravene data protection legislation.

The powers to share information under Part 5 of the DEA are supplemented by statutory codes of practice (the DEA codes). For example, there is a DEA code for public authorities sharing personal data about aspects of public service delivery. Its purpose is to achieve specified public service delivery objectives:

- to assist people experiencing multiple social or economic disadvantages, or living in fuel or water poverty;
- to reduce and manage debt owed to the public sector;
- to combat fraud against the public sector.

3.10 Memorandums of Understanding

One of the most effective ways of ensuring that the aims and objectives of each party have been agreed, and that the commitment levels have been clearly defined is by means of signing a formal memorandum of understanding (MoU).

While an MoU may not be considered a legally binding document it may protect the interests of the parties involved, and as such should outline any identifiable risks to each party involved (this includes the action or non-action of the other party involved within the agreement itself) and outline what has been put in place to counter such risk.

Such protective measures could be the inclusion of a disclaimer built into the MoU which would restrict the liability of one party due to the mistakes made by another (i.e. providing wrong or misleading information to an actioning agency in order to apply for a warrant).

Checklist—MoUs

Recommended points to include in an MOU:

- identity of those signing the MoU and their organization;
- a brief background of the circumstances leading up to the requirement of the MoU;
- main purpose that the agreement covers (shared aim/objectives);
- explanation of what each party will provide, resource, and achieve;
- data sharing arrangements;
- litigation risk regarding liability of cross-reliance on the material supplied by the other party;
- costs and funding;
- data management compliance—GDPR;
- POCA 2002 asset sharing/compensation;
- prosecution responsibilities;
- operational management and leads;
- security of evidence, communications, and operational procedures;
- disclosure under CPIA 1996;
- media management;
- health and safety considerations/policies;
- dispute resolution;
- commencement, amendment, review dates, and terms of withdrawal.

3.11 Frameworks for Scotland

Most fraud offences in Scotland will be at common law which, similarly to the 'make a gain or cause a loss' aspect of the Fraud Act requires that someone be deceived into acting in a way they would not otherwise have done called 'false pretence'. The offence requires this intention to deceive is proven and can be inferred from their actions; unsuccessful attempts to defraud are prosecutable under the common law.

Other notable criminal offences at common law include 'uttering' when someone tenders a false document to the prejudice of another. Embezzlement is the other notable offence and relates to the fraudulent appropriation of money or property without the consent of the owner.

3.12 Northern Ireland

The Department of Justice (DoJ) is responsible for the administration of the courts through the Northern Ireland Courts and Tribunals Service. DoJ is also responsible for policy and legislation relative to criminal law, legal aid policy, the police, prisons, and probation. The DoJ operates in parallel with the Police Service of Northern Ireland and Public Prosecution Office.

KEY POINTS—CRIMINAL JUSTICE SYSTEM NORTHERN IRELAND

The Criminal Justice System Northern Ireland (CJSNI) is made up of seven main statutory agencies:

(1) Northern Ireland Court Service (NICtS), www.justice-ni.gov.uk/topics/courts-and-tribunals (accessed 6 September 2023);
(2) Northern Ireland Office (NIO), www.gov.uk/government/organisations/northern-ireland-office (accessed 6 September 2023);
(3) Northern Ireland Prison Service (NIPS), www.justice-ni.gov.uk/topics/prisons (accessed 6 September 2023);
(4) Police Service of Northern Ireland (PSNI), www.psni.police.uk/ (accessed 6 September 2023);
(5) Probation Board for Northern Ireland (PBNI), www.pbni.org.uk/ (accessed 6 September 2023);
(6) Public Prosecution Service (PPS), www.ppsni.gov.uk/ (accessed 6 September 2023);
(7) Youth Justice Agency (YJA), www.justice-ni.gov.uk/topics/youth-justice (accessed 6 September 2023).

The CJSNI is responsible for investigating crimes, finding the people who have committed them, and bringing them to justice. It also works to help the victims of crime, and to rehabilitate offenders after their punishment:

The Fraud Act 2006 applies to Northern Ireland, giving statutory definition of the criminal offence of fraud, defining it in three classes—fraud by false representation, fraud by failing to disclose information, and fraud by abuse of position.

If fraud is suspected in Northern Ireland it is reported to the Police Service, who in turn work with UK law enforcement such as Action Fraud and the National Crime Agency to seek outcomes. All other crime types are investigated and responded to by the relevant law enforcement agency in the jurisdiction.

4

The Role of Fraud Risk Assessment

Blackstone's Counter Fraud Professionals' Handbook. Michael J. Betts, Laura Eshelby, and David Whitehouse-Hayes, Oxford University Press.
DOI: 10.1093/9780191996955.003.0004

4.1 **Introduction**

In this chapter we explore both the role and types of fraud risk assessments (FRAs) in countering bribery, fraud, and/or corruption. To effectively manage the bribery, fraud, and corruption threat you should start with a good understanding of how likely you are to be attacked. This remains true whether it is referring to us, as individuals, or the organizations that we are part of.

The more we understand about how people will commit fraud against our organizations, the better we will be able to defend ourselves. We can defend ourselves by making sure we have effective countermeasures (or controls), and we are actively looking for fraud (using our detection techniques) where it is most likely to be happening.

Due to the scale of fraud, it is extremely unlikely that we as individuals or an organization will be able to totally avoid fraud attacks or losses. The five principles of effective fraud management, created by the International Public Sector Fraud Forum (IPSFF), a group of leading public sector fraud experts from the Five Eyes countries, reflect this. The first principle is 'There will always be fraud'.[1] What we can do is lower the likelihood of it happening and lower the impact if and when it does.

Checklist—Five Eye Countries

The Five Eye countries are an alliance with a common purpose who share information and intelligence. They are signatories of the Charter of the Five Eyes Intelligence Oversight and Review Council,[2] the countries are:

(1) Australia;

(2) Canada;

(3) New Zealand;

(4) United Kingdom;

(5) United States.

Fraudsters have increasingly sophisticated (and evolving) techniques to attack their victims. Likewise, those who work to combat fraud and corruption have, and

[1] GOV.UK, 'Fraud in International Aid Principles for Effective Fraud Control (HTML)' (29 September 2023), www.gov.uk/government/publications/international-public-sector-fraud-forum-guidance/fraud-in-international-aid-principles-for-effective-fraud-control-html (accessed 27 January 2024).

[2] Five Eyes Intelligence Oversight and Review Charter of the Five Eyes Intelligence Oversight and Review Council, www.dni.gov/files/ICIG/Documents/Partnerships/FIORC/Signed%20FIORC%20Charter%20with%20Line.pdf (accessed 27 January 2024).

are, developing increasingly sophisticated counter measures for both prevention and detection.

Organizations with access to an effective counter fraud capability are able to draw on these countermeasures and use good FRAs to target them, to give themselves the best protection against the financial losses, and reputational damage, which result from fraud.

KEY POINT—DEFINING FRA

An FRA is a process and product that explores how an organization or entity could be defrauded and to what extent their controls reduce this risk. It helps an organization or entity understand where it is likely to be a victim of fraud, decide whether to take action to reduce this risk, and to effectively target its counter fraud resources.

4.1.1 Understanding Fraud Risk Assessments (FRAs)

The process starts with an understanding of how you are likely to be attacked. The best and most systematic way to build this understanding is through undertaking effective FRA. This codifies how an organization is likely to suffer from bribery, fraud, and corruption, and how effective the countermeasures (or controls) that they have in place are at reducing or stopping these risks. Importantly, a good FRA clearly states what the limitations of those countermeasures (or controls) are. It is in the limitations of our countermeasures (controls) that fraudsters find their opportunities.

4.1.2 The Language of Risk

In looking at risk, we turn to the language of risk; inherent risk, mitigations, controls and countermeasures, residual risk, heat maps, and tolerance. For an experienced fraud risk assessor, familiarity and use of this language is as important as their experience and knowledge of fraud and economic crime and how it transpires.

All people and organizations have some level of residual risk. As the IPSFF principles inform us, it is difficult to create a system where fraud is eliminated or designed out completely.

KEY POINTS—THE IPSFF'S FIVE PRINCIPLES

The IPSFF currently consists of representatives from organizations in the governments of the Five Eye countries. They share best and leading practice in fraud management, the five stated principles for public sector fraud are:[3]

[3] GOV.UK, 'Fraud in International Aid Principles for Effective Fraud Control (HTML)'.

(1) There is always going to be fraud.
(2) Finding fraud is a good thing.
(3) There is no one solution.
(4) Fraud and corruption are ever changing.
(5) Prevention is the most effective way to address fraud and corruption.

The role of those working to counter fraud is to understand this residual risk, and to act. Where action is taken there is a need to be mindful of effectively balancing the reduction in risk, cost, and the accessibility of a service to a customer.

Without a good FRA, there is a good likelihood that organizations will have blind spots where there is a high risk of fraud, which could lead to loss from fraud that they are unaware of and unable to act on.

4.1.3 FRA: Modernizing the Approach to Counter Fraud

The historic way to deal with fraud risk was driven by intelligence, to enable a business to gain an understanding when fraud attacks occurred. This intelligence was then often responded to by acting where fraud had happened by introducing more controls. Intelligence is still incredibly valuable, but a modern fraud response gets ahead by using FRA.

The modern fraud response is more proactive. The way it gets ahead of fraud happening is through understanding the risks by creatively looking at how an organization could be attacked, and then improving controls where it has identified vulnerabilities that it is not willing to tolerate. It enters the mindset of the fraudster, seeking out how to attack, and how to get around the controls.

Historically, there has been no standard way of undertaking FRAs. The process, expertise, and outputs were defined by those undertaking them based on their experiences and understanding. This led to FRAs being of varying quality and using lots of different methodologies and definitions. There was no common understanding of what a good FRA was, and this meant that audit and risk committees could struggle to challenge whether an FRA was accurate, informative, or effective.

4.1.4 Government Counter Fraud Profession (GCFP) FRA Standard

In 2018 the UK government developed a standard for FRA. This set expectations on how FRA should be done, and the skills, knowledge, and experience needed to undertake one effectively. This means that all FRAs that follow the standard are comparable and draw on the same method, which itself draws from best practice. This gives organizations and fraud units greater confidence in their risk assessment, and that the action that it drives will be effective.

This chapter explores how an effective FRA is undertaken and is aligned to the UK government's standard for FRA.

Further Reading

- International Public Sector Fraud Forum, 'A Guide to Managing Fraud for Public Bodies', https://assets.publishing.service.gov.uk/media/6369038cd3bf7f75553de44e/GuideToManagingFraudForPublicBodies.pdf (accessed 27 January 2024);
- GCF Professional Standards and Guidance: Fraud Risk Assessment, https://assets.publishing.service.gov.uk/media/625fd0e0d3bf7f600782fdcb/Fraud-Risk-Assessment-Standards-2022-03-25.pdf (accessed 27 January 2024);
- ACFE, 'Level-Up Your Fraud Risk Assessment' (15 June 2022), www.acfe.com/fraud-resources/fraud-examiner-archives/fraud-examiner-article?s=June-2022-Level-up-your-FRA (accessed 27 January 2024);
- Charter of the Five Eyes Intelligence Oversight and Review Council, www.dni.gov/files/ICIG/Documents/Partnerships/FIORC/Signed%20FIORC%20Charter%20with%20Line.pdf (accessed 27 January 2024).

4.2 Risk, Threat, and Intelligence

To have a common view on fraud risk, it is important that we have common usage of language. In developing our thinking on what we know about fraud (our FRA) three words are recurring: risk, threat, and intelligence.

Historically, risk and threat have been used interchangeably, as have risk and intelligence. The UK government standard on FRA has an agreed definition of risk and threat, which brings clarity to these terms. In addition, below is a definition of intelligence, showing how it is distinct to risk, and how it is complementary.

KEY POINTS—DEFINING RISK AND THREAT

The Government Counter Fraud Profession Fraud Risk Assessor Standard[4] states the following:

- **Risk**—A risk is defined as the possibility of an adverse event occurring or a beneficial opportunity being missed. If realised it may have an effect on the achievement of objectives and can be measured in terms of likelihood and impact.
- **Threat**—A risk arises out of threats. A threat is defined as a person or group, object or activity, which has the potential to cause harm to the achievement of the organisation's objectives. To understand the risk, it is important to consider and assess the capability and intent of those posing the threat.

[4] GCF Profession, 'Fraud Risk Assessment Core Discipline' (March 2022), https://assets.publishing.service.gov.uk/media/625fd0e0d3bf7f600782fdcb/Fraud-Risk-Assessment-Standards-2022-03-25.pdf (accessed 27 January 2024).

So, risk is the event that can happen (and when we assess risk, the likelihood of it happening and the impact if it does). Threat is the capability and intent of people and/or groups to make an event happen. We now turn to intelligence. Where risk is what we think could happen, intelligence is where we have gathered or received information that something has or could happen.

The intelligence we receive and have feeds our FRAs which can drive where we look to gather intelligence. For example, if we have intelligence that tells us an area of the business has allegedly been victim to a certain type of fraud—we would expect this to be seen in the FRA. Conversely, if our FRAs show an area where we have a very high risk, but we do not currently have any intelligence in that area, we may want to target some intelligence effort to proactively gather intelligence. Intelligence has exactly the same relationship (outlined above) with threat and threat assessments.

4.3 Fraud Risk Management vs FRA

When considering FRA, it is important to understand its place in the wider management of fraud risk. It is also important to understand, and have commonality, in the lexicon. FRA is part of fraud risk management. Fraud risk management is the process by which the fraud risks that an organization or entity faces are effectively managed (i.e. reduced or tolerated).

FRA is the critical first part of that process in which an organization or entity gains a deep understanding of the risks of fraud they face, the likelihood of their occurrence, the impact on the organization if they were to happen, the effectiveness of the mitigating controls or countermeasures, and the residual risk faced. This helps an organization to target, prioritize, and make effective their fraud risk management activity.

Figure 4.1 shows the fraud risk management cycle based on the Government Counter Fraud Profession standard for FRA.[5]

The FRA half of the fraud risk management cycle has two distinct steps:

(1) the identification of fraud risks;
(2) the evaluation and prioritization of fraud risks.

The end product is an improved understanding of fraud risks.

4.3.1 How Long to Spend on FRA

As we can see from the fraud risk management cycle, FRA is just a part of what should be done to tackle the risk of fraud in an organization or entity. A good (or great) FRA provides the foundation to be initiative-taking about fraud, but in and

[5] Ibid.

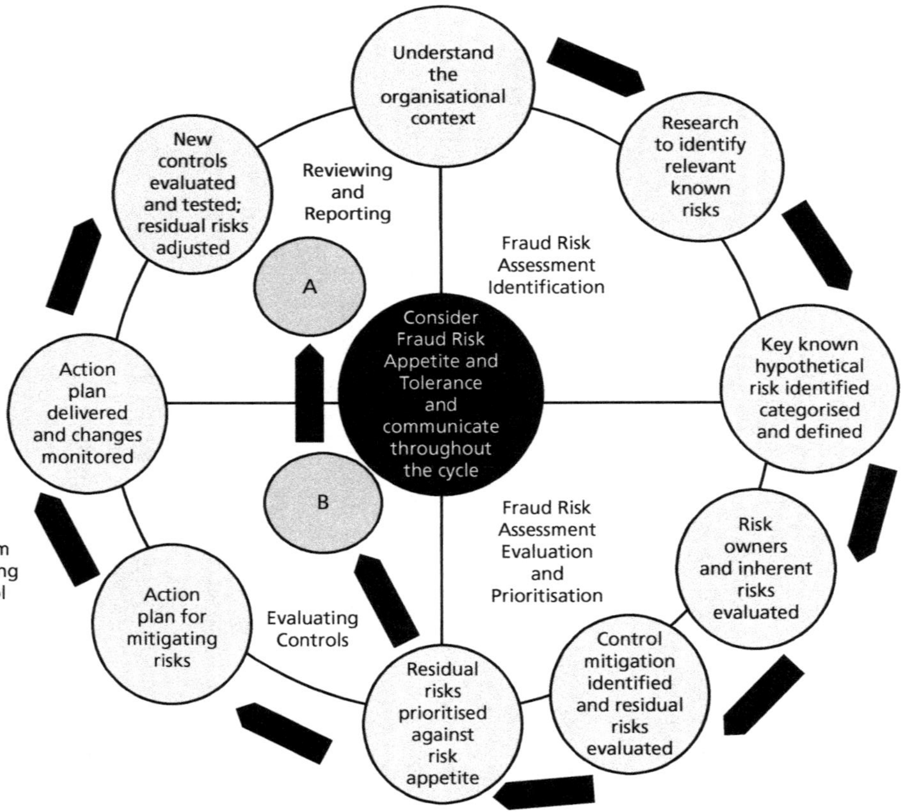

Key

A - Management Information System considered, ongoing monitoring control failures and fraud risk indicators reporting

B - Agree Controls to be tested as part of organisations assurance plan

Figure 4.1 Fraud risk management cycle

Reproduced with the kind permission of the Public Sector Fraud Authority

of itself it is only the starting point. For it to be truly effective it needs to lead to action—the fraud risk management aspect.

So, if this is the case, and in a world of finite resources, a question that is often asked is how long should be spent on FRA. This is a difficult question to answer, as it has many factors driving it, namely:

- the available resource;
- the capability of that resource;
- the complexity and breadth of the area;
- the available business time to support in the creation of the assessment (and the understanding of the area).

There is no simple answer to this question. Overall, a business or individual should commit as much time to FRA as they deem appropriate when balancing this against their other drivers, such as making sure they are acting on the assessment to reduce risk, acting on instances of fraud, assessing their controls, and, indeed, managing other corporate risks.

It is better to spend a week or a day doing an FRA than an hour (as it will be more comprehensive) but it is also better to spend an hour doing one than not doing it at all.

4.4 Different Types of FRAs

The Government Counter Fraud Profession standard for FRA[6] describes four levels of FRA:

(1) organizational (enterprise);
(2) thematic (grouped);
(3) initial fraud impact assessment (IFIA);
(4) full FRA.

The four levels are shown in Figure 4.2 which also illustrates how the assessments inform the organizational counter fraud strategy.

4.4.1 Organizational (Enterprise) FRA—Level 1

The organizational (enterprise) level FRA is essential. It is the tool which is used to communicate the level of risk, and some of the individual risks faced by the organization to the most senior members, whether they are the board or elected individuals. This enables them to make decisions based on their tolerance levels for fraud, and on the resourcing and activity they will commit to acting on countering fraud risk.

These level one FRAs can also be used across a group of organizations to give a view of their collective risk where this is helpful for those who are accountable.

[6] Ibid.

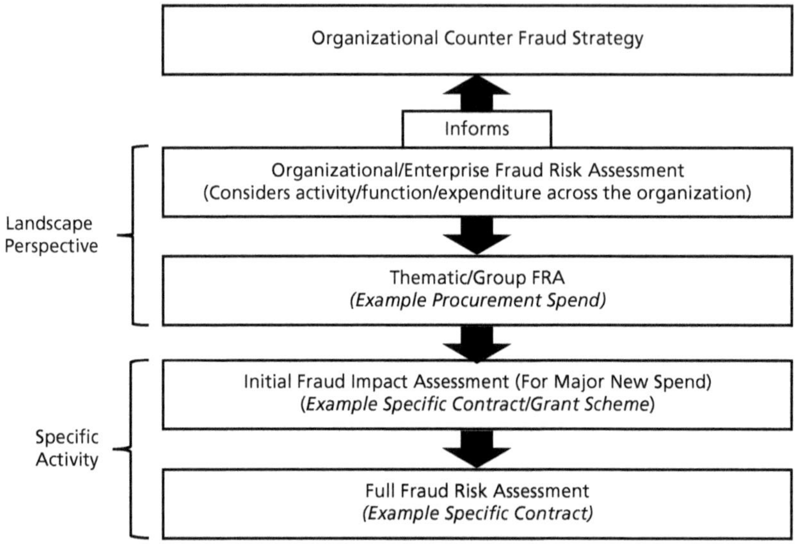

Figure 4.2 Four types of fraud risk assessment
Reproduced with the kind permission of the Public Sector Fraud Authority

4.4.4.1 Full Fraud Risk Assessments—Level 4

The next essential part is the existence of one, or some, full FRAs—Level 4 in our structure above. A full FRA considers the detail of an initiative, or area of the business and how it may be defrauded. This is what drives fraud management activity as it details the ways the organization could be defrauded and where the limitations of the controls/countermeasures are.

For smaller organizations, they may have one full FRA. Larger organizations would be expected to have several FRAs, each covering critical areas of spending/critical initiatives. Most public bodies or sizable private and third (charity) sector organizations would have a few FRAs feeding into their organizational (enterprise) level FRA.

4.4.2 Thematic (Grouped) FRAs—Level 2

A thematic (grouped) FRA looks at the overall risk faced within one of the specific activity/function/expenditure areas within the organization. The UK Government FRA standard states that these areas must be identified within the organizational (enterprise) level FRA and should make sense to the business and how the organization operates.

Organizations do not have to use thematic FRAs, but they are especially useful in larger organizations to help segment the organization's activities/payment areas/initiatives into more manageable chunks. It is essential that the 'chunks' that this divides the organization into makes sense to the business and how it operates. If this is not the case, those undertaking the assessments will find their work difficult to integrate into the organization in a meaningful way, as they will be working counter to the structures and lexicon of the organization.

Thematic (grouped) FRAs have two purposes. First, they function as an effective prioritization tool within larger organizations. They enable the organization to assess which areas of the business are most likely to be the riskiest. These can then be prioritized for full FRAs (Level 4), and the resulting fraud risk management activity.

Thematic (grouped) FRAs can also function as the equivalent of an enterprise (organizational) FRA for the next level down of management, who may have responsibility for a business directorate, an area or a group of initiatives. This helps them to understand their overall risk, think about their tolerance level, how much resource they commit to managing (and acting on) the risk of fraud, and where they target FRAs and fraud risk management.

Like the organizational (enterprise) FRAs, thematic (grouped) FRAs can also be used across organizations should this be required by those who are accountable for loss from and the risk of fraud.

4.4.3 **Initial Fraud Impact Assessments (IFIAs)—Level 3**

The IFIA is an assessment that was introduced into the UK government in 2022 as a result of experiences during the Covid-19 pandemic. It is a tool for assessing whether a new scheme or program is likely to have a high risk of fraud and irregular payments in it. It provides a risk level, and where the risk level is assessed as high, the expectation is that a full FRA (Level 4) would be undertaken to understand the risks, optimize the countermeasures and controls, and enable the senior responsible owner (SRO) for the initiative or programme to consciously set a tolerance for an acceptable level of fraud and irregular payments.

The IFIAs were designed as assessments that can be undertaken at pace, to ensure minimal delay in the creation of new schemes and initiatives. They were also designed to be able to be undertaken by non-fraud experts (although those undertaking them should consult and refer to fraud experts to improve their quality).

Theoretically, the IFIA (Level 3) can be used ahead of undertaking full FRAs (Level 4) in established areas of the business to understand the level of risk, and to prioritize the use of full FRAs, which are a more intensive undertaking.

For a larger organization, the four levels of FRA come together to create a comprehensive fraud risk framework, enabling effective communication to senior decision-makers, prioritization of resources, a detailed understanding of the fraud attacks the business faces, and the limitations of their controls in dealing with them, which enables action to reduce the residual risks that an organization always faces.

4.4.4 **Relationship with Fraud Threats**

In line with the definition of fraud threat as set out earlier in this chapter, FRAs consider the person(s) or groups that may attack the organization (or commit fraud) and their capability to do so. This provides a powerful, and helpful picture to an organization to help focus their efforts to combat fraud.

It also has an interaction with an organization's FRAs, for example:

(1) In a Level 1 Enterprise FRA, if a threat assessment has been undertaken which provides evidence that there are active threats with the capability to succeed, this should be made clear in the assessment and those threats be explicitly referenced and action taken to mitigate.
(2) In a Level 3 IFIA, if there is knowledge of capable actors in the area, or in a comparable scheme, then this will increase the likelihood that the scheme is assessed as high or very high risk.
(3) In a Level 4 full FRA, the awareness and assessment of threat drives the likelihood and impact of a fraud occurring. If an organization is aware that a capable actor is capable of attacking a system, this is likely to increase the assessed likelihood of it happening. It can also increase the impact, as it may make fraud instances more severe and long lasting.

4.4.5 Integrating the Bribery and Corruption Risk

The four levels of FRA within the framework can cover bribery and corruption risks. As the assessment focused on financial crime with its focus on financial gain or loss, it has the most success when considering corruption that has a financial outcome.

KEY POINTS—DEFINING CORRUPTION

Corruption is defined by Transparency International as:[7]

> the abuse of entrusted power for private gain.

Inherently, an FRA will cover some elements of corruption. The general offence of fraud, under the Fraud Act 2006, applicable to England, Wales, and Northern Ireland establishes three ways that the offence can be committed:

(1) fraud by false representation;
(2) fraud by failing to disclose;
(3) fraud by abuse of position.

Where fraud is committed by abuse of position, this would generally be covered by an FRA. However, when undertaking an FRA, additional care should be taken to ensure bribery risks and corruption risks are considered. To do this, the fraud risk assessor can make sure they take the additional step to consider bribery corruption

[7] Transparency International, 'What Is Corruption?' (2024), www.transparency.org/en/what-is-corruption (accessed 28 January 2024).

risk separately in the process, and then integrate these risks into the full fraud risk log.

Further Reading

- Transparency International, 'Diagnosing Bribery Risk Guidance for the Conduct of Effective Bribery Risk Assessment, www.transparency.org.uk/sites/default/files/pdf/publications/Diagnosing_Bribery_Risk.pdf (accessed 27 January 2024);
- Transparency International, 'Risk Assessment Anti-Bribery Guidance', www.antibriberyguidance.org/sites/default/files/4.%20Risk%20Assessment%20-%20Anti-Bribery%20Guidance.pdf (accessed 27 January 2024).

4.4.6 Relationship with Other Irregularities—Error

When managing the risk of fraud on a volume basis, it may be efficient to consider fraud in a wider context and include error/irregularity. This is because the difference between fraud loss and error loss is intent and when dealing with a potentially fraudulent or irregular payment or interaction it is a choice for an organization whether they invest resources in establishing the intent. Often, it can be more efficient to act, including recovery, prevention, and taking sanctions on the 'non-compliance'.

When an organization is focused on managing fraud and error collectively, it may be helpful to actively consider error risk separately and then incorporate this into the assessment. This may help to identify further fraud risks alongside risks of error.

4.4.7 Interaction with Counter Fraud Strategy

A deep understanding of the risks of fraud an organization faces drives its counter fraud strategy in dealing with fraud and related risk, which in turn drives its operational activity. Where there are critical gaps in the understanding of risk, a key part of both the strategy and the operational activity will be deepening the understanding of risk through more FRA.

4.4.8 The Use of Experts

The use of experts in FRA is highly encouraged, and a good fraud risk assessor will be looking to secure specific expertise to support and enrich the assessment. These experts should be in a diverse range of areas. Fraud expertise should be expected, but it should be complimented by expertise in the business processes and sectors/environments that are being assessed.

For example, an expert in undertaking an FRA will be able to identify fraud risks more easily as they are likely to have a deeper understanding of the types of risks that can occur as they will have experienced these when reviewing other areas. Even more risks will be identified when those with expertise from the business are engaged, as they will have an in-depth understanding of the processes. An expert from the sector will also reveal more risks. For instance, an expert in the provision of grants to charities will have some sector- specific insight that is likely to reveal more risks that they have either experienced or seen the opportunity for.

When undertaking an FRA, it is important that the fraud risk assessor considers how they draw on a range of expertise to support the assessment. This will make the assessment richer, and as such drive action that has a bigger impact in reducing the risks that the organization faces.

4.5 Getting into the Detail of Risk Assessment

Fraud is committed in the detail. When fraudsters attack, they use the specifics of processes and actions to successfully commit fraud. Whether it is creating a forged document, or failing to disclose critical information, it is in the specifics. Just as fraud is committed in the detail, it is also fought in the detail. When we consider FRA, the more specific the detail, the more impactful that risk assessment can be.

Considering a public sector example, there are initiatives that require that the citizen has savings or assets below a certain threshold to be eligible to access a service. When looking at fraud risk for this, there is a risk that an applicant misrepresents their assets, thus presenting as eligible for the service. At this level there are several ways this risk could be controlled, depending on how the individual misrepresented.

If the FRA is more detailed, the controls to reduce or remove the risk become self-evident. For example, if the fraud risk description is that the applicant does not declare property, or the applicant does not declare savings accounts the data or checks to reduce this risk are clear.

While FRA at the most detailed level of granularity can be the most impactful, it can be difficult to manage as it results in a large number of risks. As a result, a key skill of the fraud risk assessor is how to structure FRAs to balance the benefit of specific detail to drive control improvements and the requirement to make the FRA engaging for different stakeholders in the business.

4.5.1 The Nature and Mindset of FRA

It can be difficult for organizations to conduct FRA activities, as it involves adopting a mindset of how to attack and damage the business, rather than the mindset the organization encourages: how to support it and make it succeed. In the public sector this can become particularly difficult. After spending much time and effort to create an initiative that supports individuals, communities, or businesses looking at ways it can fail acts counter to the investment bias that has built up, wanting it to succeed.

For FRA to be effective, this fraudster mindset has to be adopted. Without it, risks will be argued away or underestimated.

FRA is an inherently creative process, and creativity should be encouraged. When looking at ways a business or area of spending or service could be defrauded, creativity enables the fraud risk assessor, and others involved, to adopt the mindset of the fraudster and make the assessment more comprehensive and impactful.

It also requires a very analytical mindset, for example when considering controls. Poor-quality FRAs place uncritical assurance in the existing controls and, without sufficient scrutiny, conclude that they reduce risk. Strong FRAs take an analytical approach to the controls and identify the strengths and limitations of those controls, giving clear description of the residual risk the business faces—how fraudsters could be successful.

4.6 Organizational (Enterprise) FRAs—Level 1

An organizational (enterprise) level assessment includes the organization as a whole and how susceptible to fraud it might be and is the most general of the types of assessment that can be completed. This does not mean it is not helpful, and this is for organization a key tool for briefing upwards on fraud risk at board level.

Although holistic assessments should be undertaken, those assessments should be tailored to take into consideration the specific business activity and function the organization participates in, its environment, and how susceptible this makes it to fraud.

Organizations should complete enterprise level assessments at least annually, and good practice would be to increase this with the addition of new information or other level risk assessments that can be used to assure or uplift the existing product.

Due to the continual evolution of an organization's practices, business activities, and external environmental factors, it will be necessary to continue to review and update assessments with the knowledge it will never be 'completed'. A mature environment has FRAs at all levels that continue ongoing efforts to understand risk and take action to reduce risk and loss.

Checklist—An Organizational (Enterprise) Level FRA

The Government FRA standard gives guidance on what an organizational FRA may include:

- what the organization's key business purpose is;
- how much money the organization spends or is responsible for the spending of. This should also be compared to the proportion it spends on its own administration;
- what the organization spends its money on;
- what the drivers of fraud risk are in the current context;
- where the organization receives money from;

- how many physical cash transactions are made;
- how externally facing an organization is (i.e. what the general awareness of the existence of that organization would be);
- who the organization does business with (e.g. third-party suppliers, what their normal attributes are, the variety and complexity of these interactions);
- is the organization operating overseas, if so, include fraud indices of the relevant country/countries;
- who the organization's customers are and what their normal attributes are;
- who the organization's suppliers, financiers, regulators, and other third parties are and the variety and complexity of their interactions;
- how disparate the organization is and how dependent the organization is on delivery through others;
- how specific the organization's legislation/rules are on what it can spend money on and how;
- how specific the organization's legislation/rules are on what money the organization should collect and how;
- what the levels of awareness are in the organization of the risk of fraud loss and how to report suspicions;
- how mature the organization is, or how new it is, and how established skills and ways of working to deliver the business are;
- how mature the organization's governance arrangements are, including reporting and assurance for financial management;
- what new products/significant changes, including IT projects, are planned;
- whether there are clear lines of responsibility and owners for financial loss and propriety in the key payment/service streams;
- whether the organization has a defined fraud risk appetite;
- what previous audits and audit reports have indicated.

4.7 Thematic (Grouped) FRA—Level 2

The thematic (grouped) FRAs look at the fraud risk in a specific area of the business/organization. This is a way to divide up a complex organization into smaller areas. Smaller, simpler organizations may not require thematic FRAs, and they should be considered optional.

The areas that a fraud risk assessor selects for assessment may be driven by the business taking account of how it structures itself through its accountability lines. By following this method, this will enable the business to more easily identify the owners of the risks identified, and then make progress in mitigating those risks.

A thematic FRA can either be created through a bottom-up approach (considering full FRAs that have been undertaken in that business area) or a top-down approach.

Checklist—Thematic FRA

The UK Government's Standard for FRA lays out some of the things that should be considered, namely:

- the spend level of the area, and the spend profile across the different elements/activities that make up the area;
- how high profile the area is and therefore the associated reputational risk of fraud issues;
- how much is known about potential fraud in that area:

  o whether there are clearly identified and known fraud risks;

  o whether there are reports of potential fraud or error within the spend activities;

  o whether there are similar/comparable spend areas which have had their risks assessed which can help in understanding risks relevant to this area.

  • whether there is a detection and reporting process in place for fraud and error;

  • to what extent there are controls in place to mitigate the known risks and whether there has been consideration of the effectiveness of these.

Where the thematic FRA is built from the bottom up it should:

- assess the overall level of risk that area faces—and this assessment should be comparable to the other thematic FRAs in the organization;
- draw out the key specific risks/risk areas from the full FRA;
- be clear on areas of uncertainty.

Where there is strong intelligence on instances of potential fraud, these should be a feature of a thematic assessment, including with data on volume.

4.8 IFIAs—Level 3

An IFIA is defined by the GCFP Profession in their standards for professionals on FRA[8] as:

> a fraud, bribery and corruption impact assessment that gives an overview of some of the main fraud risks and challenges facing an individual business unit, project, programme or spending area.

In 2023, the UK government in its Managing Public Money[9] guidance states that an IFIA should be completed for major expenditure and new schemes, this was a direct response to the learning of the Covid-19 pandemic.

During the Covid-19 pandemic it was imperative that fiscal support was designed and paid out at pace, but the potential impact of fraud, pre and post implementation, was not always considered. IFIA is a systemic response to mitigate this occurring for public sector administration of funding, but the approach and methodology be applied across sectors. For example, the IFIA may be applied where an organization is introducing new member benefits, company policies or change initiatives or infrastructure investments such as IT.

Like FRA, an IFIA should be introduced as early as possible in the life cycle of new major spend activity. The early analysis will help those leading the implementation of the spend/scheme/process to decide how to resource and fund counter fraud activity, which should be done in line with the proposed spend life cycle. Different fraud resourcing is required for pre-, during, and post-implementation, and will include things such as assurance activity, risk assessment, reporting routes, and investigative response.

Like with FRA, it is integral to a quality outcome that practitioners working in counter fraud participate in and inform the IFIA process. This will be supported by those subject matter experts and project managers for the system/process being introduced. They also might employ techniques such as highlighting areas, and sources, for research, and bringing together relevant experts to form and run a meeting or workshop that will inform the details of the IFIA. It is vital that the facilitator enables consideration of the different ways fraud could happen that would result in harm arising out of the spend activity.

If the counter fraud practitioner does not directly lead the assessment, they should be involved in the quality assurance of it post-completion. To inform the quality assurance, the HM Government counter fraud practitioner should:

(1) Check that the IFIA has been completed in line with the Government FRA standard.
(2) Provide a quality assurance comment based on the completeness of the IFIA as well as the level of counter fraud understanding that the IFIA demonstrates.

---

[8] GCF Profession, 'Fraud Risk Assessment Core Discipline' (March 2022).

[9] HM Treasury, 'Managing Public Money' (May 2023), https://assets.publishing.service.gov.uk/media/64c383ccf92186001486670d/Managing_Public_Money_-_May_2023_.pdf (accessed 4 February 2024).

Those undertaking an IFIA should consider how the envisaged spend can be defrauded, the following may assist in this process:

- lessons learned from other comparative spend initiatives;
- existing intelligence;
- fraud risk logs;
- risk registers;
- scenario planning.

The areas above can help to identify any known fraud risks as well as considering potential fraud risk drivers.

Checklist—Considerations Including 'Fraud Risk Drivers' for an IFIA

The Government FRA standard gives guidance[10] on IFIAs. The following is an extract from it which can be used as a guide to kickstart your IFIA document:

- who and how many organisations participate in the spend activity;
- who the funding is available to and who the end beneficiary or recipient will be;
- whether the funding has been divided across multiple initiatives or programmes;
- the extent to which the spend is new, novel or contentious;
- the anticipated speed of implementation or delivery of funding from the announced date;
- operational environment, including the delivery or the supply chain
- the value of the spend initiative;
- what the counter fraud approach is across the lifecycle of the spend;
- which inherent fraud risks need to be monitored;
- what the potential fraud impacts could be to the spend initiative;
- an initial assessment of fraud to enable prioritisation of further counter fraud activity.

4.8.1 The Outcome of the IFIA

As well as identifying the areas of fraud impacts, the IFIA will also lead to the production of an initial indicative fraud risk rating and rationale to determine the level of fraud risk that the spend activity could face relative to other spend.

[10] GCF Profession, 'Fraud Risk Assessment Core Discipline' (March 2022).

The quality of the outcome will depend on the comprehensiveness of the IFIA completed. There are many different fraud impacts that should be considered, including:

- **environmental**—e.g. pollution;
- **financial**—e.g. financial loss across the scheme;
- **security**—e.g. on a national scale, linked to funding wider criminality;
- **physical**—e.g. expose people to hazardous substances or environments;
- **policy aims**—e.g. programme objectives not met;
- **reputational**—e.g. erosion of trust in industry;
- **societal**—e.g. services being stolen—can extend beyond individuals to impact communities.

4.8.2 Giving an Indicative Assessment Score

The IFIA should have an initial indicative assessment score to understand the potential fraud risk that is posed to the spend activity as a whole. This assessment helps to determine the level of risk in comparison to other spend activity and support prioritization of counter fraud resourcing.

Each IFIA should be made up of a series of assessments. These assessments are made using the knowledge and judgement of the SRO and policy/programme/project team and should be considered in the light of the strategic context for the initiative. This differs from a full FRA, as that has a focus on assessing and scoring individual inherent risks. The IFIA is more intuitive and based on judgement and early understanding and design knowledge of those developing the scheme.

A scoring system of one to five (one being the lowest, five being the highest) should be used. Scoring definitions should be clearly articulated and explained. Assessors should ensure that the score is reflective of the impact that fraud could have on the spend activity as a whole. It is important that each assessment has a short explanatory note of the reasoning for each mark (where appropriate) to provide an audit trail of the considerations.

Checklist—Producing an IFIA

Steps that you may follow after the IFIA is produced:

- input to the design of the control framework to prevent and detect fraud, including the collection and the effective use of data and analytics from internal/external sources;
- the development and maintenance of full FRAs;
- attending fraud risk governance panels to receive expert independent counter fraud advice to strengthen fraud responses;

- employing sanctions and penalties as part of a strategy of fraud deterrence;
- linking with sources of intelligence and analysis; ensuring rights of access to inspect documents, individuals, and premises;
- the right to recover funds in cases of irregularity;
- setting fraud tolerance levels and use of fraud measurement to estimate actual levels of fraud within the spend area.

An IFIA is not a full FRA, but it can help to drive prioritization of a Full FRA. IFIAs do not evaluate in detail the effects of the controls on the specific fraud risks and the extent to which residual risk remains. A fraud risk log lists all frauds that an organization might be subject to. The IFIA provides a broad assessment of inherent risks and potential fraud impacts to an individual business unit, project, or programme.

An IFIA should inform the enterprise/organization level FRA to capture the new areas of spend which expose an organization to potential fraud to the organization.

4.9 Full FRA—Level 4

As stated earlier in the chapter, fraud is committed in the detail and, as such, the most effective action against the specific risks that are faced are driven through an understanding of the detail.

The full FRA is the tool used to drive specific control changes—to better detect, prevent, or deter acts of fraud. It does this through understanding the way an organization will be defrauded, assessing to what extent the controls in place impact this risk, clearly identifying the residual risk that remains, and then assessing the likelihood and impact of the risk happening.

From this assessment, the organization can then take choices on where to deploy controls and resources to act on fraud, and where to invest to better understand key risks and their interplay with the controls if necessary, using tools like fraud measurement and control testing.

KEY POINTS—COMPLETING THE FULL FRA

The steps to take to complete the full FRA are set out below—and there are a range of sources to obtain insight from:

- tactical intelligence that the organization receives, including whistle-blowing;
- outputs from strategic intelligence activity;
- the results of completed investigations;
- management information reports from fraud detection systems;
- interviews with key staff;
- workshops with groups of staff;

- research on an organization's unrecognized fraud risks and threats;
- research on the fraud risks and threats faced by other, comparative organizations.

When conducting the risk assessment, consideration is needed to both internal and external risks facing the organization, covering all areas of the business. The findings should be secured in a risk log, which is the sole place to maintain and review at least annually, or when new information/business changes prompt reviews. As outlined earlier, the more specific the risk can be articulated, the more insight can be gained for the business in identifying the relevant control.

Fraud risks must have a clear description of the inherent fraud risk and its consequences.

Fraud risks may be captured using the following structure:

- Actor: who commits the fraud (may be a single individual or more individuals).
- Action: what the fraudulent action is.
- Outcome: what is the resulting impact or consequence(s)? This will be financial but consider whether other aspects are relevant such as: reputational; social; physical harm; environmental; the extent to which fraud might undermine organization aims/objectives; or harm to national security.

The approach to the risk assessment should be creative and adopt the mindset of a fraudster in doing so. Best practice would be to involve a range of people from the relevant business areas to have an informative outcome. Counter fraud staff should be able to support organizing and running meetings or fraud risk workshops; arranging for walk-throughs of processes and associated controls; and providing a sense check of the assessment to ensure that the fraud risks identified are comprehensive.

All fraud risk registers can have an assessment of the inherent risk that the risk poses, which would include an assessment of the likelihood and impact of the risk occurring in the absence of the control framework.

4.9.1 Scoring Systems

There are varying approaches to scoring systems that can be deployed, but risk logs with the most meaning and utility for an organization, adopting individual scoring of the risks, with five being high and one being very low, which are then evaluated considering controls to give the residual score.

KEY POINTS—HEAT MAPS

To facilitate the reporting of risks on a 5x5 heat map by arriving at a single score for both likelihood and impact, it is suggested that assessors can add together the two scores for likelihood and also for impact and divide each by two.

- The resulting overall scores for both Likelihood and Impact are then multiplied to give an overall score for the residual risk on a 1–25 scale.

- A worked example would be: Occurrence 5 + Frequency 3 divided by 2 = a Likelihood score of 4; Duration 4 + Materiality 5 divided by 2 = an Impact score of 4.5. The total score for the residual risk is calculated as 4 multiplied by 4.5 = 18.

4.9.2 Assessing the Risk of Corruption

When assessing corruption risks as part of an FRA, the impact of corruption on both the frequency and likelihood may be considered. For example, the assessor should consider how collusion can affect the occurrence and frequency of risks happening (would it make it more or less likely to happen frequently) and whether it might make a risk more likely to succeed.

4.9.3 Reporting

In government, impact definitions will need to be agreed in advance with both the counter fraud functional lead and the overall owner for the related area of business (for other sectors, identifying who will be the lead will help to secure the long-term utility and implementation of the FRA findings).

Reporting should include clear acknowledgement of limitations of the FRA performed, including issues such as lack of accessible data or intelligence to inform the full assessment.

To conclude, the full FRA gives the most comprehensive insight for an organization, but the value of additional risk assessments is set out above. The key elements to home in on for the fraud practitioner is to:

- plan where and how to obtain the business data and insight needed;
- be as specific as possible when considering and evaluating both risks and controls;
- be creative throughout the process, which will allow you to go outside of your comfort zone and into the mind of a potential fraudster.

Further Reading

- HM Treasury, 'Managing Public Money' (2023), https://assets.publishing.service.gov.uk/media/64c383ccf92186001486670d/Managing_Public_Money_-_May_2023_.pdf (accessed 4 February 2024);
- Commonwealth Fraud Prevention Centre, 'Conduct a Fraud Risk Assessment', www.counterfraud.gov.au/access-tools-and-guidance/conduct-fraud-risk-assessment (accessed 4 February 2024);
- Charity Commission for England and Wales, 'Preventing Charity Fraud' (Fraud Risk Assessment Template), https://preventcharityfraud.org.uk/document/fraud-risk-assessment-template/ (accessed 4 February 2024).

5

Preventing Fraud

Blackstone's Counter Fraud Professionals' Handbook. Michael J. Betts, Laura Eshelby, and David Whitehouse-Hayes, Oxford University Press.
DOI: 10.1093/9780191996955.003.0005

5.1 Introduction

This chapter explores the nature of fraud prevention, the tools and techniques that can be used to effectively stop fraud. These include how legislation is shaping prevention frameworks for organizations, the role of awareness campaigns, and the use of data and analytics.

It is important to bring clarity to the purpose of fraud prevention and its relationship with fraud deterrence. Fraud prevention is one of the components that build effective fraud deterrence, others include legislation/regulation, fraud detection, response, intelligence, investigation, and sanction/redress, as shown in Figure 5.1. Deterrence is concerned with 'putting off' would-be offenders instigating a fraud attack; prevention measures are designed to stop fraud in the event of an attack.

Quantifying the value of prevention is not new: in 1736 Benjamin Franklin who was credited as organizing the Union Fire Company in Philadelphia, in the US said:

> An ounce of prevention is worth a pound of cure.[1]

Though this advice was in relation to preventing fires, the same principles apply to countering fraud.

Figure 5.1 Fraud deterrence components

[1] Independence Hall Association, 'Quick Biography of Benjamin Franklin' (1995), www.ushistory.org/franklin/info/index.htm (accessed 16 October 2023).

This same quote was repeated in the landmark Fraud Review 2006 (p. 8, para. 16). The Review was established to recommend ways of reducing fraud and its growing impact. It articulated that the government is responsible for protecting the public, consumers, and business from fraud and using the mechanisms of state to achieve that. The Review made sixty-two recommendations including the establishment of a National Fraud Reporting Centre (better known as Action Fraud); making fraud a policing priority; and the establishment of the City of London Police as the National Lead Force for fraud to act as a Centre of Excellence. With regard to preventing fraud the Review recommended:

- Ensuring public authorities proactively undertake fraud measurement and risk assessment exercises to reduce the level of fraud loss.
- National Audit capabilities should audit public bodies on the strength of their fraud controls.
- Developing and instigating public anti-fraud and warnings campaigns.
- Engaging with the press for case publicity.
- Developing and sharing best practice on fraud prevention techniques collaboratively with businesses and government.
- Coordinating fraud awareness training across sectors.

Fundamentally fraud prevention is about protecting citizens, organizations, and the public sector from criminals, who seek to steal from those who are often in most need. When fraud is committed against the public sector those who rely on it most are impacted by these crimes; less money is available to invest in supporting, protecting, and nurturing citizens. The prevention of fraud is an investment and is the best option to deter fraud offending.

KEY POINTS—FRAUD PREVENTION FACTS AND FIGURES

There are various reported facts and figures that relate to the prevented loss due to effective fraud prevention:

- Since 1996 the National Fraud Initiative programme states[2] it has made cumulative savings of £2.4 billion.
- The UK-based fraud prevention organization Cifas states[3] that since 2020 it has prevented £1.3 billion in fraudulent conduct.
- Cifas further states[4] £200 plus in savings for every £1 spent on membership.

[2] National Fraud Initiative Report (December 2022), www.gov.uk/government/publications/national-fraud-initiative-reports/national-fraud-initiative-report-december-2022-html (accessed 19 October 2023).

[3] Cifas (fraud prevention service in UK) prevents fraud for organizations/private, public, and charity, www.cifas.org.uk/fraud-prevention-community (accessed 20 October 2023).

[4] Ibid.

- UK Finance stated[5] in its 2022 Annual Report that banks and card companies prevented £1.2 billion in unauthorized fraud (equivalent to 61.5 pence in every £1 of attempted fraud being stopped).
- Association of Certified Fraud Examiners (ACFE)'s *Report to the Nation*[6] stated the most effective fraud control in reducing loss was proactive data monitoring/analysis (loss reduction of 59.7%).
- The Public Sector Fraud Authority published in 2023 the Fraud Landscape report that prevention of fraud for 2020–21 had reached £653 million across government[7] compared to £388 million in 2019–20 when including Covid-19 activity.

5.1.1 **Crime Prevention**

Though fraud is sometimes segmented from other crime, prevention techniques have universal application. Historically, preventing crime is interwoven with the development of policing in the UK. In 1829 the so called nine Peelian principles were introduced as a 'general instruction' to the newly formed Metropolitan Police; they had the prevention of crime as their number one objective. These principles took the name of Sir Robert Peel who was the Home Secretary between 1822 and 1829; he was instrumental in the introduction of the Metropolitan Police, one of the first professional police forces in England and Wales.

KEY POINTS: THE PEELIAN PRINCIPLES

The nine Peelian Principles are:[8]

(1) The basic mission for which the police exist is to prevent crime and disorder.
(2) The ability of the police to perform their duties is dependent upon public approval of police actions.
(3) Police must secure the willing cooperation of the public in voluntary observance of the law to be able to secure and maintain the respect of the public.
(4) The degree of cooperation of the public that can be secured diminishes proportionately to the necessity of the use of physical force.

[5] UK Finance, 'The Definitive Overview of Payment Industry Fraud in 2022' (2023), www.ukfinance.org.uk/system/files/2023-05/Annual%20Fraud%20Report%202023_0.pdf (accessed 20 October 2023).

[6] *ACFE Report to the Nations: 2022 Global Fraud Study*, https://legacy.acfe.com/report-to-the-nations/2022/?_ga=2.161839996.1112429651.1690183179-474221888.1688109120 (accessed 24 July 2023).

[7] Excludes tax and welfare to report on the 'rest of government' public sector fraud authority, www.gov.uk/government/publications/cross-government-fraud-landscape-annual-report-2022 (accessed 5 November 2023).

[8] HMIC, *State of Policing: The Annual Assessment of Policing in England and Wales 2013/2014* (27 November 2014), https://assets-hmicfrs.justiceinspectorates.gov.uk/uploads/state-of-policing-13-14.pdf (accessed 19 October 2023).

(5) Police seek and preserve public favour not by pandering to public opinion but by constantly demonstrating absolute impartial service to the law.
(6) Police use physical force to the extent necessary to secure observance of the law or to restore order only when the exercise of persuasion, advice and warning is found to be insufficient.
(7) Police, at all times, should maintain a relationship with the public that gives reality to the historic tradition that the police are the public and the public are the police; the police being only members of the public who are paid to give full-time attention to duties which are incumbent on every citizen in the interests of community welfare and existence.
(8) Police should always direct their action strictly towards their functions and never appear to usurp the powers of the judiciary.
(9) The test of police efficiency is the absence of crime and disorder, not the visible evidence of police action in dealing with it.

The traditional approach to crime prevention uses a number of well-established models including SARA[9] which has four stages:

(1) **Scanning**—recognizing key issues that require a response;
(2) **Analysis**—examining the issue identified to identify its root cause;
(3) **Response**—responding appropriately to the issue and tackling its causes;
(4) **Assessment**—review the effectiveness of the response and amend if required.

A second model used in this context is the so-called crime triangle or problem analysis triangle.[10] The triangle brings together three elements that often present in offending, namely:

- the **place/location**—where the offending takes place;
- the **offender**—nature of offender(s) (e.g. individual or multiple offenders, motivation, and/or enablers);
- the **victim**—profile of victim (e.g. young or older person, multiple victims).

Both these models are used to solve crime-related problems encountered, particularly in policing. They bring a useful focus on the problem, its causation, and its impact with a view to seeking ways to prevent further offending and should not be disregarded when looking to prevent fraud.

5.1.2 Policing and Fraud Prevention

A major shift in the response to fraud offending was the introduction of the excellent Fraud Investigation Model (FIM) across police forces in England and Wales. The

[9] College of Policing, 'Problem-Solving Policing' (19 October 2022), www.college.police.uk/guidance/problem-solving-policing (accessed 31 October 2023).
[10] Arizona State University, 'The Problem Analysis Triangle' (2020), https://popcenter.asu.edu/content/problem-analysis-triangle-0 (accessed 31 October 2023).

so-called FIM[11] brings a focus to prevention, disruption, and multi-agency working to the forefront of an investigation. The FIM asks four key questions, designed to drive the prevention response with the intention of reducing further harm and loss:

(1) What were the principal enablers that allowed this fraud to be perpetrated?
(2) Who else could be at risk from this or a similar fraud?
(3) What could have been done to remove or reduce the risk from this fraud?
(4) How can the lessons learned be used to prevent others from becoming a victim of a similar fraud?

The focus for policing in preventing fraud in the UK is primarily citizen and business focused. There is an increase in the number of fraud and cyber protect officers across England and Wales, with Avon and Somerset Police[12] trailblazing this initiative in the policing response to fraud and cyber-related offending.

West Yorkshire police, building on the Peelian principles, reference a ten-point approach[13] to preventing crime, which have been mapped to fraud crime (see Table 5.1).

5.1.3 **Legislation Designed to Encourage Prevention**

Even though preventing fraud and related offending is good practice; more recently legislation has been introduced to encourage organizations to ensure procedures are in place to prevent both bribery and tax evasion.

5.1.3.1 **Bribery Act 2010**

The Bribery Act 2010 came into force on 1 July 2011 and introduced liability for a commercial organization, in cases where a person so associated with the organization offers or pays a bribe (as per s. 1 and/or s. 6) in order to secure a business advantage. This is a strict liability offence, but the organization may claim a defence if it has 'adequate procedures' in place to prevent bribes being paid (based on the balance of probability). Under s. 9 of the Bribery Act 2010 the Secretary of State is obliged to publish guidance about commercial organizations preventing bribery. This led to the Bribery Act 2010 guidance document[14] published by the Ministry of Justice (MoJ); the document details six principles that organizations should use to inform their adequate procedures.

---

[11] M. J. Betts, N. Court, D. Clark, and C. Greany, *Investigation of Fraud and Economic Crime* (Oxford: Oxford University Press, 2017).

[12] Avon and Somerset Police, 'Working to Stop People Becoming Victims of Fraud and Cyber-crime' (2023), www.avonandsomerset.police.uk/news/2023/02/working-to-stop-people-becoming-victims-of-fraud-and-cyber-crime/ (accessed 31 October 2023).

[13] West Yorkshire Police, 'The 10 Principles of Crime Prevention' (2022), www.westyorkshire.police.uk/advice/10-principles-crime-prevention/10-principles-crime-prevention/10-principles-crime-prevention (accessed 22 January 2024).

[14] Bribery Act 2010, https://assets.publishing.service.gov.uk/media/5d80cfc3ed915d51e9aff85a/bribery-act-2010-guidance.pdf (accessed 31 October 2023).

Table 5.1 Prevention principles applied to fraud-related offending

Crime prevention principle	Application to fraud
Target hardening	Increase fraud defences around individuals, departments, and organizations
Target removal	Reduce the visibility of potential targets, whether individuals, organizations, or individual projects
Reducing the means	Restrict, remove, and disrupt fraud enablers
Reducing the payoff	Restrict the losses due to fraud through deterrence and prevention, and recover the proceeds of crime
Access control	Improve and implement counter fraud controls; this may be informed by fraud risk assessments
Surveillance	Amplify fraud controls, be fraud aware, and watch/monitor systems for fraud attacks
Environmental change	Design fraud out of schemes, processes, and payment systems by undertaking an initial fraud impact assessment and/or a fraud risk assessment ensuring controls are developed to mitigate the risks identified; continually monitor; and where required improve fraud controls
Rule setting	Set and communicate counter processes and procedures
Increase the chances of being caught	Ensure effective fraud detection processes are in place and the regular testing of fraud controls
Deflecting offenders	Deter fraud-related offending through a range of counter fraud measures

5.1.3.2 **Criminal Finance Act 2017 (CFA 2017)**

Following the success of the Bribery Act 2010 and the improvement in corporate behaviour, similar legislation was introduced in the CFA 2017. CFA, Part 3, ss. 44–52 introduce new offences on the part of a relevant body who fails to prevent facilitation of tax evasion by an associated person. For the purposes of Part 3, a relevant body means a body corporate or partnership (wherever incorporated or formed) and an associated person is such body's employee, agent, or person providing services to them.

Section 47 of the CFA details the requirement that guidance for relevant bodies must be prepared and published by the Chancellor of the Exchequer detailing how the facilitation of tax evasion offences may be prevented and how such prevention measures can be put in place. This guidance, entitled 'Tackling Tax

Evasion: Government Guidance for the Corporate Offences of Failure to Prevent the Criminal Facilitation of Tax Evasion'[15] (HM Customs & Revenue, 1 September 2017). Similarly to the MoJ's Bribery Act Guidance, it describes six guiding principles for relevant bodies to consider when designing or reviewing procedures and systems to prevent the criminal facilitation of tax evasion.

A comparison of the six guiding principles described in both the MoJ's Bribery Act 2010 guidance and HMRC's CFA guidance, is set out in Table 5.2.

5.1.3.3 **Economic Crime and Corporate Transparency Act**

The Economic Crime and Corporate Transparency Act 2023 was granted royal assent on 26 October 2023. The legislation was introduced to support the response to economic crime and introduces a new 'failure to prevent' offence.

Under the new offence, an organization will be liable where a specified fraud offence is committed by an employee or agent, for the organization's benefit, and the organization did not have reasonable fraud prevention procedures in place. The new offence relates to large companies and partnerships which meet at least two of the three following criteria, as at the financial year preceding the fraud offence:

- more than 250 employees;
- more than £36 million turnover;
- more than £18 million in total assets.

5.1.4 **Regulation Designed to Encourage Prevention**

5.1.4.1 **Financial Conduct Authority (FCA)**

The FCA was established on 1 April 2013 and has responsibility for the regulation of 50,000 firms and individuals[16] concerned with financial services. One of the FCA's objectives is to reduce the risk of financial crime, which includes fraud. The FCA Handbook includes rules[17] which require:

> firms to establish and maintain effective systems and controls to counter the risk that they might be used to further financial crime.

And principles, namely:

> Principles 1 (integrity), 2 (skill, care, and diligence), 3 (management and control) and 11 (relations with regulators) of our Principles for Businesses.

---

[15] HMRC, 'Tackling Tax Evasion: Government Guidance for the Corporate Offences of Failure to Prevent the Criminal Facilitation of Tax Evasion' (1 September 2017), https://assets.publishing.service.gov.uk/media/5a82aaa0e5274a2e8ab58b82/Tackling-tax-evasion-corporate-offences.pdf (accessed 31 October 2023).

[16] FCA, 'About the FCA' (2 April 2024), www.fca.org.uk/about/what-we-do/the-fca (accessed 31 October 2023).

[17] www.handbook.fca.org.uk/handbook/FCG/1/1.html (accessed 31 October 2023).

Table 5.2 Comparison of adequate procedures principles

Topic	Bribery Act 2010—MoJ Guidance[a]	Criminal Justice Act 2017—HMRC Guidance[b]
Proportionate procedures	**Principle 1—Proportionate procedures** A commercial organization's procedures to prevent bribery by persons associated with it are proportionate to the bribery risks it faces and to the nature, scale, and complexity of the commercial organization's activities. They are also clear, practical, accessible, and effectively implemented and enforced.	**Principle 2—Proportionality of risk-based prevention procedures** Reasonable procedures for a relevant body to adopt to prevent persons acting in the capacity of a person associated with it from criminally facilitating tax evasion will be proportionate to the risk the relevant body faces of persons associated with it committing tax evasion facilitation offences. This will depend on the nature, scale, and complexity of the relevant body's activities. We recognize that the reasonableness of prevention procedures should take account of the level of control and supervision the organization is able to exercise over a particular person acting on its behalf, and the proximity of the person to the relevant body. The new offences do not require relevant bodies to undertake excessively burdensome procedures in order to eradicate all risk, but they do demand more than mere lip service to preventing the criminal facilitation of tax evasion.
Top-level commitment	**Principle 2—Top-level commitment** The top-level management of a commercial organization (be it a board of directors, the owners, or any other equivalent body or person) are committed to preventing bribery by persons associated with it. They foster a culture within the organization in which bribery is never acceptable.	**Principle 3—Top-level commitment** The top-level management of a relevant body should be committed to preventing persons acting in the capacity of a person associated with it from engaging in criminal facilitation of tax evasion. They should foster a culture within the relevant body in which activity intended to facilitate tax evasion is never acceptable.

Table 5.2 Continued

Topic	Bribery Act 2010—MoJ Guidance[a]	Criminal Justice Act 2017—HMRC Guidance[b]
Risk assessment	**Principle 3—Risk assessment** The commercial organization assesses the nature and extent of its exposure to potential external and internal risks of bribery on its behalf by persons associated with it. The assessment is periodic, informed, and documented.	**Principle 1—Risk assessment** The relevant body assesses the nature and extent of its exposure to the risk of those who act in the capacity of a person associated with it criminally facilitating tax evasion offences. The risk assessment is documented and kept under review.
Due diligence	**Principle 4—Due diligence** The commercial organization applies due diligence procedures, taking a proportionate and risk-based approach, in respect of persons who perform or will perform services for or on behalf of the organization, in order to mitigate identified bribery risks.	**Principle 4—Due diligence** The organization applies due diligence procedures, taking an appropriate and risk-based approach, in respect of persons who perform or will perform services on behalf of the organization, in order to mitigate identified risks.
Communication and training	**Principle 5—Communication (including training)** The commercial organization seeks to ensure that its bribery prevention policies and procedures are embedded and understood throughout the organization through internal and external communication, including training, which is proportionate to the risks it faces.	**Principle 5—Communication (including training)** The organization seeks to ensure that its prevention policies and procedures are communicated, embedded, and understood throughout the organization, through internal and external communication, including training. This is proportionate to the risk to which the organization assesses that it is exposed.
Monitoring and review	**Principle 6—Monitoring and review** The commercial organization monitors and reviews procedures designed to prevent bribery by persons associated with it and makes improvements where necessary.	**Principle 6—Monitoring and review** The organization monitors and reviews its preventative procedures and makes improvements where necessary.

[a] Bribery Act 2010, https://assets.publishing.service.gov.uk/media/5d80cfc3ed915d51e9aff85a/bribery-act-2010-guidance.pdf (accessed 31 October 2023).
[b] HMRC, 'Tackling Tax Evasion: Government Guidance for the Corporate Offences of Failure to Prevent the Criminal Facilitation of Tax Evasion' (1 September 2017), https://assets.publishing.service.gov.uk/media/5a82aaa0e5274a2e8ab58b82/Tackling-tax-evasion-corporate-offences.pdf (accessed 31 October 2023).

The FCA has made available a document entitled *Financial Crime Guide: A Firm's Guide to Countering Financial Crime Risks* (*FCG*)[18] and provides practical assistance on prevention measures.

5.1.4.2 **HM Treasury and the management of public money**

The public sector is the guardian of the public purse and is accountable to the public through Parliament. His Majesty's Treasury (HMT) maintains control over public spending and ensures public money is managed in accordance with the standards expected of all public services.

HMT published a document entitled 'Managing Public Money'[19] which describes how public resources should be managed and includes an annex on the governance for preventing, countering, and dealing with fraud. Accounting officers have the responsibility for managing the fraud risk; the document provides a range of guidance to support the accounting officer.

Checklist—Managing Public Money: The Management of Fraud Risk

The management of fraud risk should involve:

- assessing the organizations overall vulnerability to fraud;
- identifying the area's most vulnerable to fraud risk;
- evaluating the scale of fraud risk;
- responding to fraud risk;
- detecting fraud;
- measuring the effectiveness of the fraud risk strategy;
- reporting fraud.

Further Reading

- MoJ, 'Bribery Act 2010 Guidance' (March 2011), https://assets.publishing.service.gov.uk/media/5d80cfc3ed915d51e9aff85a/bribery-act-2010-guidance.pdf (accessed 31 October 2023);

[18] *Financial Crime Guide: A Firm's Guide to Countering Financial Crime Risks (FCG)* (2024), www.handbook.fca.org.uk/handbook/FCG.pdf (accessed 9 November 2023).

[19] HM Treasury, *Managing Public Money* (May 2023), https://assets.publishing.service.gov.uk/government/uploads/system/uploads/attachment_data/file/1174979/Managing_Public_Money_-_May_2023_.pdf (accessed 23 October 2023).

- HMRC, 'Tackling Tax Evasion: Government Guidance for the Corporate Offences of Failure to Prevent the Criminal Facilitation of Tax Evasion' (1 September 2017), https://assets.publishing.service.gov.uk/media/5a82aaa0e5274a2e8ab58b82/Tackling-tax-evasion-corporate-offences.pdf (accessed 31 October 2023);
- FCA, *Financial Crime Guide: A Firm's Guide to Countering Financial Crime Risks (FCG)* (2024), www.handbook.fca.org.uk/handbook/FCG.pdf (accessed 31 October 2023);
- HM Treasury, *Managing Public Money* (May 2023), https://assets.publishing.service.gov.uk/government/uploads/system/uploads/attachment_data/file/1174979/Managing_Public_Money_-_May_2023_.pdf (accessed 23 October 2023).

5.1.5 Opportunities for Implementing Fraud Prevention

Organizationally, fraud prevention should be considered from the concept of a project, new product, or when procurement is initiated; they should be constantly monitored to ensure controls are matched appropriately to the risk.

Opportunities for implementing fraud prevention techniques during investigations include when cases are reported, during, and post-investigation. It is important for the counter fraud practitioner to identify and implement processes and strengthen controls to avoid repeat offending, thus reducing future impact and losses. The use of the range of fraud risk assessment (FRA) is also key, assessing pre-scheme or payment process design where possible. Assessing how the specific risks that may occur and how systems can be attacked will inform controls and interventions to safeguard against future loss.

Increasingly organizations are investing in the use of data and analytics allowing a view across wider populations to look for outliers, anomalies, and seek out opportunities to stop fraud occurring.

Checklist—The Benefits of Fraud Prevention

From the organizational perspective, the benefits of preventing fraud are numerous, and include:

- preventing harm, loss, and impact on businesses, the taxpayer, and wider society;
- fraud costs organizations money and losses can impact profitability and sustainability;
- demonstrating effective governance and building organizational confidence;
- fulfilling regulatory/legal responsibilities by reducing the risk of financial crime.

5.2 Understanding the Threat of Fraud

Counter fraud practitioners should understand the different types of fraud, as well as its enablers and motivators. They will also need an understanding of the specific fraud threats to their organization, as well as the wider fraud landscape in which their organization operates.

Checklist—Understanding the Fraud Threat (Organizational Resources)

Organizational resources that a counter fraud practitioner may draw on to better understand the fraud threat/risk include:

- organizational strategy, structure, and key target operating models;
- priorities, policies operating procedures, and performance data;
- intelligence and other threat assessments, risk management models, risk registers, and assessments;
- audit, compliance, investigation, and other inspection/regulatory reports;
- open and closed source reporting.

Practitioners may also draw on an organization's business process mapping to understand the processes that are applied in that organization. This approach will help to identify where fraud can enter the system and the controls that could be deployed to prevent it.

5.3 Government Counter Fraud Profession (GCFP) Fraud Prevention Standard

On the 17 July 2023, the Government Counter Fraud Profession (GCFP) published its Fraud Prevention Standard for Counter Fraud Professionals,[20] a comprehensive reference document for those looking for the tools, processes, and products required to effectively counter fraud in an organization. Its focus is on public sector organizations, but it has much wider applicability and also describes the

[20] Fraud Prevention Standard for Counter Fraud Professionals, www.gov.uk/government/publications/government-counter-fraud-profession-standards-and-guidance/fraud-prevention-standard-for-counter-fraud-professionals-html (accessed 19 October 2023).

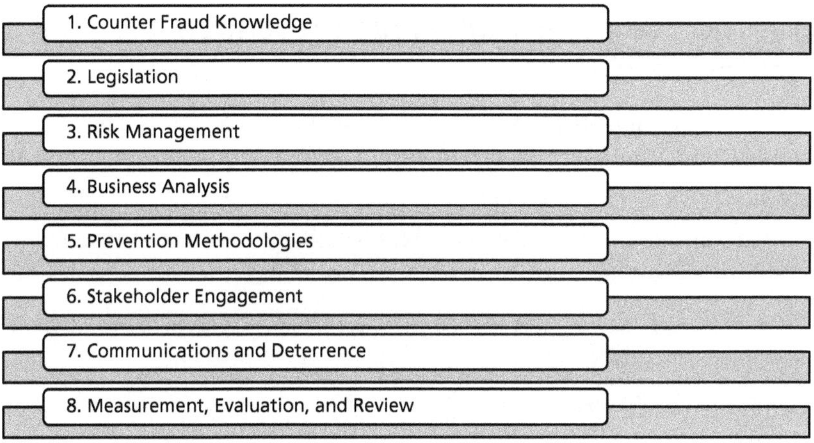

Figure 5.2 GCFP fraud prevention standard key components

knowledge and competencies needed to be an effective practitioner in fraud prevention.

The document details the competencies required by those undertaking prevention roles and a wide range of supporting guidance relating to processes, products and organizational guidance. In line with other GCFP standards, the document details eight key components that build competencies (as shown in Figure 5.2).

Further Reading

- HMICFRS, *State of Policing: the Annual Assessment of Policing in England and Wales 2013/14* (November 2014), https://hmicfrs.justiceinspectorates.gov.uk/publications/state-of-policing-13-14/ (accessed 19 October 2023);
- West Yorkshire Police, 'The 10 Principles of Crime Prevention', www.westyorkshire.police.uk/advice/10-principles-crime-prevention/10-principles-crime-prevention/10-principles-crime-prevention (accessed 19 October 2023);
- Fraud Prevention Standard for Counter Fraud Professionals, www.gov.uk/government/publications/government-counter-fraud-profession-standards-and-guidance/fraud-prevention-standard-for-counter-fraud-professionals-html (accessed 19 October 2023);
- National Fraud Initiative Report: December 2022, www.gov.uk/government/publications/national-fraud-initiative-reports/national-fraud-initiative-report-december-2022-html (accessed 19 October 2023).

5.4 The Commonwealth Fraud Prevention Centre (CFPC)

The Commonwealth Fraud Prevention Centre (CFPC) was established in 2019 and is housed in the Australian Attorney General's Department. Its stated aims are to:[21]

- identify and trial better practice approaches to mitigate fraud vulnerabilities;
- address barriers to effective fraud prevention including information sharing;
- provide support to agencies to design fraud resistant policies and programs.

The CFPC then summarizes the way effective fraud prevention measures can be undertaken, namely:

(1) raise awareness about fraud;
(2) educate people about fraud;
(3) identify fraud threats;
(4) identify control vulnerabilities or test the effectiveness of controls;
(5) identify data requirements to mitigate the common actions fraudster use;
(6) design more fraud resilient programs and functions;
(7) deter fraud through public messaging;
(8) report about fraud to your executives or risk committees.

5.5 Preventing Fraud

5.5.1 Fraud Prevention: The Basics

The basics of fraud prevention are simple steps that should be considered when developing fraud prevention controls; these four steps are shown in Figure 5.3.

5.5.2 Capability, Controls, and Testing

In this section we examine three key components of fraud prevention, as shown in Figure 5.4.

(1) **Capability**—includes training, knowledge, and culture;
(2) **Controls**—Directive, preventative, detective, deterrent, and/or corrective;
(3) **Testing**—testing controls are effective and are being applied or developing new ones as a result of lessons learned from detection activity.

[21] Attorney-General's Department (Australian government), 'Counter Fraud' (2022), www.ag.gov.au/integrity/counter-fraud#:~:text=Commonwealth%20Fraud%20Prevention%20Centre (accessed 2 November 2023).

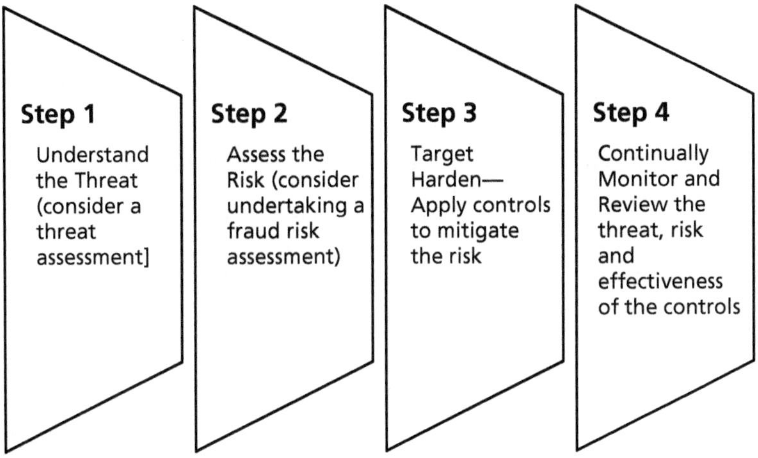

Figure 5.3 Four steps to effective fraud prevention

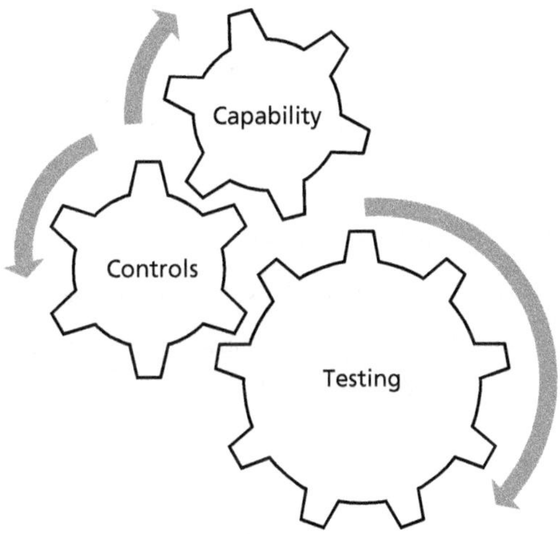

Figure 5.4 Fraud prevention components

Checklist—Organizational Capability and Controls

Typical activities to develop organizational capability include:

- fraud awareness training—consider role/risk specific sessions with anti-fraud messaging from the top of the organization;
- build a counter fraud culture embedding ethics and governance throughout the organization;

- raise the profile of the counter fraud activities within the organization;
- ensure internal counter fraud strategy, policy, and response plan ensuring clarity and understanding;
- review regularly to maintain relevance/accuracy of policy and process;
- provide easy access to fraud prevention material and reporting routes for suspicions.

Typical controls may include:

- vetting employees and those associated with the organization;
- consider rotation of responsibilities on an agreed basis;
- ensure conflicts of interest policy in place and implemented;
- provide a range of support for employees and those associated with the organizations who are in financial hardship, have habits (e.g. gambling or well-being issues);
- apply financial limits on travel and subsistence claims;
- ensure segregation of duties, typically commercial, financial, and technical;
- use automatic system prompts and warnings;
- secure processes for system and building access;
- employee claims require supporting documents that should be verified;
- analyse data of staff payments for unusual and/or duplicate transactions ensuring consistency by reconciling records;
- review delegated financial authorities in place and ensure the limits are being applied;
- restrict system access with permissions dependent on the role with authenticating access processes;
- collaborate with strategic partners and share data;
- introduce counter fraud experts into process/product development;
- strengthen system access controls with additional protection for sensitive records/information.

Testing that both capability and controls are in place and genuinely being applied is an important part of fraud prevention; testing can be undertaken in a number of differing ways.

5.5.2.1 **Desktop reviews**

Desktop reviews can be undertaken to ensure guidance is up to date, controls are in place, and that both are being implemented and are understood by employees and those associated with the organization. This is a low-cost and effective compliance activity that will provide assurance that processes are being applied or will identify weaknesses that can be addressed.

5.5.2.2 **Interviews, workshops, and surveys**

Interviews, workshops, and surveys provide a qualitative method to understand the operation of established systems and processes or any proposed new ones. They provide an understanding of the system from those who understand it best.

5.5.2.3 **System and process walkthroughs**

System and process walkthroughs allow those with knowledge of a particular system or process to understand it and assess how the fraud controls apply with a view to understanding, and preventing, any weaknesses.

5.5.2.4 **Data analytics**

Data analytics use both quantitative and qualitative data sets to assess process compliance and effectiveness of controls.

The GCFP Prevention Standard sets out the importance of the use of data analytics as part of a coherent organizational approach to fraud prevention. Effective use of data provides a dynamic tool to assure the integrity of a system against fraud. The standard sets out a number of examples of how data can be matched or analysed in this respect:

For example, matching and analysing data can be used for, but not limited to:

- risk-scoring applications to streamline processes, and directing high-risk applications to different pathways for additional checks;
- monitoring and flagging high-risk transactions, such as changes to bank details, prior to payment;
- quantifying instances of fraud and associated error being prevented and detected on an organizational, departmental scheme or service level;
- identifying and calculating the benefit from improvements to existing business processes that prevent, identify, and detect instances of fraud and associated error;
- testing for, and measuring, levels of undetected fraud and associated error and gaining further assurance of current estimated levels of fraud and associated error;
- enabling more informed and transparent conversations within the organization on its fraud risks and the material nature of the threat they present to the organization;

- testing new approaches to preventing, identifying, detecting, and measuring potential fraud and associated error.

As with any counter fraud activity, the use of analytics should be regularly reviewed and assessed against the wider organizational counter fraud strategy. This should focus on whether the current approach is delivering against stated goals, meeting key performance indicators, and is updated accordingly.

Ensuring that a data analytics programme is effective and meeting organizational needs is highly dependent on effective engagement with data teams. This means both an organization's own in-house teams and also wider cross-government teams in the case of the public sector, such as cross-government and public sector matching (including with private datasets), maximize the potential of data to detect and prevent fraud.

Again, the GCFP standard sets out example points to cover when engaging data analytics teams. Factors to consider include:

- What is the purpose of engaging?
- How are the individuals or teams identified?
- How can the engagement be mutually beneficial?
- What is the most appropriate mechanism for engagement?
- What value does the use of data analytics add?

The counter fraud practitioner should work with the data analytics team in exploring risks to understand the underlying issue(s), exploring how controls could still allow fraud to occur, highlighting where new prevention controls are required and identifying how prevention solutions could be embedded.

This activity may include, but is not limited to considering:

- How and where the fraud could occur within business processes?
- What is it about the activity that makes it fraudulent?
- How likely is the fraud to occur, and to what extent?
- Whether data analysis could be utilized to identify and prevent this fraud?

5.5.2.5 **Control testing**

Control testing can be simple testing to confirm controls are in place and being applied. This may include looking at samples to confirm that claims could not be processed by staff other than those authorized.

5.5.2.6 **Pressure testing**

The term 'pressure testing' is the process of examining processes and fraud controls under different conditions (or pressure) to fully understand their operation, assess their effectiveness, and identify any control gaps or vulnerabilities. This involves the real-world application of fraud personas to test processes and systems from the perspective of the fraudster. It also involves employing a range of different testing methods to examine how controls work, eliminate blind spots, uncover vulnerabilities, and challenge assumptions about how fraud is managed by organizations.

In some circumstances this can involve covert testing, where officials simulate methods used by fraudsters to identify how controls respond and how they could be circumvented by malicious actors. It will test assumptions about controls, and those undertaking the testing should 'think like a fraudster' and be imaginative and innovative in how they seek to circumvent controls.

This is a complex area of testing and should only be undertaken once the control landscape is understood. Further it requires close oversight and planning including objectives, scope, and any special permissions that might be required access to systems and premises. Managing stakeholders is essential as the covert nature of the testing may have negative impacts on a relationship so other testing methods must have been explored first.

5.6 Reverse-Engineering the Fraud Triangle

Though the fraud triangle illustrates the ingredients required for internal fraud, it can also be used to inform the prevention of fraud. The fraud triangle has three key ingredients:

(1) pressure;
(2) rationalization;
(3) opportunity.

By reducing these, fraud prevention can be enhanced, and an organization can be appropriately target hardened from the activities of the fraudster.

5.6.1 Relieving Financial Pressures

Pressure on individuals can be immense; it can grow steadily as financial obligations increase at the same time as expectations of lifestyle become more demanding. In the UK, according to the Money Charity,[22] individuals in the UK by the end of February 2024 owed £1,841.2 billion, the average debt per household in the UK was reported to be £65,569. In the UK, according to the Joseph Rowntree Foundation (JRF)[23] in 2022, the experience of destitution increased to 3.8 million people, this is an increase of 2.5 times from 2017.

There is a strong rationale for the correlation between pressure and the motivation for fraud. Often these pressures are hidden and not shareable. Organizations should look to relieve this pressure on individuals; they should provide a pressure

[22] Money Charity, Statistics Archive, https://themoneycharity.org.uk/money-statistics/#:~:text=People%20in%20the%20UK%20owed (accessed 2 November 2023).

[23] JRF, 'Destitution in the UK' (24 October 2023), www.jrf.org.uk/report/destitution-uk-2023 (accessed 3 November 2023).

valve. Effective fraud prevention will be enhanced through implementing the following measures:

- employee support schemes;
- confidential habits and addictions counselling support;
- debt and financial counselling;
- mental health well-being support;
- payment of a living wage;
- employee benefits including discounted goods;
- access to gyms and other physical activities;
- encouraging employees to talk through problems.

5.6.2 **Reducing Rationalization**

Rationalizing fraud as something other than crime is a feature typically seen by those committing occupational fraud. Often those perpetrators are justifying their actions by telling themselves that the monies are what they are owed, that everyone is doing it, and that they are justified in taking the money.

To mitigate these rationalizations, organizations should promote a strong ethical and cultural tone led by those at the top and in the middle of the organization. A code of conduct should be woven throughout the fabric of the organization. On occasion, fraud can be seen as a crime sitting outside the mainstream of criminality; a strong counter fraud narrative should be established explaining the threat, harm, and impact of fraud, which is theft by lying.

The use of language has an important role to play in developing the narrative and care should be taken not to use the following types of words to describe fraudsters:

- con artists;
- scammers;
- swindler;
- hustler;
- scam artist.

Linguistic meaning has a huge impact on how messages are received; stronger meaning may be taken when referring to fraud through the use of language such as 'fraud abuse' and 'fraud criminals'. Organizations should make it clear that fraud is not acceptable; it has serious implications and cannot be tolerated.

5.6.3 **Minimizing the Opportunity**

Much of the prevention activity and its link to FRA is aimed at ensuring appropriate controls are in place. Money is the target of the fraudster and where opportunity arises it will be exploited. The opportunities for exploitation should be understood; within organizations this is often through the range of FRAs and measurement exercises; these will inform the controls that should be implemented to harden the target, thus reducing the opportunity.

Other measures will include effective governance, audit/monitoring, and review of the control regime.

5.7 Behavioural Change

The GCFP Prevention Standard looks at behaviour change that addresses the rationalization aspect of the fraud triangle. To change public behaviour, the public must believe certain situations and risks outweigh any benefits. This in turn may deter someone from seeking to commit fraud as they will not be able to rationalize fraudulent behaviour relative to the risk. This can be done in a number of ways, including:

- increasing the level of perceived risk of committing fraud, for example, communicating the likelihood that they will be detected;
- reducing the perceived benefit of engaging in fraud, for example, showing the consequences if they are detected;
- influencing emotions and appealing to moral identity, for example, making them aware of the impact their actions have on others.

KEY POINTS—STRENGTHENING DETERRENCE MESSAGING

Key deterrent points to consider include:

- clear consequences of non-compliance statements communicating that fraud is an offence;
- statements communicating that the organization will consider applying sanctions, including criminal prosecutions, where appropriate;
- statements to influence emotions appealing to morals and ethics such as how fraud impacts victims.

To help prevent and deter internal fraud, it is important to build a positive workplace culture as those who are engaged and committed to an organization and its goals are less likely to defraud it.

5.8 Measuring the Impact of Fraud Prevention

The Government Functional Standard 013[24] (Counter Fraud: Management of Counter Fraud, Bribery and Corruption Activity) requires government departments to report prevented savings from counter fraud activity. It states:

[24] HM Government, *Government Functional Standard GovS 013: Counter Fraud: Management of Counter Fraud, Bribery and Corruption Activity* (August 2021), https://assets.publishing.service.gov.uk/media/612e5a8ce90e0705355a552b/6.7628_CO_Govt-Functional-Std_GovS013-Counter-Fraud_v4.pdf (accessed 2 November 2023).

> Organisations should define the outcomes they are seeking to achieve that year and should have metrics to measure whether the targeted outcome has been achieved. For organisations with a significant investment in counter fraud, bribery and corruption or a significant estimated fraud loss, these should include metrics with a financial impact. Metrics with a financial impact should be based on a targeted value of prevented and/or detected fraud against a baseline to measure improvement over time. Organisations should target an increase in the total amount of detected fraud and/or loss prevented from their counter fraud strategy.

The GCFP Prevention Standard includes methodologies and flowcharts which set out how organizations should measure the value of prevented savings and we will look at those shortly. It also states that all methodologies must be:

- clearly linked to the intervention;
- evidence based;
- logical;
- data driven (where possible);
- reasonable.

Case Study—Department for Work and Pensions Universal Credit (UC) Enhanced Checking Service

The Covid-19 pandemic saw a surge of some 2.3 million claims for Universal Credit (UC) as the pandemic led to significant job losses or reduced hours. To manage this surge, many of the upfront controls were eased to ensure money was paid to those who needed it quickly. This resulted in a significant increase in fraud and error within the system.

To address this the Enhanced Checking Service and Integrated Risk and Intelligence Service moved to focus resources and approaches to detect, correct, and prevent fraud caused by the removal of many of the front-end controls.

UC claims were reviewed for markers and inconsistencies in the claim declarations and/or the supporting evidence which suggested there may be fraudulent and/or erroneous. This assessment was based on hundreds of thousands of previous claims where overpayments were made as a result of fraud and the indicators were recorded, which can be used to indicate fraud in other claims. This led to the correction of almost 300,000 claims and saved the taxpayer around £3 billion[25] in further prevented losses as at the end 2021/22.

The value of these preventative savings are determined by a well-established evidence-based methodology called future overpayments prevented. This is based

[25] Department for Work and Pensions, 'Fighting Fraud in the Welfare System' (May 2022), https://assets.publishing.service.gov.uk/government/uploads/system/uploads/attachment_data/file/1076625/fighting-fraud-in-the-welfare-system.pdf (accessed 2 November 2023).

on the value and period of previous overpayments by fraud typology and what the average duration of time for a fraud was for them. From this, the length of time that the fraud would have continued for, but has been stopped by the intervention, can be extrapolated and a value based on the numbers of weeks this would have been can be calculated. This provides a statistically sound and independently audited basis to ascribe a value to the preventive work that allows for value for money and return on investment calculations to be made.

This evidence base supported Department for Work and Pensions to secure further funding of £613 million for preventative counter fraud work in the Spring Budget 2022 that would save a further £4 billion and 1,400 additional counter fraud staff.

5.9 **Developing Prevention Methodologies**

The GCFP Prevention Standard sets out the following key points to consider when developing a prevention methodology:

- Establish the risk to the organization:
  - understand the threat typologies;
  - assess the potential impact of fraud on the organization.
- Research organizational policies that are linked to the area of risk:
  - think about bigger policies—hone in on what the control will do, ways in which the control could affect that risk area;
  - are there any contra-indications?
- Establish the percentage chance of the fraud occurring:
  - use all available evidence to establish the likelihood of the fraud occurring.
- Seek advice from practitioners:
  - early engagement with staff working to deliver the service helps build a picture of how the service is used.
- Research all available statistics linked to the components that may make up a methodology:
  - for example, costs, frequency, and duration (national, organizational, and stakeholder groups);
  - establish all available data.
- Collate all information:
  - consider quantifying the potential savings.
- Make evidence-based assumptions on the time period to be included in the prevented fraud calculation.
- Evidence the link between the control or intervention and the saving.
- Estimate the level of savings that could be made based on the control being implemented:
  - factor in any third-party influence;
  - adjust accordingly.

- Set review dates proportionate to the control.
- Undertake retrospective testing:
  - ensure that it is the control that is making the saving.
- Review the methodology.

5.10 Fraud Prevention: Conclusion

Fraudsters are capable adversaries, and the crime of fraud is endemic in our society. The growth of fraud has been fuelled by the use of the internet and diversity and speed of payment systems. Those tasked with preventing fraud should focus their efforts in reducing the available enablers and target hardening access to the funds that fraudsters seek. The target hardening will be driven by building awareness throughout the relevant populations and using data and technical interventions that can match those being deployed by the fraudster.

6

Detecting Fraud and Measuring Loss

Blackstone's Counter Fraud Professionals' Handbook. Michael J. Betts, Laura Eshelby, and David Whitehouse-Hayes, Oxford University Press.

DOI: 10.1093/9780191996955.003.0006

6.1 **Introduction**

In this chapter we will examine how fraud is detected and how to measure fraud loss. Fraud detection and measurement are closely aligned; however, they have differing focuses and approaches, but can be used to inform and develop each other. Much fraud, by its nature, is hidden, as we saw with the fraud iceberg detailed in Chapter 1, so estimating the 'unknown' presents a number of challenges which are explored later in this chapter.

The human and cultural element of detection cannot be underestimated; organizations should invest in educating both employees and associated persons how to recognize and detect fraud; the routes to reporting their suspicions should offer confidentiality and those reporting should be confident in the process and the protections afforded.

KEY POINTS—HOW OCCUPATIONAL FRAUD IS DETECTED

The Association of Certified Fraud Examiners (ACFE) *Report to the Nation* 2022,[1] states that the top five methods of detecting occupational fraud were:

(1) whistle-blowing (tip-off) 42 per cent;
(2) internal audit 16 per cent;
(3) management review 12 per cent;
(4) documents examination 6 per cent;
(5) accident 5 per cent.

Changing the cultural attitude towards the discovery of fraud is a key first step to facilitate its detection. The two themes that support an effective counter fraud narrative in this sense are:

(1) Fraud is a constant threat: it is a fact that some individuals and organizations will look to make financial gains through fraud, where there is opportunity. Organizations need robust processes in place to prevent, detect, and respond to fraud.
(2) Discovering fraud should be considered in a positive way. If you do not find fraud, you cannot fight it. This requires a change in perspective, so the identification of fraud is viewed as a positive and proactive achievement.

The Government Counter Fraud Functional Standard GOVS013 requires that proactive detection activity, measurement, and assurance activity, or the use of data sharing and/or data analytics attempt to find fraud in a specific business area.

Measurement activity is often undertaken on the basis of anonymity; this assists in encouraging more reliable response rates. This is done by removing the

[1] *ACFE Report to the Nations: 2022 Global Fraud Study*, https://legacy.acfe.com/report-to-the-nations/2022/?_ga=2.161839996.1112429651.1690183179-474221888.1688109120 (accessed 24 July 2023).

disincentive of subsequent sanction. Once the level of loss is understood, the information can be used to inform the organizational response and counter fraud activity can then be focused on the areas where the risk is at its highest.

6.2 Fraud Detection Methods

Detecting fraud is the responsibility of all those associated with an organization; however, they should be supported by a range of specialists who have specific responsibilities to detect fraud, which these may include auditors, data scientists, and the counter fraud practitioner. Effective fraud detection is aided by an informed and motivated workforce. Both those inside and outside the organization should be able to report fraud anonymously and feel supported and protected. The organization may deploy data analytics to detect fraud; the combination of both the human effective processes and automated systems are the most effective way for an organization to detect fraud.

The range of detection methods is wide ranging and includes those working within an organization, those it connects with, and those in the wider context (examples of these are shown in Figure 6.1).

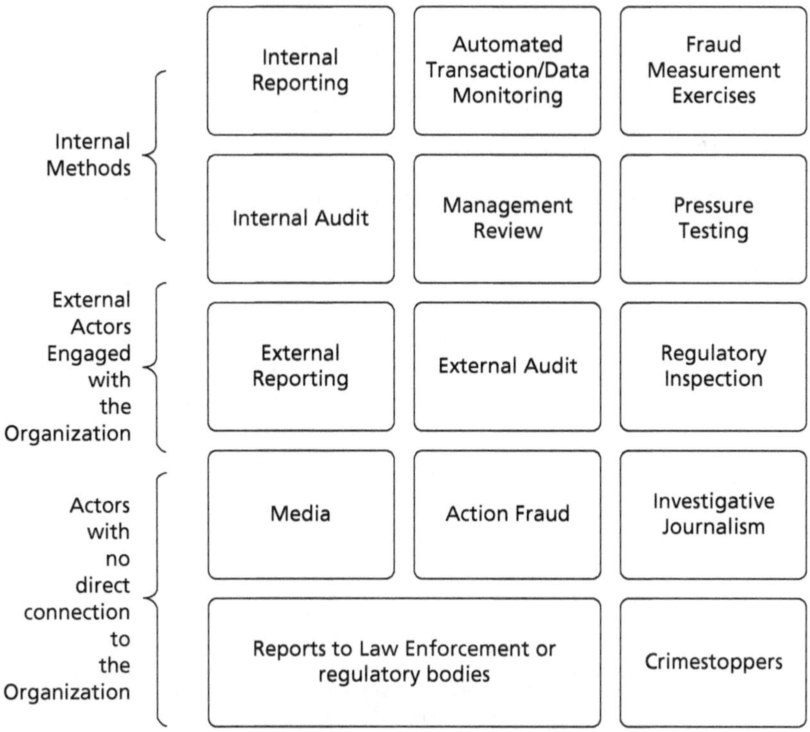

Figure 6.1 Fraud detection methods

6.2.1 Counter Fraud Culture

Developing a counter fraud culture within an organization is an essential factor in fighting fraud. The *Cambridge Dictionary* defines culture as:[2]

> the way of life, especially the general customs and beliefs, of a particular group of people at a particular time.

The culture and tone of an organization is often set by the actions and behaviour of its leaders. Though developing and changing organizational culture may need to be initiated at the top, it should gain momentum throughout the organization that is self-perpetuating if the right environmental factors are present. The Chartered Institute of Personnel and Development (CIPD)[3] states that highly engaged staff with high satisfaction levels are more likely to make 'discretionary effort' including acting on fraud risks.

Checklist—Five Levels of Organizational Cultural Maturity

The Commonwealth Fraud Prevention Centre sets out five levels of organizational cultural maturity as:[4]

(1) **interested**—explaining why counter fraud is essential activity;

(2) **invested**—move from awareness to embedding projects;

(3) **committed**—countering fraud is understood to be business critical;

(4) **engaged**—counter fraud is fundamental practice and prioritized;

(5) **embedded**—have a robust and self-perpetuating counter fraud culture.

Other recommendations by the Commonwealth Fraud Prevention Centre to build an effective counter fraud culture include:

- having a champion for your organizations code of conduct and ethics;
- connecting the counter fraud community to share best practice;
- top-level engagement in discussion and decision-making in the topics of fraud tolerance, countermeasure effectiveness, and fraud incidents;
- ensure a named person is accountable for fraud at an executive/senior management level;

[2] https://dictionary.cambridge.org/dictionary/english/culture (accessed 4 September 2023).

[3] CIPD, 'Employee Engagement' (2021), www.cipd.org/globalassets/media/knowledge/knowledge-hub/evidence-reviews/employee-engagement-discussion-report_tcm18-89598.pdf (accessed 17 July 2023).

[4] Commonwealth Fraud Prevention Centre, 'Influence Change to Develop a Strong Counter Fraud Culture' (2023), ww.counterfraud.gov.au/influence-change-develop-strong-counter-fraud-culture (accessed 4 September 2023).

- ensure all staff and contractors are aware of fraud appropriate to their role, including understanding how to identify and detect it;
- create a culture that allows all to speak freely about pressures and have mechanisms to support those associated with the organization;
- actively promote the processes in place that enable staff and contractors to safely report concerns about internal fraud;
- communicate the results of fraud investigations to raise awareness of your entity's active management of fraud risk and corrective action (where appropriate).

The effectiveness of the organization culture and the detection of fraud is linked to the wider investment in the people, services, and purpose of the organization. A wider positive organizational culture where employees are invested in their jobs and the service delivery means they are much more likely to take affirmative action when they suspect fraud. This makes any fraud awareness campaigns more likely to engage with its target audience.

6.2.2 **Effective Fraud Awareness Campaigns**

Though countering fraud is everyone's business, it requires a strong organizational counter fraud culture so that staff understand the fraud risks they may be exposed to, the indicators that might suggest there is fraud, and how to report these.[5]

As with other key aspects of any counter fraud policy an excellent starting point is the Government Function Standard (GovS 013) for counter fraud.[6] This sets out the high-level organizational requirements across a range of key counter fraud activity including awareness training:

> Organisations should ensure staff have access to and undertake fraud, bribery and corruption training as appropriate to their role. Individual staff members should ensure completion of counter fraud, bribery and corruption training as set by the organisation. The senior officer accountable for counter fraud within the organisation is responsible for the provision of fraud, bribery and corruption training. The senior officer accountable for counter fraud is responsible for the decision on what training is appropriate.

This focus on organization-specific reflects the fact that all organizations will have very different fraud risks, exposures, and appetites, as well as the legal mechanisms open to them to deal with fraud. Organization-specific training is recommended for a fully effective counter fraud culture to be developed and maintained.

---

[5] International Public Sector Fraud Forum, 'A Guide to Managing Fraud for Public Bodies' (2019), https://assets.publishing.service.gov.uk/government/uploads/system/uploads/attachment_data/file/1115931/GuideToManagingFraudForPublicBodies.pdf (accessed 17 July 2023).

[6] HM Government, *Government Functional Standard GovS 013: Counter Fraud: Management of Counter Fraud, Bribery and Corruption Activity* (August 2021), https://assets.publishing.service.gov.uk/media/612e5a8ce90e0705355a552b/6.7628_CO_Govt-Functional-Std_GovS013-Counter-Fraud_v4.pdf (accessed 2 November 2023).

Checklist—Fraud Awareness Training: The Basics

Fraud awareness training should be developed by both learning and counter fraud professionals and cover as a minimum:

- the definitions of fraud, bribery, and corruption;
- the psychology of fraud offending and the core theories;
- overview of organizational fraud landscape including key risks and their impacts;
- associated key fraud indicators and enablers for that organization;
- awareness of the policies and procedures including the gifts and hospitality policy, conflict of interest, and travel and subsistence policies;
- reporting routes for staff including whistle-blowing and the support available;
- identify those with specific responsibilities to counter the fraud threat;
- how to seek advice or support from counter fraud practitioners;
- how fraud referrals are managed from referral to disposal;
- relevant examples/case studies;
- an assessment of knowledge.

Organizations will have employees in roles that are higher risk positions, such as procurement and finance, and it is good practice to have additional bespoke training for these posts based on a proportionate response to the risks. Topics that should be covered in an enhanced module for finance may include:

- understanding mandate fraud and importance of, and compliance with, dual controls;
- sample testing of contractor billing and verification of works completion;
- expenses verification and sample testing;
- use of data matching and analytics within and between organizations.

With regard to frequency of fraud awareness learning this should be undertaken when an individual joins an organization and refreshed on annual basis.

6.2.3 **Fraud Indicators and Typologies**

As part of developing effective fraud awareness campaigns, detecting, and measuring fraud the organizational knowledge of fraud indicators and fraud typologies is important.

Checklist—Internal Fraud Indicators

Behavioural

- reluctance to take holidays;
- regularly work longer/excess hours for no discernible reason;
- unwilling to share duties or are secretive about their work;
- staff member has a clear grudge or is upset with their employer;
- behaviour changes such as becoming aggressive and defensive or bullying.

Financial

- asking questions about sensitive information (i.e. commercial) or seeking access not required for the day-to-day duties;
- lifestyle changes;
- appear to have financial difficulties;
- unusual level of cash transactions and/or customer refunds.

Procedural

- unexpected or sudden changes in suppliers or payment details/processes;
- reluctance to implement new controls;
- circumvents controls or develops 'workarounds' that do not appear necessary;
- poor record keeping;
- high volume of complaints;
- product/system failures.

External Fraud Indicators

- frequent change of directors/resurrection of dormant companies;
- lack of ID/proof of address;
- non-response to communications;
- non-renewal of applications for support/services;
- consecutive receipt numbers;

- undated records;
- failure to produce requested proofs/evidence;
- overpaying in cash for services, fines, bills then seeking refunds.

KEY POINTS—EXTERNAL FRAUD TYPOLOGIES

The Public Sector Fraud Authority (PSFA) sets categories for fraud loss typologies for the public sector as follows.

External—Expenditure

- procurement—collusion between contractors;
- procurement—mis-selling;
- procurement—other;
- means-tested payments (various);
- grant fraud (various);
- EU payments;
- loans;
- assets—theft and misuse;
- assets—written off;
- other.

External—Income

- exploiting assets and information;
- identity theft;
- post-contract fraud;
- computer hacking and unauthorized misuse;
- other.

External—Income

- charge evasion;
- fine and court costs evasion;
- tax fraud—national;
- tax fraud—local;
- other.

External—Third Party

- cheque fraud;
- mandate fraud;
- unsolicited requests for payment;
- plastic card fraud;
- computer hacking and e-enabled fraud;
- other.

6.2.4 Reporting Routes

Reporting fraud within an organization should be straightforward and the process clearly articulated and accessible. Those reporting should be able to do so in a confidential manner and have confidence that the report will be dealt with in a sensitive manner. Multiple reporting channels allow the report to be made at the appropriate level; if the report relates to internal fraud, then those reporting should be able to escalate the report to the appropriate level of seniority.

Many organizations have a fraud hotline or equivalent to encourage individuals to report their suspicions. Care and consideration should be given to the management of this information and the protection of the source.

KEY POINTS—GOVERNMENT FUNCTIONAL GOVS 013: COUNTER FRAUD (REPORTING PROCESSES)

GOV013, s. 5.2[7] prescribes the standard to be met by government bodies regarding reporting processes:

- Organizations should have well-established and documented reporting routes for staff, contractors, and members of the public to report suspicions of fraud, bribery, and corruption and a mechanism for recording these referrals and allegations.
- Reporting routes should be published and promoted.
- Organizations should monitor the usage of these reporting routes and take corrective action when needed.
- Organizations should have a mechanism or system for recording reported potential instances of fraud, bribery, and corruption.
- Instances should be recorded so the specifics of the allegations are clearly identified, including individuals and/or organizations involved and the act(s) they are alleged to have undertaken.

[7] Ibid.

6.2.5 **Data Analytics**

The use of data analytics in counter fraud detection falls into two distinct approaches. The first, and longest established, is to match different data sets from different organizations to identify suspected fraud. The second, and rapidly developing with use of artificial intelligence (AI) and machine learning, is that of data mining within a data set for patterns, anomalies, and other discrepancies that may indicate fraud. These can then be acted on to prevent, detect, and recover fraud losses.

These can never be 'evidence' of fraud in their own right and will have differing levels of likelihood. The importance of human decision-making in these processes is of critical importance.

Case Study: Data Matching—Real-Time Information

In April 2012, HM Revenue & Customs (HMRC) introduced Real-Time Information (RTI). Under RTI, information about tax and other deductions under the Pay As You Earn (PAYE) system was transmitted to HMRC by the employer every time an employee is paid.

From 2015 this was in turn matched to certain claims for welfare benefits, in particular the Department for Work and Pensions (DWP) Universal Credit (UC). Earnings reported to HMRC using PAYE/RTI are in turn reported to the DWP where they have notified HMRC that that employee is claiming UC.

This is done in 'real time' usually meaning weekly or monthly and the UC claim can be adjusted according to the earnings and disregard rules applicable to that claimant.

This significantly reduced fraud and error within welfare spending caused by earnings and are no longer the leading cause of fraud loss.[8]

The results of data analysis should always be reviewed by a human if fraud is suspected before proceedings are instigated.

6.2.6 **The National Fraud Initiative (NFI)**

The NFI remit is 'to better protect public service from fraud and error by helping to find and minimize loss'.[9] It does this through annual and biannual exercises that match electronic data within and between public and private sector bodies to prevent and detect fraud.

[8] DWP, 'Fighting Fraud in the Welfare System' (May 2022), www.gov.uk/government/publications/fighting-fraud-in-the-welfare-system/fighting-fraud-in-the-welfare-system--2#fn:1 (accessed 6 September 2023).

[9] 'National Fraud Initiative 2024 to 2025 Proposed Work Programme and Scale of Fees' (2 April 2024), https://www.gov.uk/government/consultations/national-fraud-initiative-2024-to-2025-work-programme-and-fees/national-fraud-initiative-2024-to-2025-proposed-work-programme-and-scale-of-fees-html (accessed 8 May 2024).

The NFI today sits within the PSFA as one of its operational data matching services. Since its inception in 1996 its cumulative savings are £2.4 billion. It has enabled participating organizations to prevent and detect over £1.1 billion fraud and error. By providing data matching services, the NFI helps to deliver one of PSFA's strategic objectives to innovate in intelligence and use of data, to increase the detection and fraud loss across the public sector.

Matching by the NFI includes, but is not limited to:[10]

- mortality screening to identify pensions being issued to deceased pensioners, or deferred pensioners have died;
- payroll screening to identity 'moonlighting', working while long-term sick and other undeclared conflicts that may invalidate their employment;
- housing tenant screening (social housing) by identifying if they have pre-existing social housing tenancies, only have one address, whether they are receiving housing benefit and if so for what address, verify eligibility for right to buy;
- trade creditor screening that can identify:

- overpaid VAT on invoices,
- duplicate payments,
- duplicate creditors,
- employee financial interest in a contractor;

- other bespoke matching services can be developed for the purposes of preventing and detecting fraud.

6.2.7 Pressure Testing

So-called pressure testing[11] can be applied to measure if there has been accurate reporting of measurement and detection activity. Pressure testing means testing systems and controls in place under differing circumstances (differing pressures) in order to assess their effectiveness. As stated by the Commonwealth Fraud Prevention Centre:

> This is more than just checking if countermeasures are in place or that processes are being followed. It involves considering and sometimes applying the common methods used by fraudsters to find ways around countermeasures your entity has in place. This helps you find vulnerabilities and challenge assumptions about how fraud is managed within your entity.

This assessment may identify workarounds, flaws, and other vulnerabilities that can be addressed and so reduce fraud. In this sense detection is reversed as sampling

[10] Cabinet Office, *National Fraud Initiative: Private Sector Services* (20 March 2015), www.gov.uk/guidance/national-fraud-initiative-private-sector-services#services-by-organisation-type (accessed 5 July 2023).

[11] Commonwealth Fraud Prevention Centre, 'Pressure Test Countermeasures to See If They Are Effective' (2021), www.counterfraud.gov.au/access-tools-and-guidance/i-want-pressure-test-countermeasures-see-if-they-are-effective (accessed 17 July 2023).

and detection reporting should show a fall in identified cases/values. This compared with the baseline can therefore show the value of the activity and the savings it has realized from preventing fraud.

6.2.8 Thematic Detection Activity

Thematic detection involves undertaking activities focused on specific areas of delivery and/or risk. This is based on specific fraud risks that have been identified via fraud risk assessment (FRA), measurement activity or because of a spike in existing fraud cases via typology or delivery area. Focusing efforts in this way can improve the effectiveness of detection activity and improve value for money. It can also increase the deterrent effect/deliver behavioural change that can in turn be measured via remeasuring from baseline such as has been seen with NHS dental contractors and prescription fraud levels.[12]

6.2.9 Fraud Detection by External Actors

A range of organizations, professionals, and individuals external to an organization play a significant role in the detection of fraud. Professionals such as auditors have responsibilities which are detailed in the 'International Standard on Auditing' of the Financial Reporting Council (FRC):[13]

> An auditor conducting an audit in accordance with ISAs (UK) is responsible for obtaining reasonable assurance that the financial statements taken as a whole are free from material misstatement, whether caused by fraud or error.

The revised standard was published in response to a review conducted by Sir Donlad Brydon who examined the quality and effectiveness of audit. The final report dated December 2019 titled 'Assess, Assure and Inform Improving Audit Quality and Effectiveness'[14] made a total of sixty-four recommendations, many relating to the strengthening of counter fraud activity.

Investigative journalism has proven to be essential in the detection and reporting of fraud and bringing it to the attention of both the public and victim organizations. The International Consortium of Investigative Journalists (ICIJ) regularly reports on financial crime matters and was responsible for the Panama Papers, Paradise Papers, and Pandora Paper, all of which were linked to exposing various forms of economic crime.

---

[12] NHSCFA (NHS Counter Fraud Authority), 'Influencing Behavioural Change', https://cfa.nhs.uk/fraud-prevention/fraud-prevention-reports/preventing-procurement-fraud-in-the-NHS/pp-influencing-behavioural-change (accessed 6 September 2023).

[13] FRC, 'The Auditor's Responsibilities Relating to Fraud in an Audit of Financial Statements' (May 2021), www.frc.org.uk/getattachment/e48499f2-b69b-4f45-8bef-762583eab1cd/ISA-(UK)-240_Revised-May-2021_Updated-May-2022.pdf (accessed 5 September 2023).

[14] D. Brydon, 'Assess, Assure and Inform Improving Audit Quality and Effectiveness' (December 2019), https://assets.publishing.service.gov.uk/government/uploads/system/uploads/attachment_data/file/852960/brydon-review-final-report.pdf (accessed 5 September 2023).

Further Reading

- *ACFE Report to the Nations: 2022 Global Fraud Study*, https://legacy.acfe.com/report-to-the-nations/2022/?_ga=2.161839996.1112429651.1690183179-474221888.1688109120 (accessed 24 July 2023);
- Commonwealth Fraud Prevention Centre, www.counterfraud.gov.au/ (accessed 4 September 2023);
- PSFA, 'Guide to Managing Fraud for Public Bodies' (2023), www.gov.uk/government/publications/international-public-sector-fraud-forum-guidance (accessed 4 September 2023);
- HM Government, 'Government Functional Standard: GovS 013: Counter Fraud' (version 2, August 2021), www.gov.uk/government/publications/government-functional-standard-govs-013-counter-fraud (accessed 17 July 2023);
- NFI, www.gov.uk/government/collections/national-fraud-initiative (accessed 4 September 2023);
- Digital Economy Act 2017, ch. 4 Fraud Against the Public Sector, www.legislation.gov.uk/ukpga/2017/30/part/5/chapter/4/enacted (accessed 5 September 2023);
- FRC, 'The Auditor's Responsibilities Relating to Fraud in an Audit of Financial Statements' (May 2021), www.frc.org.uk/getattachment/e48499f2-b69b-4f45-8bef-762583eab1cd/ISA-(UK)-240_Revised-May-2021_Updated-May-2022.pdf (accessed 5 September 2023);
- ICIJ, www.icij.org/about/ (accessed 5 September 2023).

6.3 Fraud Measurement

The Government Counter Fraud Professions Fraud Measurement Standard[15] sets out the objectives for fraud measurement activity:

- establish the vulnerabilities of the organization to fraud;
- identify, quantify, and report instances of fraud and error being prevented and detected through the business processes and controls operated by the organization;
- test for and measure levels of undetected fraud and error to gain additional insights into, and assurance over, current estimated levels of fraud and error across the organization;
- be able to calculate the value of fraud and error prevented, including future savings from the implementation of additional controls or ways of working;
- enable more informed and transparent conversations within the organization on its fraud risks and the material nature of the threat they present to the organization;
- measure the effectiveness of the organization's counter fraud strategy.

[15] Cabinet Office, 'Fraud Investigation Core Discipline Standard (2018)' (available from the Government Counter Fraud Profession gcfp@cabinetoffice.gov.uk).

For the purposes of counter fraud, it is important to understand the difference between the general testing of systems and processes, and specific fraud measurement assurance as one evolved out of the other. The former is testing the effectiveness and application of controls such as compliance with financial processes or contracts using a statistically valid sample.

Distinguishing between the error and fraud is sometimes clear from the outset, but more often than not requires investigative or compliance resources which is not the objective of the exercise. However, the organization may wish to refer cases identified as error for further inquiry, if they have such resources available, and their measurement approach did not provide anonymity assurances to anyone interviewed to improve engagement and reliability aspects of the exercise.

It has been noted by both the National Audit Office (NAO) and at Public Accounts Committees (PACs) over time that historically measurement activity to estimate the levels of fraud and error levels within the public sector has focused on tax, welfare, and health. It is also notable that these areas are where that the majority of counter fraud resources are focused.

Figure 6.2 sets out the high-level approach to the Government's Counter Fraud Function and Profession's Fraud Measurement and Assurance three gate approach. Selecting an area of spend can be drawn from the organization's FRA or by considering the following points:

- any recent cases of fraud confirmed or expected;
- any areas which are most likely to be subject to fraud;
- areas with perceived highest risk.

Measurement requires data that can be tested to confirm the validity of each attribute or item within the sample. Testing for fraud requires each item to be rigorously verified

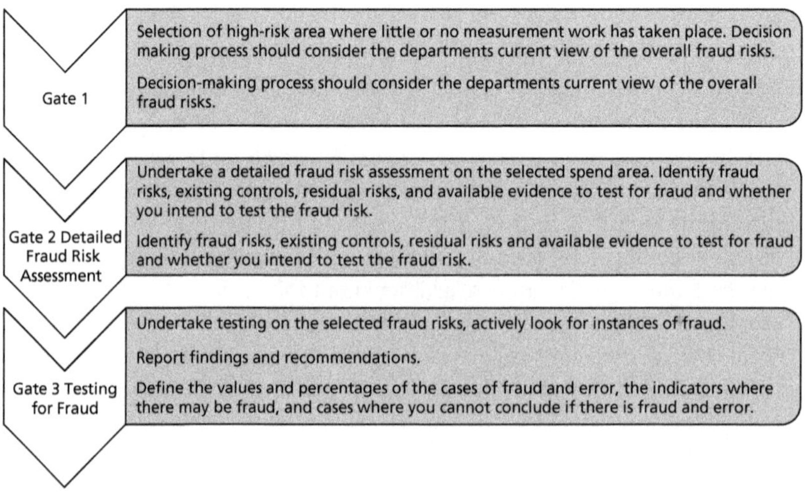

Figure 6.2 GCFP's Fraud Measurement and Assurance process

by examining all information accessed via legal gateways to confirm that the data and information held within the area of spend/income can be measured for fraud. Comparator data is also required to validate existing data and identify inconsistencies and anomalies which can be an indicator of fraud or error. This can be evidence taken from within the particular spend area that relates to key decision points, as can be identified on a process map, and the evidence and information required to make that decision.

This data should then be compared to secondary or external data sources that can be used to test the accuracy and reliability of the application data. If this comparison is not made, the process would only be testing controls and process compliance, not taking the additional step of testing the data provided itself. This is the key difference between control testing and fraud measurement. Such data may come through use of the Digital Economy Act 2017 gateways or the NFI that can be used to prevent and detect fraud by matching data sets from different sources and organizations.

The PSFA assessment of the fraud landscape each year shows there is a large area where the actual fraud loss is unknown.[16] The rationale for this is described in the PSFA 'Fraud Landscape Annual Report 2022' as:

> Due to the nature of fraud as an inherently hidden crime, with a high degree of uncertainty, the government uses an estimated range for it.[17]

6.4 Impact of the Covid-19 Pandemic on Fraud Measurement

The UK government spent hundreds of billions of pounds[18] during the Covid-19 pandemic, this included £46 billion in Bounce Back Loan support to businesses and sole traders. The fraud losses that followed in the BBL scheme had a significant impact on both the fraud landscape and how the government responds to fraud. Key publications that resulted from the pandemic included:

In March 2021, the NAO published its 'Fraud & Error Good Practice Guidance', and a key focus was the need to undertake effective detection activity:

> Organisations need cost-effective controls to detect and rectify fraud and error.

In May 2021, the NAO stated that[19]:

> government needs to do more to measure exactly how much fraud and error there is in the system, put in place cost-effective counter-fraud and error controls, and

[16] Public Sector Fraud Authority, 'Cross-Government Fraud Landscape Annual Report 2022' (21 March 2023), https://assets.publishing.service.gov.uk/government/uploads/system/uploads/attachment_data/file/1145111/2974_Fraud_Landscape_Annual_Report_2022_.pdf (accessed 17 July 2023).

[17] Ibid.

[18] P. Brien and M. Keep, 'Public Spending during the Covid-19 Pandemic' (12 September 2023), https://researchbriefings.files.parliament.uk/documents/CBP-9309/CBP-9309.pdf (accessed 24 July 2023).

[19] National Audit Office (NAO), 'Good Practice Guidance: Fraud and Error—NAO Insight' (2021), https://www.nao.org.uk/insights/good-practice-guidance-fraud-and-error/ (accessed 26 April 2024).

> detect and pursue overpayments to protect the taxpayer's interest. This is now more important than ever.
>
> The same month the Public Accounts Committee (PAC) recommended that government 'introduce mandatory (initial) fraud impact assessments...for all Government Major Projects Portfolio (GMPP)'.

These reports and hearings changed the political landscape for public sector fraud with a recognition that more had to be done across all aspects of counter fraud but with a particular focus of effective detection activity to inform wider counter fraud responses.

As a result, in March 2022 HMT formally adopted the PAC recommendation for initial fraud impact assessments (IFIAs) and updated the Green Book and Managing Public Money to include the need for an IFIA. This comes early in the life cycle of proposed new major spend activity. The purpose is to provide early assessment of the need to resource counter fraud activity, including mapping out counter fraud requirements throughout the spend area life cycle. It should also identify when the proposed design of a spend activity needs to be adapted or changed in relation to counter fraud concerns.

This assessment includes the need for effective future use of measurement and detection activity, maintenance of detailed FRAs, and the need to improve controls to reduce fraud and error. The government FRA standard[20] that covers IFIAs and full FRAs specified that management reports from fraud risk detections systems must be reported.

Further Reading

- International Public Sector Fraud Forum, 'A Guide to Managing Fraud for Public Bodies' (2019), https://assets.publishing.service.gov.uk/government/uploads/system/uploads/attachment_data/file/1115931/GuideToManagingFraudForPublicBodies.pdf (accessed 17 July 2023);
- GOV.UK, 'Cross-Government Fraud Landscape Annual Report 2022' (21 March 2023), www.gov.uk/government/publications/cross-government-fraud-landscape-annual-report-2022 (accessed 17 July 2023);
- HM Treasury, *Whole of Government Accounts, 2020–21* (20 July 2023), www.gov.uk/government/publications/whole-of-government-accounts-2020-21 (accessed 22 July 2023).

[20] https://assets.publishing.service.gov.uk/government/uploads/system/uploads/attachment_data/file/1069745/Fraud-Risk-Assessment-Standards-2022-03-25.pdf (accessed 22 June 2023).

7

Using Intelligence to Counter Fraud

Blackstone's Counter Fraud Professionals' Handbook. Michael J. Betts, Laura Eshelby, and David Whitehouse-Hayes, Oxford University Press.

DOI: 10.1093/9780191996955.003.0007

7.1 Introduction

In this chapter we explore the intelligence gathering landscape, identify sources of intelligence, review how it can be analysed and shared to counter fraud. We will explain the intelligence cycle explaining the difference between information and intelligence. The National Intelligence Model (NIM) will be critically analysed to see how it can be used effectively in a counter fraud environment. We will summarize how the NIM works and explain how it can be used to inform fraud prevention and detection. The intelligence handling codes and methods of sharing between organizations are described. We will detail how the NIM can be applied effectively across the public sector and beyond.

Countering fraud relies on several key factors and intelligence gathering is critical to success, whether it is used to develop a strategic intelligence assessment, responding to a suspicious activity report (SAR)[1] or developing a financial profile. The counter fraud practitioner is required to understand the numerous sources of intelligence, how to gather it lawfully, how it should be analysed, and, where appropriate, shared. All this must be undertaken with a view to fulfilling the requirements of a range of legislation including in England and Wales, the Criminal Procedure and Investigations Act 1996 and its associated Codes of Practice.[2]

Intelligence is a multidimensional concept; it incorporates material from a wide range of sources including human, open, and closed sources (information held in confidence requiring a level of authority to access). Intelligence is gathered by governments on a routine basis. These include geospatial (objects reproduced electronically or by optical means)[3] and communications data. This material is often sensitive in nature.

The management of intelligence requires a significant degree of competency and should only be undertaken by an appropriately trained practitioner. The protection of the sources of intelligence, depending on its sensitivity, should always be at the forefront of a counter fraud practitioner's mind. The management of intelligence deals with sensitive information much of which is personal data and covered by the Human Rights Act 1998, Data Protection Act 2018, and General Data Protection Regulations.

---

1 National Crime Agency, 'Suspicious Activity Reports', www.nationalcrimeagency.gov.uk, www.nationalcrimeagency.gov.uk/what-we-do/crime-threats/money-laundering-and-illicit-finance/suspicious-activity-reports (accessed 16 July 2023).

2 Ministry of Justice (2020), Criminal Procedure and Investigations Act 1996 (s. 23(1)) Code of Practice, https://assets.publishing.service.gov.uk/government/uploads/system/uploads/attachment_data/file/931173/Criminal-procedure-and-investigations-act-1996.pdf (accessed 16 July 2023).

3 USNWC, Intelligence studies: imagery/geospatial intelligence, https://usnwc.libguides.com/c.php?g=494120&p=3381562 (accessed 16 July 2023).

Table 7.1 Data/information to product

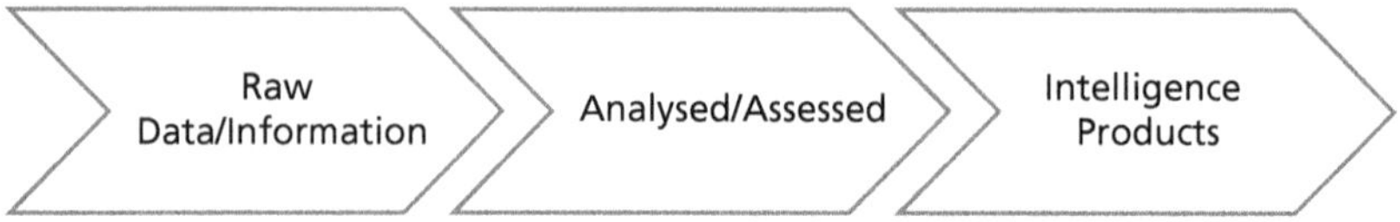

7.1.1 **What is Intelligence?**

For the purposes of this chapter, when referring to intelligence we mean information and/or data that is analysed and subject to a defined evaluation; when effectively managed its processing results in products that can lead to the effective prevention and detection of fraud and ultimately the prosecution of offenders (see Table 7.1).

Intelligence allows those tasked with counter fraud and associated offending to see beyond the boundaries of an organization, assess fraudsters' capabilities, methods, and attack vectors. This knowledge should inform the counter measures including the assessing of risk.

7.1.2 **An Information-Rich World**

We live in a world where information is all around us—in this digital age we are saturated with information. Making sense of information is vital to those countering fraud, bribery, and corruption. We live in an increasingly data-rich society which presents a wide range of intelligence sources accessible through digital devices by both human and artificial intelligence.

KEY POINTS—AN INTELLIGENCE-RICH WORLD

- Google is visited 89.3 billion times every month;[4]
- 2020—467.65 billion purchase transactions for goods and services worldwide;[5]
- 2020—there were reported to be 4.8 billion internet users across the globe;[6]
- 2022—the global human population reached 8.0 billion;[7]
- 129 million different books have been published;[8]
- around 1.01 billion credit card transactions occur daily.[9]

[4] M. Mohsin, '10 Google Search Statistics You Need to Know in 2023' (infographic) (13 January 2023), Oberlo, www.oberlo.com/blog/google-search-statistics (accessed 16 July 2023).

[5] Nilson Report, https://nilsonreport.com/research_featured_chart.php (accessed 16 July 2023).

[6] SeedScientific, 'How Much Data Is Created Every Day?' (2021) (27 Powerful Stats), https://seedscientific.com/how-much-data-is-created-every-day (accessed 16 July 2023).

[7] United Nations, Population (2023), www.un.org/en/global-issues/population (accessed 16 July 2023).

[8] J. Jackson, 'Google: 129 Million Different Books Have Been Published', *PCWorld* (6 August 2010), www.pcworld.com/article/508405/google_129_million_different_books_have_been_published.html (accessed 16 July 2023).

[9] Nilson Report.

In the digital era, the volume of accessible information is almost overwhelming. Information needs to be transformed into a usable product that can be used to inform counter fraud activity. Turning information into an intelligence product requires it to be analysed and evaluated. Once this process has been undertaken it can be used to inform a range of activities including informing fraud risk assessments, instigating, and supporting fraud investigations.

The process of managing intelligence-led activity in the UK is undertaken in compliance with the NIM, which is detailed later in the chapter. The process of converting information in the UK uses an intelligence management evaluation method, based on grading the source, evaluation, and dissemination (further detailed later in this chapter).

Checklist—Types of Intelligence

There are three key types of intelligence:

- **Strategic intelligence**—typically provides insight into the wider threats a country or organization faces, it may identify the threat actors, crime trends, and hotspots; it is often used to inform the development of a national strategic assessment or strategic intelligence assessment. This type of intelligence details current and future trends; it identifies at a strategic level the 'what' and 'why'. It is used to inform the strategic response to the threats identified.
- **Tactical intelligence**—provides insight into the methods used by offenders; it can be used to develop the response and often describes the wider when, where, who, and how of potential threats.
- **Operational intelligence**—is more granular in nature and may relate to a specific person and/or crime group. It may describe associations, methods of offending, and used to inform the response to future actions.

7.2 History of Intelligence Gathering

Gathering intelligence has an interesting history and is not a new phenomenon, in Tudor England one of Queen Elizabeth I's advisers, Sir Francis Walsingham, established an effective spy network to protect the queen; the acquisition of intelligence was central to the Queen's reign from 1558 until she died in 1603. Oliver Cromwell relied on John Thurloe who excelled at intelligence gathering; in 1653 he became head of intelligence. Thurloe was responsible for a network of national and international intelligence gathering using spies and experts including a mathematician to break codes.

In 1878, the first Criminal Investigation Department (CID), was formed by the Metropolitan police force and was led by Howard Vincent, a barrister by profession. The gathering of intelligence was fundamental to its success.

In 1909, MI5, the UK's national security service was founded to protect the country from threats to national security. At the heart of the organization is intelligence gathering.

During conflict between nations intelligence gathering has been paramount to defending nations; the range of methods and their intrusive nature continued to expand. Today we are the most surveilled and monitored society: we live in an era where intelligence has never been so prolific but the challenges for the counter fraud practitioner are in identifying, accessing, and analysing the material.

7.3 Intelligence and Confidentiality

Breaches of intelligence security can result in significant issues for those providing material, the methods of collection, and harm to the reputation of the organization involved. An example of the harm caused by the leaking of intelligence was the case of Edward Snowden[10] which was first reported by the *Guardian* newspaper in 2013. Snowden, a systems analyst, was employed as a contractor working for the US Central Intelligence Agency (CIA), he was responsible for the largest leak of intelligence from the US National Security Agency.[11] It is reported that he accessed 1.7 million files, the downloaded amount unknown, but more than 7,000 top-secret documents were released by journalists in both the UK and US by a range of media outlets including the *Guardian* and *Washington Post* newspapers. The release of this top-secret intelligence detailing the US and UK surveillance programmes caused significant reputational harm and criticism from those who had been subject to the intelligence gathering activity.

Case Study—Insider Threat Charles Fletcher

The insider threat should not be underestimated by those managing intelligence. The case of Colin Gunn[12] and Temporary Detective Constable Charles Fletcher of Nottinghamshire constabulary is a useful reminder of the ever-present threat.

Gunn led an organized crime group in Nottingham and was jailed for life in 2006 for conspiring to murder Joan and John Stirland in Trusthorpe, Lincolnshire.

---

[10] 'NSA', *The Guardian*, www.theguardian.com/us-news/nsa (accessed 16 July 2023).

[11] P. Szoldra, 'This Is Everything Edward Snowden Revealed in One Year of Unprecedented Top-Secret Leaks', *Business Insider* (2016), www.businessinsider.com/snowden-leaks-timeline-2016-9?r=US&IR=T (accessed 16 July 2023).

[12] R. Sherdley, 'Colin Gunn Told Jury Who Convicted Him "Thank You, You Scumbags"' (2022), www.nottinghampost.com/news/local-news/moment-colin-gunn-told-jury-7590696 (accessed 16 July 2023).

Fletcher provided access to police intelligence reports on Gunn and his associates, which were sent via faxes to an associate of Gunn. Fletcher was jailed for seven years for misconduct in a public office.

He was jailed for nine years for the corruption of Charles Fletcher, a serving officer in the Nottinghamshire constabulary.

Intelligence should be kept confidential and on a strict need-to-know basis. Those involved in intelligence gathering, its analysis, and sharing should be suitably trained to ensure its sources are protected.

Checklist—Maintaining Confidentiality

- consider enhanced vetting for those managing intelligence;
- ensure physical locations are secure;
- use of sterile corridors;
- ensure documents are appropriately security marked;
- restrict access to databases holding intelligence;
- ensure audit records are maintained of access to intelligence;
- monitor the well-being of those concerned with the management of intelligence;
- maintain a duty of care to sources of intelligence;
- only share on a need-to-know basis;
- undertake regular security briefings with staff handling intelligence;
- undertake regular risk assessments of sources of intelligence;
- use approved forms to share intelligence (intelligence report 3 x 5 x 2);
- implement effective security procedures.

7.4 Intelligence Landscape

The international and national intelligence landscape is complex; some organizations are purely intelligence focused; others have an intelligence capability blended with an investigative function.

7.5 International Intelligence Gathering Organizations

Organizations with international reach and relevance include the following.

7.5.1 International Criminal Police Organization (Interpol)

Interpol was established in 1923 and is an international organization with its headquarters in France. It has 195 member countries including the UK. It undertakes a range of activities including the collection and sharing of intelligence to its member organizations. It has a powerful secure intelligence database used for criminal analysis. The organization also issues a range of alert notices which are international requests for cooperation or alerts to share critical crime-related information.

7.5.2 Financial Action Task Force (FATF)

FATF was established in 1989 and is based in France. It is an intergovernmental organization with a focus on countering money laundering and terrorist financing. It develops, maintains, and publishes international standards. It has thirty-nine[13] member countries within excess of two hundred jurisdictions applying the standards. It has a global network and nine regional bodies. FATF maintains both high-risk jurisdictions subject to a call for action[14] and jurisdictions under increased monitoring; these designations indicate countries with strategic deficiencies.

Further Reading—International Intelligence Gathering Organizations

- Interpol, www.interpol.int (accessed 16 July 2023);
- FATF, www.fatf-gafi.org/en/home.html (accessed 16 July 2023).

7.6 National Intelligence Gathering Organizations

There are a range of organizations that gather intelligence in the UK as part of their function. However, several organizations focus more on intelligence gathering.

[13] FATF suspended membership of the Russian Federation on 24 February 2023.

[14] This statement (previously called 'public statement'), identifies countries or jurisdictions with serious strategic deficiencies to counter money laundering, terrorist financing, and financing of proliferation. For all countries identified as high-risk, the FATF calls on all members and urges all jurisdictions to apply enhanced due diligence, and in the most serious cases, countries are called upon to apply countermeasures to protect the international financial system from the ongoing money laundering, terrorist financing, and proliferation financing risks emanating from the country.

7.6.1 **Security Service (MI5)**

The role of MI5, is defined in the Security Service Act 1989:

> the function of the Service shall be the protection of national security and, in particular, its protection against threats from espionage, terrorism and sabotage, from the activities of agents of foreign powers and from actions intended to overthrow or undermine parliamentary democracy by political, industrial, or violent means.[15]

The organization counters four key areas of threat: terrorism, espionage, cyber, and the proliferation of weapons of mass destruction.

7.6.2 **UK Secret Intelligence Service (SIS)**

SIS is also known as MI6, and has three main aims:

(1) to work internationally to counter terrorism;
(2) to disrupt hostile states;
(3) to give the UK a cyber advantage.

KEY POINTS—SECURITY SERVICES INTELLIGENCE COLLECTION

The methods of intelligence collection by the security services include:

- covert human intelligence sources (CHIS);
- directed surveillance;
- interception of communications;
- communications data;
- accessing bulk personal data;
- intrusive surveillance;
- equipment interference.

7.6.3 **GCHQ**

Formed in 1919 following the recognition of the importance of signals intelligence gathered during the First World War, it was originally called the Government Code & Cypher School. Following its move to Bletchley Park, it changed its name to GCHQ. During the Second World War there, it became home to Alan Turing, a leading cryptanalyst,[16] who is famed for leading the project to break the German navy Enigma code machine.[17] In 1946, GCHQ moved to Cheltenham where it

[15] Security Service Act 1989, www.legislation.gov.uk/ukpga/1989/5/section/1 (accessed 16 July 2023).
[16] An expert in deciphering coded messages without prior knowledge of the key.
[17] Alan Turing, www.gchq.gov.uk/information/alan-turing (accessed 16 July 2023).

continues to be located. GCHQ is the UK's national intelligence, cyber, and security agency. It has five focus areas:

(1) counter terrorism;
(2) cyber security;
(3) strategic advantage (including promoting the UK's prosperity);
(4) serious and organized crime;
(5) supporting the Ministry of Defence.

As an agency it gathers substantial amounts of communications data and has extensive analysis capability.

7.6.4 Joint Intelligence Committee (JIC)

The JIC is located within the Cabinet Office. It is intelligence focused and produces assessments and briefings on matters that may impact on the national interest, primarily security, defence, and foreign affairs. Its members include the National Security Advisor and representatives from the Cabinet Office, Foreign and Commonwealth Office, the Ministry of Defence, the Home Office, the Department for International Development, HM Treasury and the heads of GCHQ, SIS, and MI5. It also maintains oversight of the intelligence community's analytical capability through a Professional Head of Intelligence Analysis.[18]

7.6.5 National Crime Agency (NCA)

The NCA is responsible for protecting the UK from serious and organized crime, through disruption and prosecution and providing specialist capabilities. It collects intelligence and publishes the National Strategic Threat Assessment of serious and organized crime. The NCA operate the National Economic Crime Centre (NECC) which is a collaborative body to coordinate the response to economic crime. It houses the UK Financial Intelligence Unit (UKFIU) whose responsibilities include managing the flow of financial intelligence gathered from SARs. The NCA has the Home Office-funded International Corruption Unit which has responsibility for undertaking inquiries into allegations of international bribery and the linked money laundering offence.

Further Reading

- UK Security Service (MI5), www.mi5.gov.uk/ (accessed 16 July 2023);
- UK Secret Intelligence Service (SIS), www.sis.gov.uk (accessed 16 July 2023);
- GCHQ, www.gchq.gov.uk (accessed 16 July 2023);

[18] JIC, www.gchq.gov.uk. www.gchq.gov.uk/information/joint-intelligence-committee (accessed 16 July 2023).

- JIC, www.gchq.gov.uk/information/joint-intelligence-committee (accessed 16 July 2023);
- NCA, www.nationalcrimeagency.gov.uk (accessed 16 July 2023);
- NECC, www.nationalcrimeagency.gov.uk/what-we-do/national-economic-crime-centre (accessed 16 July 2023);
- UK Financial Investigation Unit (UKFIU), https://nationalcrimeagency.gov.uk/what-we-do/crime-threats/money-laundering-and-illicit-finance/ukfiu (accessed 16 July 2023).

7.7 The National Intelligence Model (NIM)

In 2000, the NIM was introduced into law enforcement in England and Wales (Figure 7.1). It was the result of work undertaken by the then National Criminal Intelligence Service (NCIS) and the Association of Chief Police Officers (ACPO).[19] The model is a framework that promotes an intelligence-led response to offending and is used at both the strategic and tactical levels. It introduced a consistent

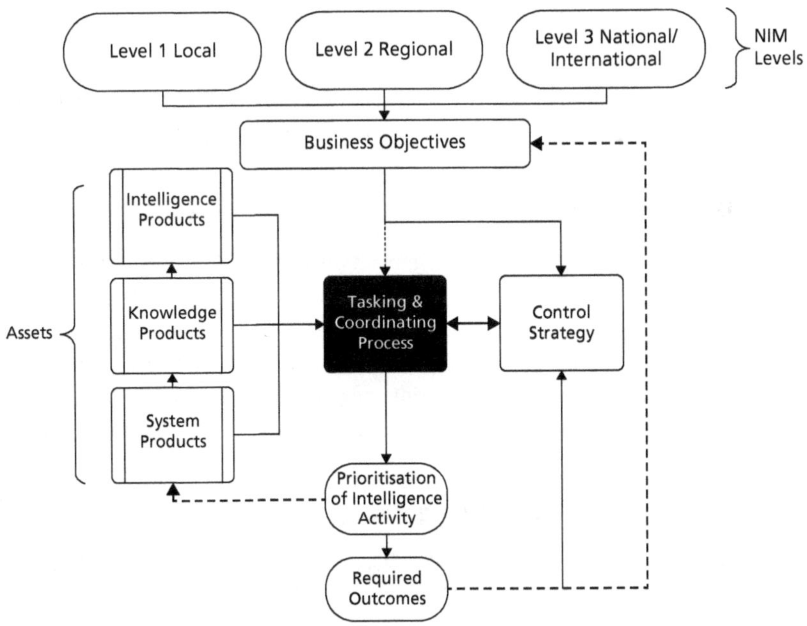

Figure 7.1 NIM overview

[19] National Criminal Intelligence Service (2000); NIM, p. 8, www.intelligenceanalysis.net/National%20Intelligence%20Model.pdf (accessed 16 July 2023).

Table 7.2 NIM levels

Level	Descriptor	Description
1	Local	Local issues impacting on a force area often linked to volume crime offending
2	Cross border	Cross border impacting on several forces and/or agencies
3	National/international	Serious and organized crime often requiring a national proactive response

and professional approach to the resourcing, collection, and dissemination of intelligence.

Figure 7.1 illustrates the key components of the NIM, central to its coordination is the tasking and coordinating process. This process is linked to the business objectives and fed by intelligence assets which are reviewed against the control strategy and required outcomes. The NIM can operate effectively at any of the three levels being local, regional (cross boarders), and national.

7.7.1 NIM Levels

Table 7.2 describes each of the NIM levels. While the processes and products are similar, they may vary in detail and complexity.

7.7.2 NIM Control Strategy

The NIM control strategy details the organizational priorities to counter fraud and may relate to detection, prevention, and enforcement. It provides a framework for those attending the tasking and coordinating meetings to prioritize resources and inform the decision-making process. The control strategy should be developed in a collaborative manner engaging with a wide range of stakeholders.

The control strategy can be amended by those attending the strategic tasking group.

Further Reading—Control Strategies

- College of Policing, 'Governance' (23 October 2013), www.college.police.uk/app/intelligence-management/governance (accessed 16 July 2023).

Table 7.3 T&CG activities

Tasking and Coordination meetings	Production of intelligence products	Prioritisation of intelligence activity

7.7.3 **Tasking and Coordinating Process**

The Tasking and Coordinating Group (T&CG) process has three key areas as shown in Table 7.3.

7.7.4 **Tasking and Coordination Meetings**

The tasking and coordination meeting is key to success, and should be chaired by a senior manager with the appropriate authority level to make decisions and deploy resources. The meetings are 'driven' by four main intelligence products, namely the strategic assessment, tactical assessment, target profiles, and problem profiles. Two tasking and coordination meeting types may take place:

(1) Strategic—meets every 3–6 months and considers the control strategy, setting the priorities for the intelligence, prevention, disruption, enforcement priorities, and resource control.
(2) Tactical—meets weekly to review the tactical assessment and reviews the current plans are fulfilling their objectives. It uses a tactical menu to respond to emerging issues.

Checklist—Tactical Menu

The tactical menu includes four key responses:

(1) targeting of offenders;
(2) management of crime hotspots;
(3) investigation of linked offending;
(4) application of prevention measures.

7.7.5 **Intelligence Products**

These products should be collaborative, and their design and content should involve all key stakeholders. Typically these will include both intelligence officers and analysts. Those involved have responsibility for the collection, analysis, and presentation of information which inform decisions. Such products include:

- strategic assessments;
- tactical assessments;
- target profiles;
- problem Profiles.

7.7.6 **Strategic Assessment**

A strategic assessment provides insight into its topic area; it tends to be a higher-level document detailing both the current situation but also future trends and in particular threats. On counter fraud, it will review at a strategic level the current threat landscape in the required area and predict the medium and long-term issues. The assessment should inform the prioritization of resources, assist with business planning, and the development of policies. It should be used to develop the control strategy for the organization and link to supporting activities including fraud investigation, disruption, and prevention.

The strategic strategy should be reviewed on a regular basis.

KEY POINTS—FORMAT OF STRATEGIC ASSESSMENT

- foreword—details the content of the assessment and its key features;
- executive summary;
- aim/scope—articulates the scope of the assessment;
- current situation—to include a summary of the previous assessment and any key changes;
- emerging areas—describes contemporary trends and threats;
- recommendations;
- conclusions.

The NCA produces a National Strategic Assessment of serious and organized crime. The document provides a comprehensive assessment of threats facing the UK. The report covers child sexual abuse, modern slavery, and human trafficking, organized immigration crime, drugs, firearms, organized acquisitive crime, cyber-crime, fraud, money laundering, bribery corruption, and sanctions evasion.[20]

[20] NCA, 'Crime Strategic Assessment' (2021), https://nationalcrimeagency.gov.uk/who-we-are/publications/533-national-strategic-assessment-of-serious-and-organised-crime-2021/file (accessed 16 July 2023).

The National Health Service Counter Fraud Authority (NHSCFA) publishes a strategic intelligence assessment which identifies potential losses, threats, enablers, and vulnerabilities. The document directly informs the risk to the organization and pinpoints where mitigations are required.

Further Reading

- NCA National Strategic Assessments can be viewed at: https://nationalcrimeagency.gov.uk/component/finder/search?q=%22National+Strategic+Assessment%22&Itemid=101&Itemid=101 (accessed 16 July 2023);
- NHS Counter Fraud Authority Strategic Intelligence Document can be viewed at: https://cfa.nhs.uk/about-nhscfa/corporate-publications/strategic-intelligence-assessment (accessed 16 July 2023).

7.7.7 Tactical Assessments

The primary purpose of a tactical assessment is to assess issues that are having current impact, to help gain an understanding of the root causes, and to assist in the early intervention of the threat. The assessment may report on the prevalent situation and be used to inform the deployment of resources. It may identify the causes, offender profiles, and provide options for the response to limit harm and loss.

7.7.8 Target Profiles

Target profiles provide an analysis of a person of interest.[21] The profile may detail a wide-ranging set of intelligence drawn from a range of sources including:

- previous convictions;
- associations and network;
- use of communications;
- vehicles;
- a financial profile.

It is used to inform decision-making and assist in operational management.

Checklist—Financial Profiles

Financial profiles are an essential intelligence tool; they can be commissioned for a variety of reasons including the need to identify criminality, identify the proceeds of crime, identify motives, associations, and links to people and places, and to provide

[21] Person of interest in this context means suspected offender or convicted offender.

information on a suspect's movements. The accredited financial investigation or intelligence officer will gather material from a range of sources, including:

- criminal records and organizational intelligence systems;
- SARs;
- utility companies;
- retailers, including loyalty cards;
- financial information including credit reference agencies;
- classified information held on a range of financial databases;
- open source including Land Registry and Companies House;
- regulatory information held by organizations including the Financial Conduct Authority (FCA) and Competitions and Markets Authority;
- information held by government departments including His Majesty's Revenue & Customs and Department for Work and Pensions;
- local authorities;
- Passport Office.

7.7.9 Problem Profiles

Problem profiles are helpful in establishing the scale and cause of specific crime hotspots or trends. They are important in understanding the root cause of problem areas and can assist in developing an appropriate response. Problem profiles often include an analysis of the background issues, their scale, a profile of the offenders, and their related potential impact. The profile should be used to consider the range of responses and drive crime reduction activity, which could include prevention, disruption, and enforcement activity.

7.8 The Intelligence Cycle

The intelligence cycle is used to present the process of gathering and analysing material at both strategic and tactical levels (Figure 7.2). It is often presented in six stages detailing a methodological approach to this process. This process links directly to the NIM and forms a fundamental component of informing the model's assets (intelligence, knowledge, and system).

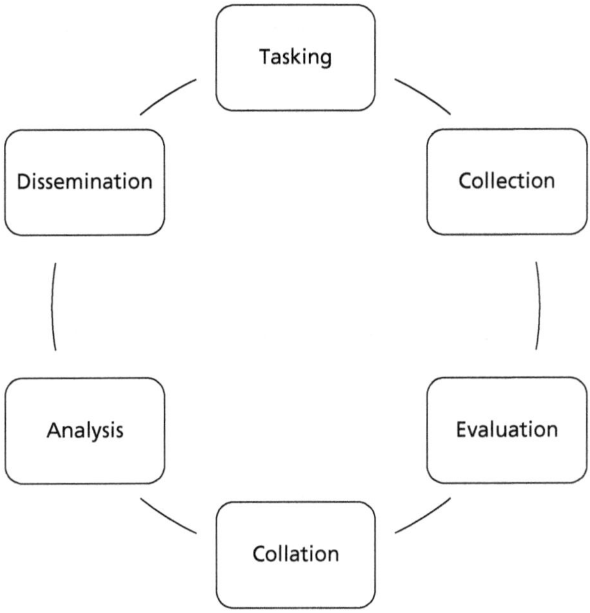

Figure 7.2 The intelligence cycle

Checklist—The Intelligence Cycle Stages

Direction/Tasking

- Direction and tasking are the responsibility of those attending the strategic and tactical coordination meetings.
- Meetings are chaired by those who have the authority to make decisions and can deploy resources.
- Direction and tasking should take account of the control strategy.
- Problems, patterns, and trends should be discussed, and resources tasked in response.

Collection

- Collection plans are used to structure the gathering of intelligence.
- These plans describe the information needed and the means of acquisition; the format usually includes:
    - the problem definition;
    - project aim and scope.

- Intelligence analysts are specialists who gather and analyse the intelligence.
- The analyst should select the information sources relevant to the collection plan; these range from open source, closed/confidential, or classified sources.

Evaluation

- The information that is collected is subject to evaluation.
- Evaluation assesses the reliability and quality of the information gathered.
- In the UK, the method used to evaluate intelligence is the 3 x 5 x 2 classification method:
  - the acquisition through the source of the evaluation (3);
  - the intelligence evaluation (5);
  - the conditions for handling the intelligence (2).
- Other systems are used internationally; these include a 4 x 4 system that grades the source evaluation and information evaluation.[22]

Collation

- Collation describes the process of organizing the information gathered into a system where it can be accessed and analysed.
- An extensive range of digital platforms are available for this purpose.

Analysis

- Integrating the intelligence gathered is fundamental to building the intelligence picture.
- The visual representation of the information gathered is a crucial factor in maximizing the value of the intelligence.
- A range of commercial and bespoke software is available to automate the analysis and for use by analysts to chart the intelligence.

Dissemination

- Once the intelligence has been analysed, the analytical products need to be shared with the relevant stakeholders.

[22] UNODC (UN Office on Drugs and Crime), *Criminal Intelligence: Manual for Analysts* (UN, New York, 2011), www.unodc.org/documents/organized-crime/Law-Enforcement/Criminal_Intelligence_for_Analysts.pdf (accessed 16 July 2023).

- Intelligence products include:
  - strategic assessment;
  - tactical assessment;
  - target profiles;
  - problem profiles;
  - network analysis;
  - criminal business profiles;
  - financial profile.

7.8.1 **Intelligence Reports (3 x 5 x 2)**

In the UK, the 3 x 5 x 2 intelligence report grading system was introduced to ensure material gathered is assessed and shared using a standardized system; the grades and codes used provide differing levels of confidence and credibility in the information. Intelligence reports are used extensively across the UK by a variety of organizations including law enforcement and those in the public sector. If the intelligence report contains multiple pieces of information each should be appropriately graded.

There is a standard template for the intelligence report. It is important to note that these intelligence reports should be allocated the appropriate security marking particularly as the data may contain sensitive information.

Checklist—Security Classifications

The UK government has a three-level security classification system which indicates the sensitivity of the information. Each level requires an appropriate level control to mitigate the risks; the levels are:

(1) **Official**—this is the lowest level and includes routine business operations.

(2) **Secret**—this relates to sensitive information that compromise could cause severe damage.

(3) **Top Secret**—the most sensitive information where compromise may cause loss to life or the economic well-being of the nation.

Additional descriptors are permitted to identify certain categories of information which are 'subcategories' linked to the three levels of security classification. An example being where the access to personal data could have damaging consequences—this may be recorded as 'official-personal'.

Table 7.4 Intelligence report grades

Acquisition		Exploitation
Source	**Intelligence Evaluation**	**Handling**
1. Reliable 2. Untested 3. Not Reliable	A. Known directly B. Known indirectly but corroborated C. Known indirectly D. Not Known E. Suspected to be false	P. Lawful sharing Permitted C. Lawful sharing with conditions

The gradings relate to the acquisition and exploitation of the intelligence shared (Table 7.4).

7.8.2 **Source Evaluation**

This grading relates to the originator of the information; the source is normally protected and the identity of those providing the intelligence remains confidential. Originating organizations are responsible for the protection and safeguarding of the information.

KEY POINTS—SOURCE EVALUATION

There are three gradings available for the source evaluation, which relates to the credibility of the source:

(1) Reliable
- the source is competent;
- the information from this source is reliable.

(2) Untested
- the source has not previously provided information;
- the information should be treated with some caution;
- appropriate steps should be considered before acting on this information;
- an example of untested in the UK may include information from Crimestoppers.[23]

[23] Crimestoppers is an independent charity that provides a reporting facility to report crime anonymously.

(3) Not reliable

- used when there are reasonable grounds to doubt the source's reliability;
- a risk assessment may be incorporated into the report detailing the risks and mitigation required when considering using this information;
- an example of not reliable information may be sources known to make false allegations.

7.8.3 **Intelligence Evaluation**

Intelligence evaluation relates to the confidence that can be taken from the information and if it is personally known to the source.

KEY POINTS—INTELLIGENCE EVALUATION

There are five gradings available for the intelligence evaluation:

(1) Known directly to the source
- information is first hand, known directly by the source.

(2) Known indirectly to the source but can be corroborated
- information is not known directly by the source but is confirmed by other information that has the A grading;
- this confirmation may come from a range of sources including technical and investigations.

(3) Known indirectly to the source
- information is not known directly to the source.

(4) Not known
- this may include anonymous information and there is no method available to assess the information.

(5) Suspected to be false
- there are reasons to believe the information may be false;
- the reason for this should be recorded on the intelligence report.

7.8.4 **Handling Codes**

Handling codes are used to inform how the intelligence report can be shared. Those with responsibility for the completion and management of the intelligence report should risk-assess the impact of disseminating the intelligence. These codes are linked to conditions for sharing the intelligence.

Further Reading

- Government security classifications, https://assets.publishing.service.gov.uk/government/uploads/system/uploads/attachment_data/file/715778/May-2018_Government-Security-Classifications-2.pdf (accessed 16 July 2023);
- College of Policing, intelligence reports, www.college.police.uk/app/intelligence-management/intelligence-report (accessed 16 July 2023).

7.9 Gathering Intelligence Lawfully

The lawful gathering of intelligence is essential, and a variety of gateways allow for this to take place. Those tasked with the gathering of intelligence need to demonstrate both the knowledge and competence to do this in a lawful and proportionate manner. Counter fraud professionals should be aware of the responsibilities of those who use the wide range of powers and the subsequent impact of the intrusion on the private lives of citizens.

Investigators should always consider the principles of the Human Rights Act 1998 when undertaking enquiries, in particular Article 8 which protects an individual's right to a private life including family life, their home, and correspondence.[24]

KEY POINTS—HUMAN RIGHTS CONSIDERATIONS

When considering the rights of an individual under investigation the following mnemonics JAPAN-PLAN are helpful to consider when making decisions about gathering intelligence:

- **J**—Justification
- **A**—Authority
- **P**—Proportionality
- **A**—Auditable
- **N**—Necessity
- **P**—Proportionality
- **L**—Legality (legal basis for the actions)
- **A**—Accountability
- **N**—Necessity

[24] Equality and Human Rights Commission (2021), Article 8 (respect for your private and family life), www.equalityhumanrights.com/en/human-rights-act/article-8-respect-your-private-and-family-life (accessed 16 July 2023).

7.9.1 Intelligence Sharing Gateways

There are a range of gateways and legislation that allow the lawful sharing of intelligence. These vary depending on the organization and jurisdiction. Often the more intrusive the gathering of intelligence, the higher the level of authority required to access the information. Mechanisms for sharing information include:

- Memorandum of understanding—a non-binding agreement signed between two or more organizations describing the reasons for sharing data and the safeguards in place.
- Data sharing agreements—an agreement between organizations detailing the roles, the purpose of the data sharing, and the management of the data.[25]
- Data Protection Act 2018 (Part 3)—competent authorities are permitted to process data for the prevention, investigation, detection, or prosecution of criminal offences or the execution of criminal penalties, including the safeguarding against and the prevention of threats to public security.[26]
- Specified anti-fraud organization—can share information for the purposes of preventing fraud and is specified by an order made by the Secretary of State.
- Digital Economy Act 2017, s. 56—deals with the disclosure of information to combat fraud against the public sector.
- Court orders—including Police and Criminal Evidence Act, s. 9, schedule 1 (special procedure material) and Proceeds of Crime Act 2002 orders.
- Financial Crime Information Network—this organization operates under the umbrella of the FCA and facilitates the sharing of information between law enforcement and regulators on specific individuals and entities.[27]

Further Reading

- Information Commissioner's Office (ICO) (lawful data sharing), https://ico.org.uk/ (accessed 16 July 2023);
- Crown Prosecution Service (MOUs and protocols), www.cps.gov.uk/national-protocols-and-agreements-other-agencies (accessed 16 July 2023);
- Home Office, 'Data Sharing for the Prevention of Fraud: Code of Practice' (25 March 2015), www.gov.uk/government/publications/data-sharing-for-the-prevention-of-fraud-code-of-practice (accessed 16 July 2023);
- Police and Criminal Evidence Act 1984, www.legislation.gov.uk/ukpga/1984/60/contents (accessed 16 July 2023);

[25] ICO, Data sharing agreements, https://ico.org.uk/for-organisations/uk-gdpr-guidance-and-resources/data-sharing/data-sharing-a-code-of-practice/data-sharing-agreements (accessed 16 July 2023).

[26] ICO, Scope and key definitions, https://ico.org.uk/for-organisations/guide-to-le-processing/scope-and-key-definitions/ (accessed 16 July 2023).

[27] HM Treasury, 'Call for Information: Anti-Money Laundering Supervisory Regime' (16 March 2017), www.gov.uk/government/consultations/call-for-information-anti-money-laundering-supervisory-regime/call-for-information-anti-money-laundering-supervisory-regime#information-sharing (accessed 16 July 2023).

- Proceeds of Crime Act 2002, www.legislation.gov.uk/ukpga/2002/29/contents (accessed 16 July 2023);
- Digital Economy Act 2017, www.legislation.gov.uk/ukpga/2017/30/section/56/enacted (accessed 16 July 2023).

7.9.2 Gathering Intelligence on the Internet

The intelligence gathering opportunities using the internet are extensive and easily accessible; most use the internet daily and will be familiar with accessing social media sites, webpages, and conducting internet searches. The ease of accessibility can be problematic for the counter fraud practitioner as unlawful intrusion can have a devastating impact on the victim, suspect, and the investigation. In some cases such actions can lead to disciplinary action and/or prosecution.

Practitioners should remember that internet investigations leave a 'trace' which can be exploited by potential offenders; often organizations have digital media investigators and specialist trained officers who specialize in covert internet investigations. Identifying the nature of the information and the conditions under which it may be accessed are paramount. As previously stated in this chapter the higher the level of confidentiality normally the higher level of authority required to access that data.

Many organizations concerned with countering fraud have a range of policies and procedures that articulate by who and how intelligence should be gathered from digital sources. Paramount to this activity is knowledge and competence to undertake this form of investigation. At all times, the counter fraud practitioners should be aware of their organizational approach. In addition, the counter fraud practitioner should understand the relevant codes of practice and legislative framework governing the gathering of intelligence.

KEY POINTS—LEGISLATION AND CODES OF PRACTICE RELEVANT TO GATHERING INTELLIGENCE

The range of legislation impacting on the gathering of intelligence in England and Wales includes:

- Regulation of Investigatory Powers Act 2000 (RIPA);
- Human Rights Act 1998;
- Data Protection Act 1998;
- Police and Criminal Evidence Act 1984;
- Investigatory Powers Act 2016;
- covert surveillance code of practice;
- code of practice for the investigation of protected electronic information;
- Covert Human Intelligence Sources Code of Practice 2022;
- Communications Data Code of Practice 2018;
- Criminal Procedure and Investigations Act 1996;

- Criminal Procedure and Investigations Act 1996, s. 23(1);
- Code of Practice 2020.

7.9.3 Categories of Digital Intelligence

The categorization of digitally accessible intelligence has a variety of naming conventions depending on the organization:

- internet open source intelligence (OSINT)—this is information that is openly available;
- internet closed sources—this is information that has restricted access.

The National Police Chiefs' Council (NPCC) usefully categorizes the gathering of this intelligence into four specific areas[28] (see Table 7.5).

Table 7.5 Internet investigations categories

Descriptor	Data Types
Core internet use	Overt enquiries using online resources including Companies House, local authority planning departments, and maps. These investigations do not require username and passwords to access the information. Recording the rationale for the checks undertaken, the date and time, and by whom are the minimum requirements for recording this activity.
Internet investigations (not covert)	Overt enquiries made in task-driven and structured way may require the use of advanced search techniques; access to the site may require profiles to be created and access gained via restrictions. The profiles created should not be covert and should reflect the account that is being used for the organizational purpose.[a] Systematic monitoring of a profile will be considered directed surveillance and the appropriate authorities should be put in place.
Covert internet investigations	Used to access covert access to closed and private groups. To covertly gather information and conduct online surveillance. This activity normally requires, in England and Wales, authorization under the Regulation of Investigatory Powers Act (2000).
Authorized undercover online activity	A specialist activity undertaken by undercover online operatives. They are trained to maintain a personal or other relationship to access information in a covert manner. Significant levels of authorization[b] are required to undertake this activity.

[a] Systematic monitoring of a profile will be considered directed surveillance and the appropriate authorities should be put in place.
[b] The authorizing officer is an officer of at least assistant chief constable rank or equivalent.

[28] NPCC, https://library.college.police.uk/docs/NPCC/Internet-Intelligence-and-Investigation-v1.5.pdf (accessed 16 July 2023).

Further Reading

- NPCC Internet Intelligence & Investigations Strategy, https://library.college.police.uk/docs/NPCC/Internet-Intelligence-and-Investigation-v1.5.pdf (accessed 16 July 2023).

7.10 Useful Sources of Intelligence

There are many sources of information that may provide useful intelligence.

7.10.1 Internet Search Engines and Archives

The internet has many search engines, each with its own unique search capability; the counter fraud practitioner should note that the advanced search features on the search engines are useful in narrowing searches. To search archived webpages, the Wayback Machine website is a useful resource as it has captured a vast array of webpages, books and texts, audio recordings, and images. A range of the most common search engines are shown in Figure 7.3.

7.10.2 Companies and People

There are a range of open source websites that provide information on people and companies. The following are some of the most common.

Companies House—company details, including:

- company information, for example registered address and date of incorporation;
- current and resigned officers;
- document images;
- mortgage charge data;
- previous company names;
- insolvency information.

Historic Company and Business Records—are held at the National Archives; the information held may include records of dissolved companies and business names.

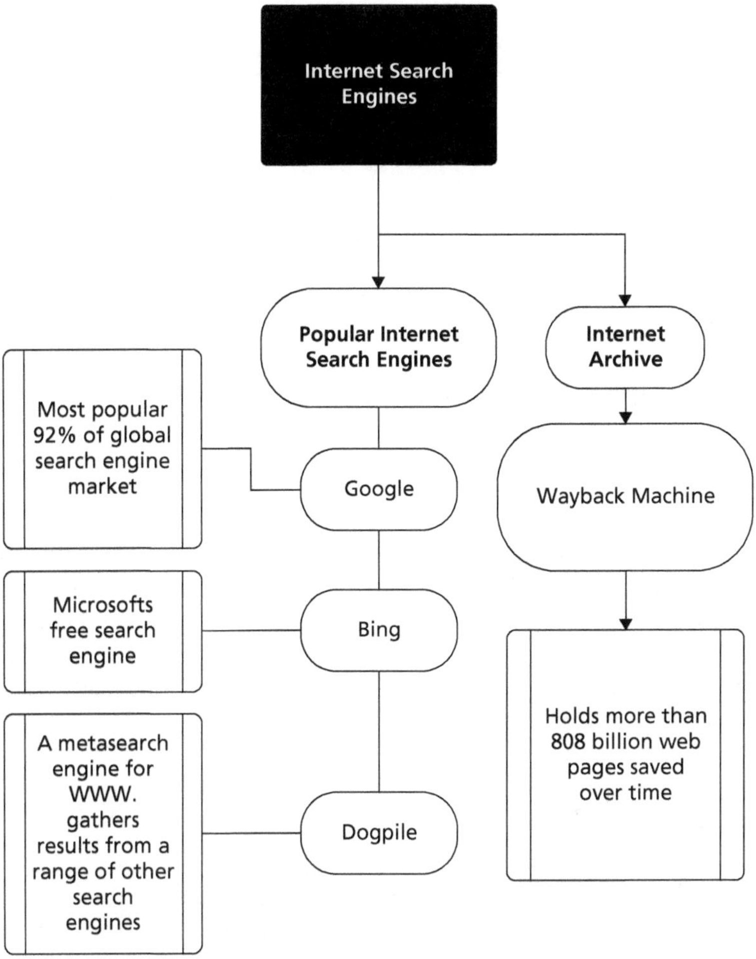

Figure 7.3 Internet search engines

7.10.3 Flight and Ship Trackers

There are a range of flight and ship trackers that allow the real-time monitoring of both flights and ship. Figure 7.4 has links to two trackers.

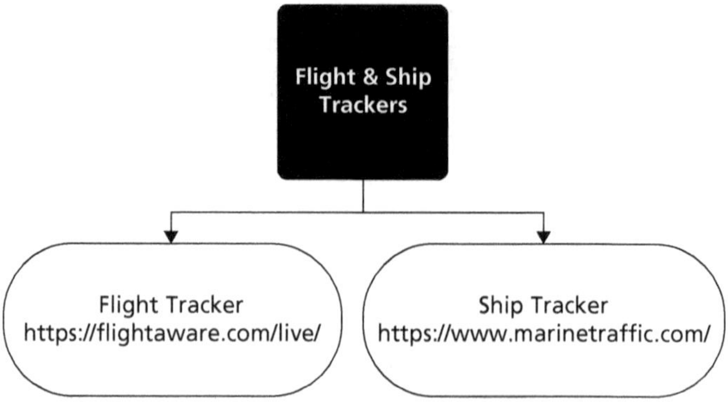

Figure 7.4 Flight and ship trackers

7.10.4 **Other Useful Websites**

- The International Consortium of Investigative Journalists (ICIJ)—this website contains several leaked resources including the Panama Papers, Paradise Papers, and Pandora Papers. The website has both a search and charting capability.
- TinEye is a reverse-image search: by uploading an image or URL it is possible to see if the image is used elsewhere on the website. In 2024 it was reported to have an index of over 67.5 billion images.[29]

Further Reading

- Companies House, www.gov.uk/government/organisations/companies-house (accessed 16 July 2023);
- National Archives, www.nationalarchives.gov.uk/help-with-your-research/research-guides/companies-and-businesses/ (accessed 16 July 2023);
- ICIJ, www.icij.org/ (accessed 16 July 2023);
- TinEye, https://tineye.com/ (accessed 16 July 2023).

7.10.5 **Covert Human Intelligence Sources (CHIS)**

The gathering of covert human intelligence is regulated by the RIPA 2002. There is a code of practice which is issued under s. 71 of the Act. The management of CHIS is a specialist area and the counter fraud practitioner should be fully conversant with their organizational policies and procedures when engaged with a CHIS.

[29] TinEye, 'TinEye Reverse Image Search' (n.d.), https://tineye.com/ (accessed 16 July 2023).

KEY POINTS—CHIS

Under the 2000 Act, a person is a CHIS if:

- they establish or maintain a personal or other relationship with a person for the covert purpose of facilitating the doing of anything falling within s. 26(8)(b) or (c);
- they covertly use such a relationship to obtain information or to provide access to any information to another person; or
- they covertly disclose information obtained using such a relationship or because of the existence of such a relationship.

A relationship is established or maintained for a covert purpose if and only if it is conducted in a manner that is calculated to ensure that one of the parties to the relationship is unaware of the purpose.

A relationship is used covertly, and information obtained is disclosed covertly, if and only if the relationship is used or the information is disclosed in a manner that is calculated to ensure that one of the parties to the relationship is unaware of the use or disclosure in question.[30]

The CHIS revised Code of Practice relates to the use of CHIS by public authorities and provides guidance on the authorization relating to the conduct of the CHIS. The Code describes when a human source activity does not meet the definition of a CHIS:

- Public volunteers—cases where information is volunteered, and the source has not established or maintained a relationship for a covert purpose for example a call to a confidential reporting telephone line.
- Professional or statutory duty—cases where individuals have a professional or legal responsibility to report matters, for example reporting an SAR to the authorities.
- Tasking not involving relationships—the example given in the Code describes the example where a member of the public is asked to record details of vehicles; this could be undertaken by a member of a neighbourhood watch scheme.

The tasking of a CHIS requires an authorization from the authorizing officer, from a relevant authority listed in Schedule 1 of RIPA 2002. The underpinning principles for the tasking include the necessity and proportionality of the conduct.

Where the conduct authorized is to take place in Scotland authorizations should be sought under the Regulation of Investigatory Powers (Scotland) Act 2000, a separate Code of Practice covers this process.

[30] www.gov.uk/government/publications/covert-human-intelligence-sources-code-of-practice-2022/covert-human-intelligence-sources-revised-code-of-practice- (accessed 16 July 2023).

Further Reading

- Covert Human Intelligence Sources revised Code of Practice December 2022, www.gov.uk/government/publications/covert-human-intelligence-sources-code-of-practice-2022/covert-human-intelligence-sources-revised-code-of-practice-accessible#:~:text=Definition%20of%20a%20covert%20human,)(b)%20or%20(c)%3B (accessed 16 July 2023);
- RIPA 2000, www.legislation.gov.uk/ukpga/2000/23/contents (accessed 16 July 2023);
- Regulation of Investigatory Powers (Scotland) Act 2000, www.legislation.gov.uk/asp/2000/11/contents (accessed 16 July 2023).

7.11 Government Counter Fraud Profession (GCFP) Intelligence Core Discipline Standard

The GCFP Intelligence Core Discipline was originally made accessible to members of the counter fraud profession in February 2018. It details the agreed professional standards and guidance for the implementation of a consistent approach to counter fraud intelligence and is part of the wider government counter fraud standards and guidance. The standard is consistent with the NIM.

Like other GCFP standards, this one describes the knowledge, skills, and experience needed for an individual to achieve practitioner level and helps set out career routes. The roles it references include the intelligence analyst and intelligence manager. It contains guidance for those using the standards on the relevant intelligence-related processes and products. It describes the guidance an organization should have in place to support the counter fraud intelligence activity for those with that specialist capability.

The key components of the standard are:[31]

- intelligence manager or senior intelligence analyst/officer;
- legislation and departmental policy;
- analysing diverse types of fraud information;
- developing judgements and recommendations;
- understanding and communicating threats;
- stakeholder engagement;
- preparing intelligence to start an investigation;
- recording and evaluation;
- disseminating intelligence;

[31] At a high level, components outline the knowledge, skills, and experience required for each core and subdiscipline. There are thirteen components for intelligence highlighting the knowledge, skills, and experience required for effective intelligence activity.

- intelligence products;
- quality, performance, and capability;
- collecting and developing intelligence;
- evaluating the effectiveness of processes and products.

8

Fraud Investigation Fundamentals

Blackstone's Counter Fraud Professionals' Handbook. Michael J. Betts, Laura Eshelby, and David Whitehouse-Hayes, Oxford University Press.

DOI: 10.1093/9780191996955.003.0008

8.1 Introduction

In this chapter we explore the fundamentals of the investigative process. This includes the underpinning knowledge relating to the principles of material attrition, the investigative mindset, effective decision-making, how to develop a case theory, and the art of planning and managing an investigation. We explain the use of techniques and models that will help support consistent-quality investigative outcomes. The key challenges and risks are examined, and mitigation techniques are discussed in the pursuit of ethical and effective investigations.

The skill of investigating fraud should not be underestimated; the adversary is often cunning and skilled in concealing their true identity, location, and the fraudulent activity. The use of technology as an enabler adds to the complexity of the investigation, along with the diversity of payment systems. Complex fraud investigations require a multiskilled team who can collaborate to identify, secure, and present the relevant material to the appropriate authority.

The Government Counter Fraud Profession's (GCFP) Counter Fraud Investigator Standard is referenced within the chapter. This standard is a really useful resource providing a range of products and guidance, which directly supports the counter fraud practitioner.

KEY POINTS—GCFP COUNTER FRAUD INVESTIGATOR STANDARD

The GCFP Counter Fraud Investigator Standard[1] describe the knowledge, skills, and experience required to effectively investigate fraud and related offending in the public sector. This standard identifies eight key components against which an effective investigator should demonstrate knowledge and competency:

(1) **Case initiation**—has technical and investigation competency to plan and address issues raised in accordance with organizational procedures and legislation.
(2) **Evidence gathering**—ability to identify, gather, retain, and reveal material in accordance with relevant legislation and organizational policy.
(3) **Stakeholder engagement**—establish a network of counter fraud stakeholders both internally and externally to the investigation organization.
(4) **Quality, performance, and review**—recognize and review training and development opportunities to increase knowledge and capability and apply performance/productivity management and skills to perform quality control.
(5) **Legislation and departmental policy**—conduct investigations in accordance with relevant legislation and organizational policy.

[1] Government Counter Fraud Professional Standard and Guidance: Counter Fraud Investigator, www.gov.uk/government/publications/professional-standards-and-guidance-investigation/government-counter-fraud-professional-standards-and-guidance-counter-fraud-investigator-html (accessed 14 September 2023).

(6) **Investigative interviewing**—ability to undertake a range of investigative interviews including planning, conducting, and evaluation.
(7) **Case progression**—has report writing skills, articulating evidence, and progressing cases to conclusion in accordance with relevant legislation and organizational policy;
(8) **Parallel/multitrack approach**—ability to undertake civil, disciplinary, regulatory, and criminal investigations to relevant standards in accordance with legislation and organizational policy.

8.2 Purpose of an Investigation

An investigation is a process to establish the facts of an allegation under investigation. Criminal Procedure and Investigations Act 1996 (CPIA 1996) (s. 23(1)) Code of Practice[2] (the Code), paragraph 2.1 defines a criminal investigation as:

> an investigation conducted by police officers with a view to it being ascertained whether a person should be charged with an offence, or whether a person charged with an offence is guilty of it. This will include:
> - investigations into crimes that have been committed;
> - investigations whose purpose is to ascertain whether a crime has been committed, with a view to the possible institution of criminal proceedings;
> - investigations which begin in the belief that a crime may be committed, for example when the police keep premises or individuals under observation for a period of time, with a view to the possible institution of criminal proceedings;
> - charging a person with an offence includes prosecution by way of summons or postal requisition.

Though 'the Code' refers to police officers it has a wider application as it applies to investigators other than police officers who are charged with the duty of investigating as defined in the Act.

[2] Criminal Procedure and Investigations Act 1996 (s. 23(1)) Code of Practice Revised in accordance with section 25(4) of the Criminal Procedure and Investigations Act 1996, https://assets.publishing.service.gov.uk/media/5a80d491e5274a2e8ab5267c/code-of-practice-approved.pdf (accessed 16 October 2023).

Checklist—CPIA Code of Practice 1996

For those undertaking criminal investigations in England and Wales compliance with the CPIA 1996 Code of Practice is critical. Counter fraud practitioners need to understand the terms, roles, responsibilities, and material disclosure detailed. These include:

- definitions of:
    - criminal investigation;
    - investigations;
    - officer in charge of an investigation;
    - the disclosure officer;
    - prosecutor;
    - material and relevancy;
    - sensitive material;
- general responsibilities:
    - investigator, officer in charge of the investigation and disclosure officer;
    - chief officer of police;
- recording of information;
- retention of material;
- preparation of material for the prosecutor;
- action by the disclosure officer;
- certification by the disclosure officer;
- disclosure of material to the accused.

An especially important section contained within the Code is paragraph 3.5 which states that:

> In conducting an investigation, the investigator should pursue all reasonable lines of inquiry, whether these point towards or away from the suspect. What is reasonable in each case will depend on the particular circumstances.

An investigator needs to consider this when developing an investigative plan and/or strategy; it is crucial to follow lines of inquiry that point towards or away from any suspect.

Further Reading on Disclosure

- Attorney General's Guidance on Disclosure 2022, https://assets.publishing.service.gov.uk/media/628ce5efd3bf7f1f3b19efa7/AG_Guidelines_2022_Revision_Publication_Copy.pdf (accessed 30 October 2023);
- Code of Practice issued under s. 23 of the CPIA 1996 ('the Code of Practice'), https://assets.publishing.service.gov.uk/media/5f9af5e6d3bf7f1e3a29321b/Criminal-procedure-and-investigations-act-1996.pdf (accessed 30 October 2023);
- Covert Surveillance and Covert Human Intelligence Sources Code of Practice, https://assets.publishing.service.gov.uk/media/5ba37401e5274a55cdb89bce/201800802_CSPI_code.pdf (accessed 30 October 2023).

8.3 Exclusion of Evidence

The Police and Criminal Evidence Act 1984 (PACE) details when evidence may be excluded if gathered unfairly or through an abuse of process. Indeed, a significant number of challenges in fraud cases are based on procedural failures rather than the evidence of the case. Section 76 (2) of PACE details when confessions may be excluded from proceedings, it states:

(1) If, in any proceedings where the prosecution proposes to give in evidence a confession made by an accused person, it is represented to the court that the confession was or may have been obtained—
   (a) by oppression of the person who made it; or
   (b) in consequence of anything said or done which was likely, in the circumstances existing at the time, to render unreliable any confession which might be made by him in consequence thereof, the court shall not allow the confession to be given in evidence against him except in so far as the prosecution proves to the court beyond reasonable doubt that the confession (notwithstanding that it may be true) was not obtained as aforesaid.

Section 78(1) PACE states that:

> In any proceedings the court may refuse to allow evidence to be given on which the prosecution proposes to rely if it appears to the court that, having regard to all the circumstances, including the circumstances in which the evidence was obtained, the admission of the evidence would have such an adverse effect on the fairness of the proceedings that the court ought not to admit it.

8.4 Core Skills and Knowledge

The core knowledge and skills to undertake an effective fraud investigation are wide ranging, they include an understanding of the relevant legislation, frameworks, and Codes of Practice. These are essential to ensure that the relevant material is gathered in a proportionate, legal, accountable, and necessary manner. This will ensure any subsequent proceedings are safe and that judicial outcomes are free from challenge. Investigators have a wide range of responsibilities and powers; these should be used wisely, and due regard should be paid to the rationale for their use. The worst outcome possible is the misuse of power leading to unsafe convictions and significant trauma for all those involved.

Case Study—Post Office Horizon IT Scandal

In 1999 the Post Office introduced a new point of sale and accounting computerized system called Horizon, across its branches. Horizon included both the hardware and software required to process accounting information.[3] Over a period of time a number of software 'fixes' were made to the Horizon system.

Following the introduction of the Horizon system, in 2015 a significant number of Post Office branch operatives were prosecuted, and some convicted for fraud-related offences. This had significant impact on those both investigated and convicted whose lives were devastated.

It was subsequently discovered that Horizon contained several software errors which contributed to the suspected shortfalls and discrepancies in the accounting systems at different branches. Subsequently action was taken by those affected by the cases, appeals instigated, and several convictions quashed.

The Horizon scandal has been reported as 'the most widespread miscarriage of justice in UK history'.[4]

In September 2020, the Post Office Horizon IT Inquiry was established as a non-statutory inquiry; in 2021 it was converted to a statutory inquiry led by retired High Court judge Sir Wyn Williams.

Experience of investigating fraud is also a factor in investigative success; understanding the range of fraud typologies, modus operandi and the fraudster's mindset can aid the investigative process.

[3] Post Office Horizon IT Inquiry, www.postofficehorizoninquiry.org.uk/ (accessed 20 September 2023).

[4] M. Sweney, 'Post Office: Horizon Scandal Victims to Receive £600,000 Compensation Each', *The Guardian* (18 September 2023), www.theguardian.com/business/2023/sep/18/post-office-horizon-scandal-victims-compensation (accessed 21 September 2023).

8.5 Effective Decision-Making

At the centre of any investigation is effective decision-making; an investigation is a series of decisions which inform the direction of the investigation, the development of the case theory, strategy areas, and the lines of inquiry. Historically, poor decision-making has impacted on the investigative process, a number of notable case reviews have highlighted this issue; in some cases, these have led to injustices.

Case Study—Serious Fraud Office and the *Unaoil* Case

On 19 October 2022, the Director of the UK Serious Fraud Office (SFO) apologized to the House of Commons Justice Select Committee[5] during an oral hearing into the work of the SFO.

The apology was in relation to a meeting during the Unaoil case. The Director said: 'It was a damaging relationship. I appreciate and apologize for the fact that we had that meeting.'

The apology related to a case investigated by the SFO concerning alleged corruption at oil and gas consultancy Unaoil. In 2021/22 the Court of Appeal overturned three convictions[6] in the case after ruling the SFO had denied the convicted former oil and gas executive the right to a fair trial. During the appeals, the staff at the SFO were criticized for disclosure failures.

An independent review into the SFO's handling of the *Unaoil* case—*R.* v. *Akle & Another*, was undertaken by Sir David Calvert-Smith and published in July 2022. The review was critical of the actions of the SFO and made a number of recommendations. Among the findings the following were reported:

- A senior member of staff using her personal mobile phone and failing to take contemporaneous notes of meetings and conversations.
- The chief investigator who failed to maintain complete and proper records of his contact with a third party non-legal representative and promptly share them with the case team.
- A head of division who did not undertake formal case assurance processes; a case team which did not maintain an up-to-date disclosure strategy document.

The review stated:

It was not a lack of policy or guidance which caused the issues that came to the fore in this case, it was the fact that some individuals were willing and able to ignore it.[7]

---

[5] https://committees.parliament.uk/oralevidence/11382/pdf/ (accessed 29 September 2023).

[6] SFO, Unaoil, www.sfo.gov.uk/cases/unaoil/ (accessed 29 September 2023).

[7] Sir David Calvert-Smith, *Independent Review into the SFO's Handling of the Unaoil Case—R v Akle & Anor* (July 2022), https://assets.publishing.service.gov.uk/government/uploads/system/uploads/attachment_data/file/1092872/DCS_report_-__FINAL_-_21_July_08.31_.pdf (accessed 29 September 2023).

Further Reading

- Sir David Calvert-Smith, *Independent Review into the SFO's Handling of the Unaoil Case—R v Akle & Anor* (July 2022), https://assets.publishing.service.gov.uk/government/uploads/system/uploads/attachment_data/file/1092872/DCS_report_-_FINAL_-_21_July_08.31_.pdf (accessed 29 September 2023);
- Post Office Horizon Inquiry website, www.postofficehorizoninquiry.org.uk/ (accessed 20 September 2023).

8.5.1 Understanding Bias

Bias is an intrinsic part of our personality; it forms our personal view of the world and can result in fundamental error. Recognizing and mitigating bias while making decisions is an essential ability for the counter fraud practitioner. Unconscious bias is a natural process: humans operate on a daily basis with about 95 per cent of processing being unconscious; the conscious processing is used for thought tasks. However, each individual has a frame of reference against which thoughts and decisions are mapped. Though generally an effective life skill, during an investigation this can be inherently problematic and may adversely impact on the decisions that are made by investigators. The counter fraud practitioner should recognize these biases and take active steps to mitigate their impact. A range of biases are shown in Table 8.1.

Table 8.1 Bias

Bias	Description
Confirmation	An unconscious desire to search and/or interpret material to confirm the preconceptions held by the counter fraud practitioner
Anchoring	The propensity to rely on previous experiences or material during the decision-making process
Cultural	Personifying decision-making based on own cultural beliefs and attitudes
Bandwagon	A tendency to follow the crowd and allow the beliefs of others to impact on the decision-making process
Framing	Taking a too narrow approach and not considering the wider context or material
Working rules	Making decisions based on previous experiences made in similar circumstances which are accepted as a way of working within, for example, a team or organization. The way things are always done; a set of unwritten rules.

8.5.2 **Mitigating Bias**

A number of strategies may be adopted to mitigate the impact of bias on an investigation. The first and most obvious is to understand that all human beings are subject to bias in their decision-making. To negate the impact, practitioners should adopt a critical thinking approach to their decision-making. Critical thinking is the ability to check the logic of an argument or statement—it is a very conscious act and takes time and energy. It assists in analysing, evaluating, and building the rationale for any decision to be made. It should result in logical decisions which are supported by reason. The elements of critical thinking are:

- clarity—have you established a clear 'picture' of the matter?
- accuracy—have you taken every effort to verify the information?
- precision—are you in possession of the specific details required?
- relevance—is the information you are relying on to make decisions relevant?
- depth—is the information you have sufficient depth and detail?
- breadth—have you taken into consideration the broader aspects and wider context?

Counter fraud practitioners should be looking to make logical decisions; this occurs when there is a combination of thought and evidence which is unaffected by bias, resulting in a sound rationale for the decisions made based on the best information available at that time.

Other strategies for mitigating bias include peer conversations and reviews; this can help challenge the underpinning rationale for decision-making. Collaborative decision-making can assist in managing bias by bringing together a range of experts to critically analyse a problem.

8.5.3 **Investigative Reasoning**

Linked to the topic of bias is reasoning and how information is processed by the brain. Understanding the processes involved in how information is received and processed is beneficial to the investigative process. There are two relevant types of reasoning which impact the process of investigation; inductive and deductive reasoning. Inductive reasoning is the absorbing of information, looking for patterns, and developing a tentative hypothesis; much of this process is unconscious. Figure 8.1 illustrations inductive reasoning.

Deductive reasoning requires conscious thought, and leads to case theories being developed, the collection of relevant material instigated resulting in confirmation of the hypothesis. Figure 8.2 illustrates deductive reasoning.

8.5.4 **Material Attrition**

A key factor in the investigation of fraud and related offending is material attrition which should be at the forefront of the investigator's mind. At the time when the

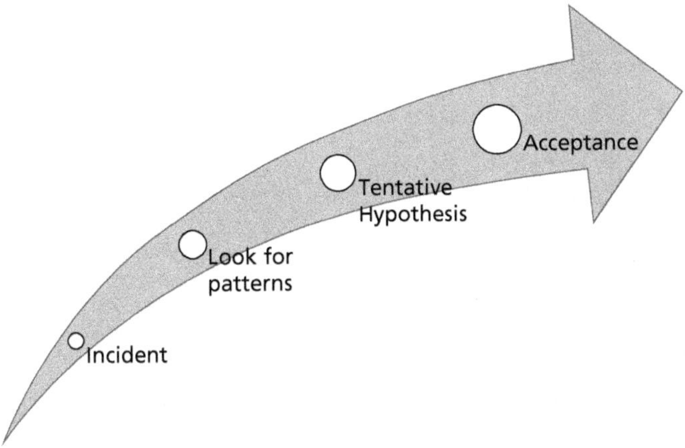

Figure 8.1 Inductive reasoning

Figure 8.2 Deductive reasoning

crime is committed, material is at its most abundant and rich. Memories of those who were the victims, witnessed or indeed committed the offence will be at their fullest the nearer to the crime they are examined (interviewed). As time progresses, material starts to dissipate. Data may only be stored for a short period. A good example of this is closed-circuit television (CCTV) which may only be retained for just a few hours (Table 8.2).

The investigator needs to plan and prioritize the recovery of all relevant material. Informed decisions need to be made with regard to the ordering of recovery of material and securing that at most risk first within the context of the investigation. There is a natural process of attrition during an investigation. This should be limited, as should only a percentage of the material gathered be presented to any subsequent proceedings, the management of attrition will maximize the material available to establish the facts of any case.

Table 8.2 Typical material retention periods

Material	Typical retention length
Data relating to telephone usage	12 months
Mobile phone location data	12 months
Bank statements and records	7 years
Automatic number plate recognition (ANPR) records	12 months
Internet service provider (ISP) records of internet usage	12–36 months
Close circuit television (CCTV)	1 month
His Majesty's Revenue & Customs (HMRC) business records	6 years

8.5.5 Investigative Curiosity

Investigative curiosity is an attitude to the investigative process and has more recently been highlighted after a number of failed investigations particularly relating to vulnerable persons.

Case Study—The Stephen Port Murders

On 27 April 2023, HM Inspectorate of Constabulary and Fire & Rescue Services (HMICFRS) issued a report[8] into the Metropolitan Police's flawed investigation into Stephen Port who was responsible for the murder of four males in East London between June 2014 and September 2015. This report detailed several failings including:

- insufficient training on the investigative mindset;
- poor supervision;
- poor record keeping;
- policy and guidance were outdated and confusing;
- intelligence and crime analysis processes were inadequate.

In response, the College of Policing issued guidance to those undertaking investigations. Investigators should keep an open and inquiring mind during the course of an inquiry, making every effort to avoid assumption and stereotyping. They should continue to question the material presented to them and when developing the investigative hypothesis reflect on:

[8] HMICFRS, 'An Inspection of the Metropolitan Police Service's Response to Lessons from the Stephen Port Murders', https://hmicfrs.justiceinspectorates.gov.uk/publication-html/inspection-of-the-metropolitan-police-services-response-to-lessons-from-the-stephen-port-murders/ (accessed 16 October 2023).

(1) what is known by the investigation;
(2) what is not known within the investigation;
(3) consistencies with the material;
(4) conflicts within the material;
(5) what the investigation needs to know.

Checklist—Developing an Investigative Mindset

It is important for the investigator to seek to confirm material presented to them. The investigative mindset aids with this process. The five principles of the investigative mindset are:

(1) understanding the source of the material;

(2) prepare and plan for the examination of the material;

(3) examination of the material;

(4) record and collate the information following the examination;

(5) evaluate the information and act accordingly.

8.6 Investigation Planning

Those leading an investigation are like the conductor of an orchestra: they need to identify the range of experts to support the investigation and coordinate their activities to best effect. Planning an investigation is a key skill of the counter fraud practitioner: the process includes developing the case theory (hypothesis); an investigative policy supported by strategies and investigative actions. These should be underpinned by the supporting rationale; the key decisions made; and rationale should be recorded in a durable form. This process is shown in Figure 8.3.

Those leading an investigation may want to consider the following responsibilities based on the mnemonic HOLMES, which of course has its origins in the fictional character Sherlock Holmes:

- **H**—Hypothesis: develop a case theory to maximize investigative opportunities;
- **O**—Offences: identify the offence that has been committed;
- **L**—Leadership: provide effective leadership;
- **M**—Material: Gather relevant material and manage its disclosure;
- **E**—Experts: engage with Subject Matter Experts;
- **S**—Strategy: develop an effective strategy and lines of inquiry.

Figure 8.3 Investigative process

8.6.1 Commencing an Investigation

Once an investigation has commenced there are several key considerations these will include:

(1) identifying who is in charge of the investigation;
(2) identifying who has responsibility for disclosure;
(3) identifying the expertise required to progress the investigation;
(4) maintaining investigation records;
(5) developing the investigative hypothesis;
(6) identifying and securing the relevant material;
(7) preventing further harm and loss;
(8) identifying the fast-track actions;
(9) liaising with the relevant stakeholders;
(10) managing risk within the investigation;
(11) safeguarding the victim;
(12) looking after the welfare of the investigation team and those connected to the investigation;
(13) securing assets that are at risk of dissipation.

8.6.2 Developing a Hypothesis

The starting point for any investigative planning is the hypothesis. This is often referred to as a working hypothesis and allows those leading an investigation to consider the known facts and identify the possible explanations which should in turn lead to an investigation policy that is sufficiently broad to gather material to further establish the facts of the case. The considerations for those developing a hypothesis include:

- accessing the initial material gathered for relevance and reliability;
- possessing the knowledge (or access to experts) to interpret the material correctly;

- having the experience to produce a 'best fit' to the material and consider all explanations to produce a range of hypotheses; it is common at the start of an investigation to have multiple possibilities to explain the actions of a potential suspect; these may include mistake, error, or indeed fraud.

Once the hypothesis has been developed, plans should be made to gather further relevant material and pursue all reasonable lines of inquiry. The sequencing of the recovery of material should be considered and actions taken to secure the material at most jeopardy.

KEY POINTS—SEQUENCING OF GATHERING MATERIAL

The gathering of relevant material needs sequencing based on jeopardy and risk of dissipation; investigators should consider the following approach.

(1) What are the offences under investigation—what are the points to prove, where will the relevant material be located?
(2) Who are the victims, witness, and suspects? What approach should be taken towards each?
(3) Where is the location of the relevant material?
(4) When should the material be recovered and in what order, what are the available powers?
(5) How will the examination take place and what is the best method?
(6) Why should those actions be undertaken? The rationale should be recorded.

8.6.3 Decision Books/Logs

Those leading an investigation should maintain records of their key decisions and in particular the supporting rationale. Often such information is recorded in a key decision log (KDL) or policy book; this may be in paper form or digital format. Such a record is an important record of the direction of the investigation and should be kept secure. If sensitive matters or techniques are being deployed, then two logs may be retained; this assists in the management of material at a later date for disclosure considerations. The KDL is used to record the investigation policy and supporting strategies. The policy will outline the who, what, and why; the strategies detail the how, when, and where (see Figure 8.4).

8.6.4 Investigative Strategies

A fraud investigation will require several individual strategies to enable the focus, direction, and control of the investigative process. These strategies should be developed with subject matter experts who can either advise on or write the required strategy. Though it should be remembered that the ownership of the risk will be the responsibility of the officer in charge of the investigation. Typical strategies

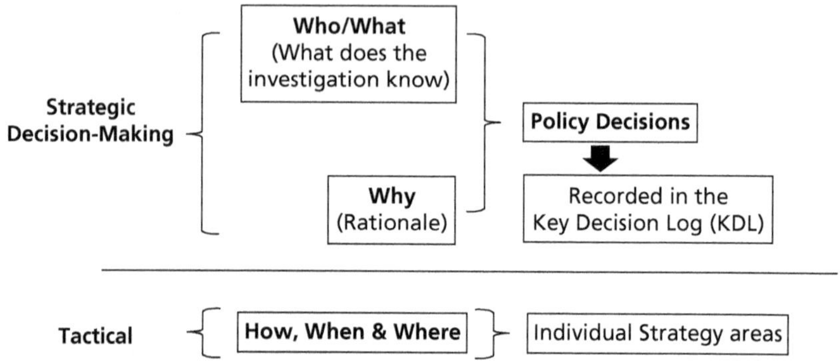

Figure 8.4 Strategic decision-making

required will include financial investigation including asset recovery, digital forensic, interview and search. The key considerations for each of these is shown in Table 8.3.

8.6.5 Investigation Plans

In cases when a senior investigating officer is not appointed, the officer in the case should develop an investigation plan. The plan is a living document that should be kept up to date as the investigation progresses, the key headings and content are detailed below.

8.6.5.1 Identification of offence(s) or issue under investigation (instigation)

If commencing a criminal fraud investigation, a fundamental is understanding the offence(s) being investigated. This will inform the points to prove for the offence, the lines of inquiry that may be needed, and the possible options to obtain the relevant material. On the latter, many options to obtain material may require specific offences to be the focus of a case to allow the use of various bespoke powers specific to it or related to the level of offence. If the offender(s) is known at this time this should be recorded with the accompanying rationale.

8.6.5.2 Investigation roles, responsibilities, and resourcing

It is essential to consider who is involved in undertaking the investigation and ensuring the roles and responsibilities are recorded and aligned to fulfil the CPIA obligations. The available resource should also be recorded, including access, when appropriate to a financial investigator; digital media investigators; and other specialist support that may be required. Forensic accountants can offer significant value if the investigation concerns company structures and/or accounts.

Table 8.3 Strategies and considerations

Strategy type	Considerations
Search	The search strategy should consider the roles of those involved which may include search adviser, crime scene investigators, crime scene manager, scene coordinator, and forensic specialists. For complex or multiple scenes searches it is strongly advised that a search adviser should be consulted and actively engaged in writing the search strategy. There are three different types of searches each requiring a different approach. There is a visual check used when limited resources are available, a non-specialist search undertaken by non-specialist search officers, and specialist searches undertaken by trained and often licensed officers. For specialist searches a five-stage approach to planning should be considered each stage should be described. The five stages are planning, searching, discovery, securing, and evaluating. Those leading the investigation should clearly identify the scenes to be searched and the rationale and legal basis for the search. Underpinning the search strategy should be a risk assessment, this should include environmental hazards and any threat to those conducting the search, any identified risk should be mitigated to allow the search to be conducted. The use of search dogs should be considered; two types are particularly relevant in fraud inquiries, namely cash dogs (who can locate cash) and electronic detection dogs who can identify chemicals in digital devices. Any briefing to those who are to undertake the search should include an outline of the circumstances of the case and be informed what is being searched for; a model for such briefings is the IIMARCH, this is effective for briefing down, its components are: • Information; • Intention; • Method; • Administration; • Risk assessment; • Communication; • Human rights.

(continued)

Table 8.3 Continued

Strategy type	Considerations
Digital Forensic	The digital forensic strategy is more effective if written by a specialist. The strategy should encompass five stages: • data capture at crime scenes; • open source research and social network sites; • data examination; • data interpretation; • recording and reporting the findings. It is important to consider the approach to interviewing witnesses, victims, and suspects. Interviewers should include questions around use of encryption, names of contacts, use of devices, and identification of the internet service provider. If an individual refuses to give a password to a device, then s. 49 of Regulation of Investigatory Powers Act 2000[a] should be considered. This section enables a notice to compel a suspect to disclose their password to access any electronic device (subject to the required criteria).
Financial investigation	Financial investigation is a powerful tool in any fraud-related inquiry. Financial inquiries can establish the motives, associations and links to people and places as well as typically identify the movements of money and the proceeds of criminal conduct. The strategy should set clear objectives for example to follow the financial trail to prove or not the offences under investigation; it could identify offences in relation to the Proceeds of Crime Act 2002 including the offence of money laundering. The financial intelligence requirement should also be considered as access to the suspicious activity reports is a powerful tool.
Interview	Interview strategies are often best developed by interview advisers. They can advise of the method, location, and timing of any interviews particularly if there are multiple suspects. The selection of the interviewers is an important aspect as trained officers are required who should be familiar with the core interview skills of knowledge and understanding, planning and preparation, building a rapport, listening, and questioning skills. In financial investigation interviews, it is crucial to gather as much relevant information as possible. This will include the suspect's income, expenditure, assets, and liabilities.

[a] Regulation of Investigatory Powers Act 2000, www.legislation.gov.uk/ukpga/2000/23/section/49 (accessed 28 September 2023).

8.6.5.3 **Summary of the case**

This will set out the case to date, referral source, and pre-existing evidence or intelligence that may already have been obtained. Some cases may be sufficiently developed to progress on a fast-track procedure straight to a formal interview under caution, requiring nothing more than a review of the material to be satisfied that reasonable suspicion has been demonstrated under PACE.

8.6.5.4 **Asset recovery**

The considerations of early restraint should be considered to fulfil any potential confiscation following conviction.

8.6.5.5 **Case reviews/key stages**

As all cases will vary and the lines of inquiry will change, depending on the nature and facts of the specific case, regular case reviews between the investigator and their manager are essential. These should be both at agreed stages, that is when a disposal decision is required, but if aligned to other major investigation types, 7-, 14-, and/or 28-day reviews may be particularly beneficial.

Case reviews serve a number of purposes, including:

- Sense-checking the approach of the investigator with their manager by discussing the case, lines of inquiry, and alternative approaches as well as seeking to clear blockers or solve other challenges.
- From the manager's perspective can ensure cases are being progressed in a timely and competent manner.
- Undertaking some quality assurance and feedback on things such as interviews to ensure compliance with legislative and organizational guidance.
- This can in turn inform any development/capability needs (but these are not to be confused with performance meetings but will feed into those).
- Help determine if additional resources are required and authorize them.
- Alternatively ensure cases that are unlikely to achieve a positive outcome are identified and closed promptly to maximize efficiency of resources.

8.6.5.6 **Case closure and/or disposal decision (evidential evaluation/charge)**

All cases will reach a closure, whether because of no further action or following a formal disposal mechanism (criminal, civil, or regulatory). For straightforward closures key points that need to be considered are:

- Have all reasonable lines of inquiry been pursued and on balance it is unlikely the case could be progressed?
- Ensure all legal requirements are complied with (e.g. disposal of data relating to individuals where no offence can be demonstrated).
- Are there any learnings from the case that might improve organizational processes?
- Even if no sanction action, have any reports been issued to other departments such as to raise invoices or stop services?

Cases where sanction or redress has been applied:

- application of disposal/sanction policy;
- sanction recommendation and reason including aggravating and mitigating factors set out;
- referral to the Crown Prosecution Service/prosecutor;
- case completion notes and subsequent formal notification to Police National Computer or instruction of debt recovery agents.

8.6.5.7 **Operational learning**

Some cases may have highlighted system control failings, exposed the organization to reputational damage, or other significant or unique factors that mean a post-case report or other review is appropriate. The GCFP Counter Fraud Investigator Standard states: provide insight from investigations to identify and facilitate improvements to policy and processes to assist prevention, deterrence, and increased future detection. Produce full and accurate post-investigation assessments.

This may seek to cover areas such as:

- identify control failings and make recommendations for changes;
- recommend changes in training and/or resourcing.

Further Reading

- CPIA 1996 (s. 23(1)) Code of Practice, https://assets.publishing.service.gov.uk/government/uploads/system/uploads/attachment_data/file/447967/code-of-practice-approved.pdf (accessed 27 September 2023);
- Government Counter Fraud Professional Standard and Guidance: Counter Fraud Investigator, www.gov.uk/government/publications/professional-standards-and-guidance-investigation/government-counter-fraud-professional-standards-and-guidance-counter-fraud-investigator-html (accessed 14 September 2023);
- Regulation of Investigatory Powers Act 2000, s. 49 Notices requiring disclosure, www.legislation.gov.uk/ukpga/2000/23/section/49 (accessed 28 September 2023).

8.7 The Caution

The use of the caution is described in PACE Code C.[9] It must be given to a person for whom there are grounds to suspect of an offence before any questions about the offence. The words of the caution are:

[9] PACE Code C 2019, www.gov.uk/government/publications/pace-code-c-2019/pace-code-c-2019-accessible#bookmark30 (accessed 29 September 2023).

> You do not have to say anything. But it may harm your defence if you do not mention when questioned something which you later rely on in Court. Anything you do say may be given in evidence.

A person need not be cautioned if questions are to establish their identity or ownership of any vehicle, to obtain information in accordance with any relevant statutory requirement, or in furtherance of the proper and effective conduct of a search. The caution which must be given on arrest, or occasions before a person is charged, or informed they may be prosecuted. After any break in questioning under caution, the person being questioned must be made aware they remain under caution.

The Code states that 'minor deviations from the words of any caution given in accordance with this Code do not constitute a breach of this Code, provided the sense of the relevant caution is preserved'.

KEY POINTS—ADVERSE INFERENCES AND SPECIAL WARNINGS

The Criminal Justice and Public Order Act 1994, ss. 34, 36, and 37 (amended by the Youth Justice and Criminal Evidence Act 1999, s. 58) detail the circumstances when inferences may be drawn from the failure of a suspect to fail to mention facts when questioned; fail to account for objects, marks, or substances; or fail to account for their presence in a particular place. PACE Code C details how the so-called special warning should be administered in interview to enable adverse inferences to be drawn in proceedings. These warnings have some complexity. The key points are summarized below.

Criminal Justice and Public Order Act 1994, ss. 34, 36, and 37

- **Section 34—Effect of accused's failure to mention facts when questioned or charged**. This relates to the accused's failing to mention any fact relied on in their defence in proceedings, that they could reasonably have been expected to mention before being charged with an offence (or informed they might be prosecuted for it).
- For further detail, see the Criminal Justice and Public Order Act 1994, s. 34, www.legislation.gov.uk/ukpga/1994/33/section/34 (accessed 30 October 2023).

Note: This section applies in relation to questioning by persons (other than constables) charged with the duty of investigating offences or charging offenders as it applies in relation to questioning by constables.[10]

- **Section 36—Effect of accused's failure or refusal to account for objects, substances, or marks.** This applies to where a person is arrested by a constable and fails or refuses to account for any objects, marks, or substances, or marks on such objects found:
  - on their person; or
  - in or on their clothing or footwear; or

[10] Criminal Justice and Public Order Act 1994, www.legislation.gov.uk/ukpga/1994/33/section/34 (accessed 29 September 2023).

- otherwise in their possession; or
- in the place they were arrested.
- The officer dealing must inform the arrested person they believe the presence of the object, substance, or mark may be attributable to the commission of a specified offence, and must request the person to account for the presence of these.
- For further detail, see the Criminal Justice and Public Order Act 1994, s. 36 www.legislation.gov.uk/ukpga/1994/33/section/36 (accessed 30 October 2023).
- **Section 37—Effect of accused's failure or refusal to account for presence at a particular place**. Where the arrested suspect was found by a constable at a place at or about the time the offence for which that officer has arrested them, and the arrested person fails or refuses to account for their presence there.
- For further detail, see the Criminal Justice and Public Order Act 1994, s. 36, www.legislation.gov.uk/ukpga/1994/33/section/37 (accessed 30 October 2023).
- **Section 39—Power to apply ss. 34–38 to armed forces**.
- For further detail, see www.legislation.gov.uk/ukpga/1994/33/section/39 (accessed 30 October 2023).
- **Section 39—Power to apply ss. 36 and 37 in relation to food crime officers**.
- For further detail, see www.legislation.gov.uk/ukpga/1994/33/section/39A (accessed 30 October 2023).

PACE 1984 Code C 2019, s. C (updated 4 November 2020)

- When a suspect is interviewed at a police station or authorized place of detention after arrest fails to or refuses to answer certain questions or to answer them satisfactory after due warning a court or jury may draw an inference.
- For an inference to be drawn when a suspect fails or refuses to answer a question about one of these matters or to answer it satisfactorily, the suspect must first be told in ordinary language:
  - what offence is being investigated;
  - what fact they are being asked to account for;
  - this fact may be due to them taking part in the commission of the offence;
  - a court may draw a proper inference if they fail or refuse to account for this fact;
  - a record is being made of the interview and it may be given in evidence if they are brought to trial.[11]
- **Note:** There are a number of restrictions on drawing adverse inferences (as detailed in Annex C of the Code).
- For further information, see PACE 1984, Code C Annex C, www.gov.uk/government/publications/pace-code-c-2019/pace-code-c-2019-accessible#bookmark65 (accessed 30 October 2023).

[11] PACE Code C 2019.

Further Reading

- Criminal Justice and Public Order Act 1994, www.legislation.gov.uk/ukpga/1994/33/contents (accessed 30 October 2023);
- PACE 1984 Code C, www.gov.uk/government/publications/pace-code-c-2019/pace-code-c-2019-accessible#bookmark65 (accessed 29 September 2023).

8.8 Multi-Agency Investigations and MOUs

The Serious Crime Act 2007, s. 68 enables specified organizations to disclose information to prevent fraud with public bodies. Further data sharing for law enforcement purposes (including fraud) between organization that are remitted to investigate crime defines these bodies as 'competent authorities' that fall under Part 3 of the Data Protection Act 2018 (DPA 2018) for law enforcement (data) processing.[12]

Data protection legislation specifically supports and facilitates information sharing to prevent and detect crime (fraud), but it ensures that this is done in a compliant and proportionate way. Most public bodies and police forces are competent bodies and listed under DPA 2018, Schedule 7. If they are not, data can still be shared so long as they are remitted to investigate crime (even if specific areas) and so data can be shared under s. 31 of DPA for:

> the purposes of the prevention, investigation, detection, or prosecution of criminal offences or the execution of criminal penalties, including the safeguarding against and the prevention of threats to public security.

When there is more than one organization investigating and/or prosecuting criminal offences jointly on a regular basis, leading practice encourages that the bodies will sign a joint memorandum of understanding (MoU). An MoU is an agreement between organizations setting out how they will work together on the case(s). These MoUs can be between two organizations (bilateral) or multiple organizations (multilateral).

The process of creating an MoU therefore means the organizations entering into, or formalizing existing relationships, can work through and set out the legal gateways authorizing the sharing of information, and what information is to be shared. This means that during disclosure, or responding to any challenge to the legality of data sharing, the organizations and investigators will be able to refer to the MoU and respond to such challenges.

Common features might include:

- details of the parties/organizations included;
- reason for the agreement;

[12] DPA 2018, www.legislation.gov.uk/ukpga/2018/12/part/3/enacted#:~:text=The%20third%20data%20protection%20principle%20is%20that%20personal%20data%20processed (accessed 20 October 2023).

- date it will come into force;
- purpose of the agreement;
- roles and responsibilities;
- use of powers;
- data sharing provisions;
- onward sharing and disclosure;
- case decision-making mechanisms;
- monitoring of the agreement.

8.9 Financial Investigation

A financial investigation is at the heart of fraud investigations; indeed, a fraud investigation is financial investigation. Care should be taken when using the terms 'financial investigation' and 'accredited financial investigator' (AFI) as often the meanings are misunderstood, which can lead to a lack of clarity and understanding.

Investigators can undertake a financial investigation into the predicate offence. Depending on the powers available to the investigator this will define the range of material that can be sought; following the money is key to apprehending the fraud offender. These powers are available to a range of investigators including the police, National Crime Agency (NCA), officers of His Majesty's Revenue & Customs, officers of the Welsh Revenue Authority, Labour Abuse Prevention officers (Gangmasters and Labour Abuse Authority), and foods crime officers (Foods Standards Agency).

KEY POINTS—KEY PACE SEARCH AND SEIZURE POWERS

The following is a summary of the key PACE powers used to search for and/or seize relevant material:

- s. 1—power to stop and search persons and vehicles.;
- s. 8—power of Justice of the Peace to authorize entry and search of premises;
- s. 9—provisions to access excluded material or special procedure material;
- s. 17—powers of entry for the purpose of arrest;
- s. 18—power of entry and search after arrest;
- s. 19—general power of seizure;
- s. 32—power to search upon arrest.

The Proceeds of Crime Act 2002 (POCA 2002) was introduced to take the proceeds of crime away from criminals. Most of the powers are available to police officers and NCA officers, but to increase the capability to deprive criminals of the proceeds of crime an accredited status was introduced for those that did not have access to powers under the proceeding legislation. Thus, the AFI was introduced. Normally the focus of the AFI is restraint and confiscation (civil powers) or money laundering investigations.

8.9.1 Accredited Financial Investigator (AFI)

AFIs were created by POCA and significantly expanded those public bodies that could undertake powers under POCA. POCA empowers the Secretary of State to designate investigators that have the description as an AFI who are employed or engaged by law enforcement authorities or, crucially, in a law enforcement capacity (so including counter fraud) by various public bodies as scheduled.

There are a large number of bodies and persons who qualify as AFIs for the purposes of POCA and who undertake activities in this area. Home Office guidance sets out how public sector organizations can apply for staff to become AFIs which is overseen by the NCAs who are responsible for the training and accreditation of AFIs.

8.10 Investigative Interviewing

In England, Wales, and Northern Ireland, the PEACE model is the preferred model for investigative interviewing (as detailed in Figure 8.5). This model is used across investigations to support high-quality interviews in all case types and all types of interviews (victims, witnesses, and suspects). It was developed in the 1990s to move to a more non-confrontational approach as a number of investigations were shown to have used 'aggressive' techniques that were not consistent with a fair and appropriate approach to interviewing with a detrimental impact on the case and individuals concerned. This is also a key competency within the interviewing component of the GCFP standard as seen previously.

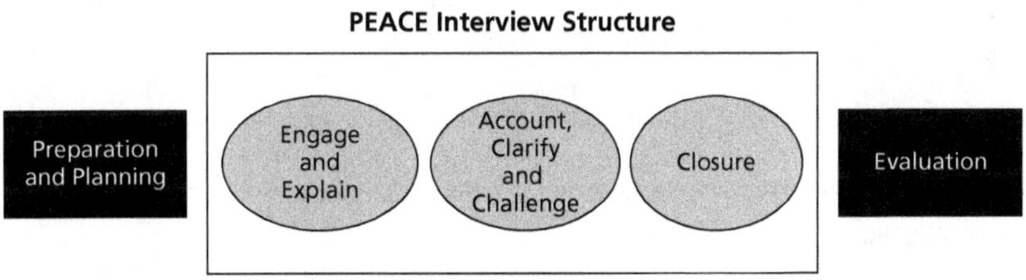

Figure 8.5 PEACE model

Checklist—PEACE Interview Model

Planning and preparation

Investigators at this stage should be creating an interview plan and consider the following:

- What offence or issue is being investigated? What are the points to prove/focus of the interview?

- Who and what order should suspects/witnesses be interviewed?
- Assess what is known by the investigation.
- Understand what the investigation needs to know.
- Logistical considerations such as location, reasonable adjustments, and equipment.
- Any third parties such as solicitors or union representatives?

Engage and explain

- seek to engage with the interviewee and develop a rapport;
- explain the reason for the interview and the process (use an aide-mémoire);
- explain the interview process;
- if appropriate, caution the suspect;
- explain role of the notetaker/second interviewer.

Account, clarify, and challenge

- encourage natural conversation style;
- reflect back explanations and statements;
- probe, confirm, and clarify;
- use varies question types appropriate to the point being explored (e.g. closed, open, forced choice, multiple, and leading).

Closure

- Summarize interview and seek confirmation from interviewee; do they have any questions? (e.g. next steps).
- Confirm with any second interviewer no further questions.
- Complete any PACE or equivalent recording conclusion procedures.

Evaluation

- Any further action/next steps?
- How does the interview fit with the known case? What is its impact?
- A sample of interviews may be used as part of ongoing case reviews and performance management processes.

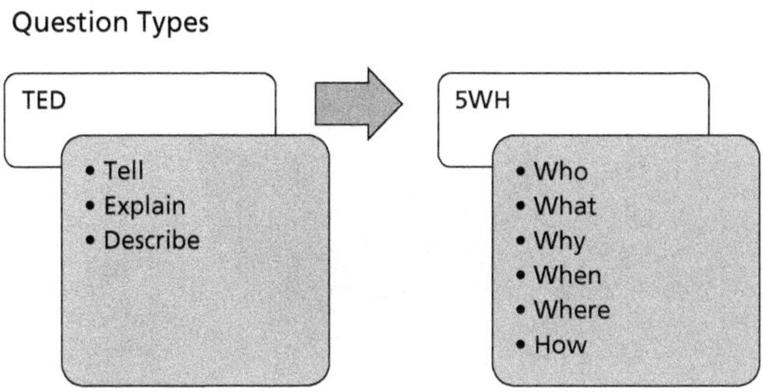

Figure 8.6 Question types

8.10.1 Question Types

The purpose of an interview is to gather as much relevant material to establish the facts of the case. Interviewing officers should consider the use of question types with care and must avoid contaminating the person they are interviewing with knowledge known to the interviewer but not the interviewee. The memory is susceptible to contamination; the use of TED questions help avoid such contamination as they are open instructions:

- T—tell me
- E—explain to me
- D—describe to me

These questions may be followed by more granular questions of 5WH; the 5WH questions are who, what, when, why, where, and how. These question types are illustrated in Figure 8.6.

The use of these question types acts like a funnel which aims to be effective in gathering fine grain information. The interview funnel is shown in Figure 8.7.

8.11 Counter Fraud Framework

In Chapter 1 we introduced the counter fraud framework (detailed in Figure 8.8). In this chapter we take a deeper dive to explore its elements in detail and look at the strategic and tactical options for each topic area. As described in Chapter 1 the role of those leading or undertaking a fraud investigation is more than just pursuing an offender; it is to focus on pursuing with actively considering preventing further harm and loss. It harnesses a range of options and specialists to deny fraud criminals access to further victims.

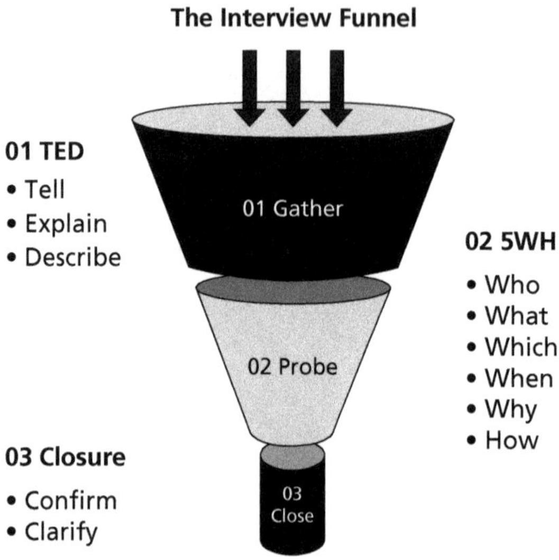

Figure 8.7 Interview funnel

8.11.1 **Case Acceptance Criteria**

Organizations should have a case acceptance criterion, to ensure transparency and clarity in the decision-making process. It helps focus the organizational resources of the crimes that represent the highest threat and harm.

KEY POINTS—SFO CASE ACCEPTANCE: STATEMENT OF PRINCIPLE

The SFO have published their case acceptance, which states:[13]

> The Director may investigate any suspected offence which appears to her on reasonable grounds to involve serious or complex fraud, bribery or corruption.
>
> In considering whether to authorise an investigation the Director will take into account the actual or intended harm that may be caused to:
>
> - the public, or
> - the reputation and integrity of the UK as an international financial centre, or
> - the economy and prosperity of the UK
> - and whether the complexity and nature of the suspected offence warrants the application of the SFO's specialist skills, powers, and capabilities to investigate and prosecute.

[13] SFO, Statement of Principle, www.sfo.gov.uk/publications/guidance-policy-and-protocols/sfo-statement-of-principle/ (accessed 1 October 2023).

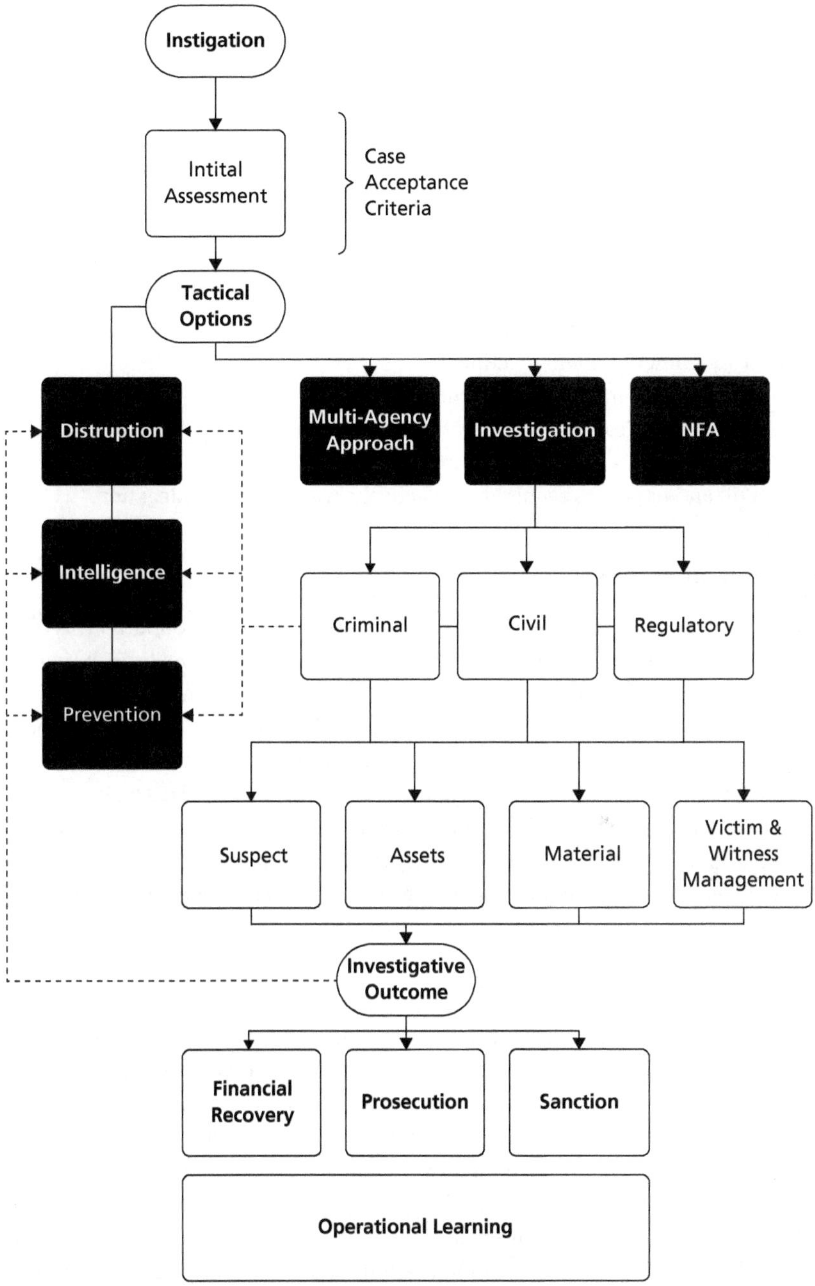

Figure 8.8 Counter Fraud Framework

Organizations will typically use a scoring matrix to quantify the value of the referral to enable it to be prioritized and considered against competing demands; factors to be considered may include:

(1) victim vulnerability/susceptibility;
(2) crime in action (call for service);
(3) linked offending;
(4) offender known;
(5) investigative opportunities (clear lines of inquiry);
(6) value of loss/gain;
(7) organizational jurisdiction;
(8) cross-border offending/victims;
(9) international inquiries required;
(10) case of significant public interest;
(11) priority offence (i.e. bribery of a public official);
(12) skill and/or powers required to effectively investigate the allegation.

8.11.2 Tactical Options

The Counter Fraud Framework presents a number of tactical options. These are considerations for the investigator, which can be revisited at any time during the investigation and should not 'dictate' investigative actions. However, a number of options may be combined: for example, an investigation may be launched though at the same time actions may be taken to prevent further harm and loss by target hardening the victims—whether an individual or organization. This may be undertaken by deploying a fraud prevention officer or commissioning a fraud risk assessment. The investigator may consider suggesting a fraud measurement exercise be undertaken to assess the potential loss to the organization and to gain improved understanding of the issues.

8.11.2.1 Multi-Agency Working

When considering the appropriate response to the referral, consideration should be given to which investigative organization has the most appropriate jurisdiction and/or powers to respond appropriately to the allegation. Across the public sector there is an extensive range of organizations with complementary investigative powers; it may be a preferred option to refer the allegation in its totality or seek to work together on the case. Often multi-agency working can be highly effective and the use of complementary powers aids the efficiency of the investigative process. Table 8.4 provides a summary of organizations, their focus, and available powers.

8.11.2.2 Prevention and Disruption

This is the most important aspect countering fraud; from the policing perspective, it reflects the Peelian principles where the number one principle was described as preventing crime (and disorder). Those investigating fraud offending should

Table 8.4 Public sector organizations: focus and powers

Organization	Focus	Relevant statutes
Serious Fraud Office	Serious and complex fraud and bribery	Criminal Justice Act 1987
Competition Markets Authority	Promoting competitive markets and tackling unfair behaviour (e.g. cartels)	Competition Act 1998; Enterprise Act 2002
Financial Conduct Authority	Abuse in the financial markets	Financial Services Act 2012
Department for Work and Pensions	Benefits abuse	Social Security Administration Act 1992
His Majesty's Revenue and Customs	Tax and excise abuse	Commissioners for Revenue and Customs Act 2005; Police and Criminal Evidence Act (PACE) 1984
National Crime Agency	Organized crime; human, weapons, and drug trafficking; cybercrime; economic crime	PACE 1984; Courts and Crime Act 2013

analyse the case to identify the enablers that permitted the offender access to the victim and any subsequent transfer of money. Once the enablers have been identified the investigator should seek to disrupt them where possible thus denying the offender the opportunity to re-offend.

Prevention techniques include education of the at-risk communities through awareness campaigns, identifying and implementing further controls, and limiting or closing communication routes being used by the offenders.

Disruption of fraud offending should also be considered. The options include working with domain providers to remove websites, working with the financial sector to reduce the opportunity for using bank accounts as an enabler of fraud, and working with the telecommunications sector to limit the use of devices by fraudsters.

9

Prosecution, Sanctions, and Redress

Blackstone's Counter Fraud Professionals' Handbook. Michael J. Betts, Laura Eshelby, and David Whitehouse-Hayes, Oxford University Press.
DOI: 10.1093/9780191996955.003.0009

9.1 Introduction

In this chapter we explore the UK organizations who prosecute fraud offenders and those that have the power to impose civil sanctions. This chapter is primarily focused on what can be done by public sector organizations and the way they can use the resources and options at their disposal to the best effect. We will explain the importance of early consultation with prosecutors, the recording of decisions, and the supporting rationale. The range of routes available for sanctions and redress are detailed in Figure 9.1—each comes with its own considerations and possible outcomes.

The different routes shown in Figure 9.1 are triggered by differing criteria: the burden of proof differs in civil and criminal proceedings.

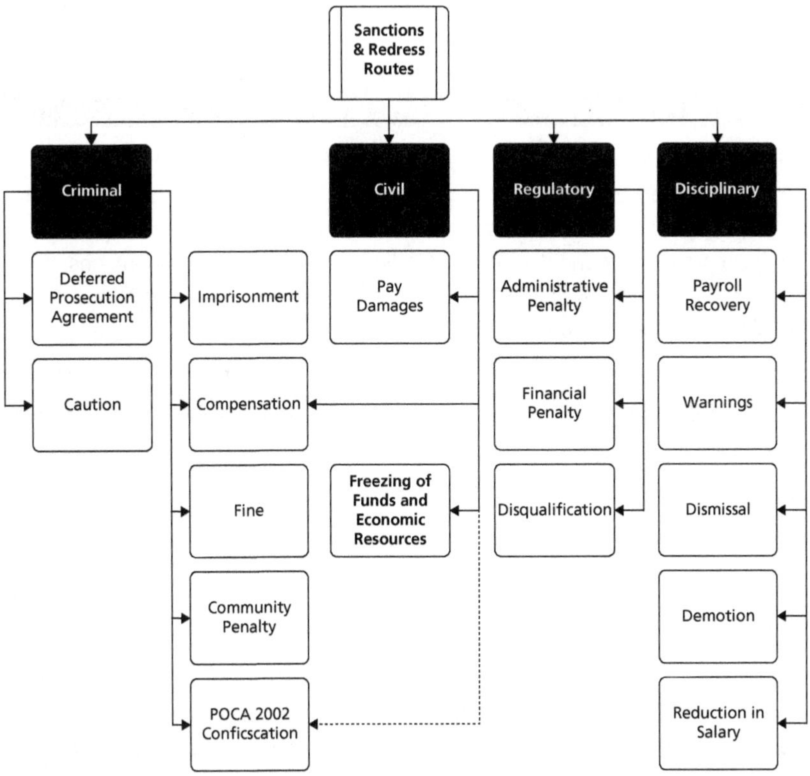

Figure 9.1 Sanctions and redress routes and options

KEY POINTS—BURDEN OF PROOF

There are two 'burdens of proof' that are routinely applied in disposal matters, these are the civil and criminal standard:

- The civil test essentially asks 'is it more likely than not' (known as the balance of probabilities).
- The criminal test is that it is 'beyond reasonable doubt' (that you are sure).

9.2 Prosecuting Authorities

9.2.1 Crown Prosecution Service (CPS)

The CPS prosecute criminal cases in England and Wales that have been investigated by a range of investigative bodies including the police. The decisions they make are done independently of government.

KEY POINTS—INTRODUCTION OF THE CPS

- The CPS was created by the Prosecution of Offences Act 1985.[1]
- This was part of these wider reforms to the criminal justice system that was mired by considerable evidence of bias and discrimination.
- It separated charging decisions from those that investigated them, ensuring these were made by independent prosecutors applying a two-tier test of sufficient evidence and public policy.

The CPS apply a two-stage test, to determine whether a case should be prosecuted:

(1) Is there enough evidence against the defendant?
(2) Is it in the public interest for the CPS to bring the case to court?

Checklist—Public Interest Factors

In all cases where the evidential test is met prosecutors are required to consider whether a prosecution is in the public interest. The considerations for this test are detailed in the Code for Crown Prosecutors,[2] questions to be considered include:

[1] Prosecution of Offences Act 1985, www.legislation.gov.uk/ukpga/1985/23 (accessed 18 April 2023).

[2] CPS, *The Code for Crown Prosecutors* (2018), www.cps.gov.uk/publication/code-crown-prosecutors (accessed 18 April 2023).

- the seriousness of the offence committed;
- the level of culpability of the suspect;
- the circumstances of and the harm caused to the victim;
- the suspect's age and maturity at the time of the offence;
- the impact of the offending on the community;
- whether a prosecution is a proportionate response;
- if sources of information require protecting.

Early consultation with the prosecuting authority is highly recommended, particularly in complex cases, they may advise on:

(1) advice on points of law;
(2) post-arrest guidance on what offences might be appropriate for charging;
(3) additional evidence requirements needed.

The CPS will assess whether there is sufficient evidence and whether it is in the public interest to prosecute. Alternatives to this route are a simple or conditional caution. If the case does not reach this threshold, the CPS may determine the case requires further evidence or may recommend that it should be closed 'no further action'. The rationale for this decision may be because there is no public interest and/or insufficient, and unlikely to be sufficient evidence for there to be a 'reasonable prospect of conviction'.

KEY POINTS—CODE FOR CROWN PROSECUTORS

The factors that prosecutors must apply is set out in the Code for Crown Prosecutors which is issued by the Director of Public Prosecutions (DPP). This sets out in broad terms the factors that should be considered when deciding to prosecute.[3]

Summary of key principles include:

- Prosecutors' independence is paramount to the criminal justice system, and they must operate without political or other undue or improper interference.
- A decision to charge is based purely on the factors set out before and in no way indicates guilt as only a court can make a determination.
- Equally, a decision not to prosecute does not mean someone has not been the victim of crime (and civil remedy may still be pursued and looked at later).
- All decisions must be fair, considered, and balance rights of victims and suspects against interests of justice, also factoring in Human Rights Act 1998 considerations.

[3] Ibid.

9.2.2 Crown Office and Procurator Fiscal Service (COPFS)

The COPFS is a department of the Scottish government headed by the Lord Advocate and is Scotland's' public prosecution service and death investigation authority. They are sponsible for investigating alleged criminal conduct by the police.

COPFS is an independent prosecuting authority (pre-dating the CPS) and applies the Prosecution Code to make disposal decisions.[4] They explicitly outline their remit as being to provide decisions on cases free of political or other pressure. Further, disposal decisions are made in an effective and consistent way applying the full range of prosecution and alternatives to prosecution as appropriate.

Like the CPS they apply this code considering factors such as the gravity of the offence, impact on the victim, personal circumstances of the suspect, and mitigating circumstances.

9.2.3 Public Prosecution Service (PPS) Northern Ireland

The PPS is the prosecuting authority in Northern Ireland, with similar responsibility disposal decisions including all cases investigated by the police as well as other public sector bodies. As with the others it is an independent body and applies a code. The PPS was formed in June 2005, and is led by the Director of Public Prosecutions (DPP) for Northern Ireland and the Deputy Director of Public Prosecutions who has the same powers as the Director but must exercise these subjects to the DPP's direction and control.

Section 37 of the Justice Act (NI) 2002, sets out the Code for Prosecutors. The Code details the organization's values such as independence and integrity as well as openness and respect, among others. It also sets out an evidential and public interest test that must be met in a comparable way to the CPS. It details the considerations that either increase the appropriateness of prosecution or reduce it. Examples are offenders in a position of authority and/or premeditation, among others in favour of prosecution.

Further Reading

- CPS, www.cps.gov.uk (accessed 16 August 2023);
- Code for Crown Prosecutors, www.cps.gov.uk/publication/code-crown-prosecutors (accessed 16 August 2023);
- Public Prosecution Service Northern Ireland, www.ppsni.gov.uk (accessed 16 August 2023);
  Code for Public Prosecution Service Northern Ireland, www.ppsni.gov.uk/publications/code-prosecutors (accessed 16 August 2023);
- Crown Office and Procurator Fiscal Service (COPFS), www.copfs.gov.uk/ (accessed 16 August 2023).

[4] The Code explains the factors that prosecutors consider including legal, evidential, and public interest considerations.

9.2.4 Other Prosecuting Authorities

A range of other organizations have the capability to directly prosecute criminal cases through the criminal courts. These tend to be organizations that have the required knowledge and competency to undertake inquiries in a specialist field of investigation and can focus on that area of criminality.

Many of these organizations have signed the CPS's Prosecutors' Convention. This agreement details the principles prosecution agencies should follow when both have a shared interest in the prosecution.

Checklist—Other Prosecution Bodies

There are a range of prosecuting bodies who have a bespoke responsibility for prosecuting cases these include:

- **Serious Fraud Office (SFO)**—is a specialist prosecuting authority and has authority in England, Wales, and Northern Ireland. It has responsibility for the investigation and prosecution of complex fraud, bribery, and corruption cases.
- **Service Prosecuting Authority (SPA)**—prosecutes cases within the Armed Forces that are brought before the service courts.
- **Competitions Markets Authority (CMA)**—responsible for investigating a range of competition offences and bringing criminal proceedings against individuals who commit cartels offences.
- **Civil Aviation Authority (CAA)**—The CAA is an arm's-length body of the Department for Transport. It investigates and prosecutes breaches of aviation safety rules as well as some aviation-related consumer protection and health and safety requirements.
- **Department for Environment, Food & Rural Affairs (DEFRA)** and its arm's-length bodies, such as the Environment Agency and Food Standards Agency, have extensive and broad powers of investigation and criminal sanction powers. These can range from investigating and prosecuting fraudulent farming subsidy claims using powers including evidence from spy satellites to the fraudulent breaches of the prohibition of the sale of ivory and consumer food safety and counterfeiting offences.
- **Financial Conduct Authority (FCA)**—the FCA can prosecute criminal matters such as money laundering under the Proceeds of Crime Act 2002 (POCA 2002). Its primary purpose is as a regulator of financial services firms, and, as such, authorized and registered firms in this sector of the economy.

Further Reading

- CPS's Prosecutors' Convention, www.cps.gov.uk/legal-guidance/relations-other-prosecuting-agencies-and-prosecutors-convention (accessed 16 August 2023);
- SPA, www.gov.uk/guidance/service-prosecuting-authority (accessed 16 August 2023);
- CMA, www.gov.uk/government/organisations/competition-and-markets-authority (accessed 16 August 2023).

9.3 England, Wales, and Northern Ireland Offence Types

In England, Wales, and Northern Ireland offences are classified and may be heard in the appropriate court:

- **Summary only**—these are the lower level of offence and are limited to the magistrates' court and the sentencing is usually limited to six months in prison but range from three to twelve months, as well as limited fines and community payback orders. Examples of fraud-specific offences in this category are failure to notify a change in circumstances under s. 112 Social Security Administration Act 1992.[5]
- **Either-way**—these offences can be heard in either the magistrates' court or the Crown Court. The magistrates can decide to refer a case to the Crown Court due to its seriousness, or for sentencing after a summary trial if they feel their sentencing power is insufficient. The defendant can also elect a Crown Court trial.
- **Indictable only**—these offences are the most serious and can only be heard in the Crown Court.

Deferred Prosecution Agreements (DPAs) came into force in February 2014 under the Crime and Courts Act 2013. They are only available to the DPP and Director of the SFO. They can be applied in certain types of fraud such as conspiracy to commit fraud, money laundering, failure to prevent bribery, and tax evasion offences at the corporate level.

9.4 Sentencing Guidelines

The Sentencing Council provides guidelines for magistrates and judges to follow when considering the sentencing for a range of economic crime including fraud. This is in accordance with the Coroners and Justice Act 2009. It applies to all offenders aged 18 or over. The guideline specifies the range of sentences appropriate for each type of offence. Within each offence, the Council has specified several categories which reflect varying degrees of seriousness and considers the level of harm and culpability.

[5] Social Security Administration Act 1992, www.legislation.gov.uk/ukpga/1992/5/section/112 (accessed 18 April 2023).

KEY POINTS—OFFENCE TYPES INCLUDED IN THE SENTENCING COUNCIL'S GUIDELINES

- fraud by false representation;
- fraud by failing to disclose information;
- fraud by abuse of position—Fraud Act 2006;
- conspiracy to defraud at common law;
- false accounting—Theft Act 1968 (s. 17);
- possession of articles for use in frauds—Fraud Act 2006 (s. 6);
- making or supplying articles for use in frauds—Fraud Act 2006 (s. 7);
- revenue fraud;
- Fraud Conspiracy to defraud (common law);
- fraudulent evasion of VAT;
- false statement for VAT purposes; conduct amounting to an offence—Value Added Tax Act 1994 (s. 72).

9.5 Alternatives to Prosecution

Simple and conditional cautions: simple cautions are most often issued by the police. However, several other public bodies can also issue them such as local authorities who have the power under the Local Government Act 1972. The CPS sets out that simple cautions can be considered for dealing with low-level, usually first time, offending where prosecution would not be the best disposal in the public interest.

Checklist—Criteria for a Simple Caution

The criteria that must be met to issue a simple caution are:

- the offender has admitted the offence;
- the offender is willing to accept the caution;
- there must be sufficient evidence to provide a realistic prospect of a conviction if the offender were to be prosecuted;
- the offence is not one where a prosecution is required in the public interest.

Simple cautions form part of the offender's criminal record. They may be referred to in future legal proceedings and may be revealed as part of a criminal record check.[6]

[6] CPS, 'Cautioning and Diversion' (2 August 2022), www.cps.gov.uk/legal-guidance/cautioning-and-diversion (accessed 18 April 2023).

9.6 Range of Other Fines and Penalties

Many public bodies have other alternatives to prosecution that are specific to their organization and area of responsibility. These include, but are not limited to:

- welfare fraud administrative penalties under Social Security Administration Act 1992, set at 50 per cent of the value of the prosecutable loss;
- HMRC Tax Credits penalty charge under Tax Credit Act 2002, for overpayments of £4,000 or more;
- prescription and dental charge fraud (England and Wales) can attract penalty notices under NHS (Penalty Charge) Regulations 1999 and is five times the value of the original evaded charge to a maximum of £100.

9.7 Public Sector Organizations' Powers and Sanctions

9.7.1 Department for Work and Pensions (DWP)

The DWP has a significant capability to undertake investigations and can take enforcement action if social security benefit fraud is suspected; these investigations are undertaken by DWP's Counter Fraud & Compliance Directorate (CFCD) and includes an Economic & Serious Organised Crime division (ESOC).

KEY POINTS—DWP BENEFITS IN CFCD SCOPE

There are a range of benefits in scope which DWP may investigate:

- Universal Credit;
- Jobseeker's Allowance;
- Pension Credit;
- Employment and Support Allowance;
- Personal Independence Payment;
- Disability Living Allowance;
- State Retirement Pension;
- bereavement benefits;
- Maternity Allowance;
- War Pensions paid by the Veterans Agency.[7]

There are also non-benefits that are DWP's remit including:

- access to Work payments.

[7] DWP, 'Penalties Policy: In Respect of Social Security Fraud and Error' (14 August 2017), www.gov.uk/government/publications/penalties-for-social-security-fraud-and-error/penalties-policy-in-respect-of-social-security-fraud-and-error (accessed 2 May 2023).

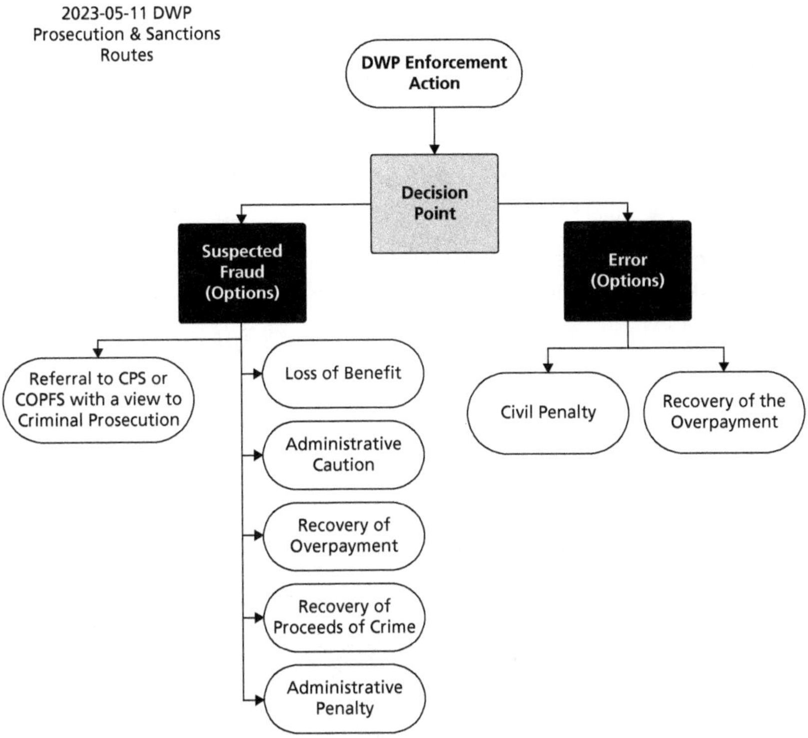

Figure 9.2 DWP prosecution and sanctions routes

The prosecution and sanctions routes available to DWP are detailed in Figure 9.2.

9.7.2 DWP Criteria for Referrals for Prosecution

Where one or more of the following factors are revealed in an investigation, DWP will normally refer the case to the CPS or the COPFS:

- the recoverable overpayment determined as 'fraud' or 'claimant error' as decided by the decision-maker (including Housing Benefit and Council Tax Benefit and Tax Credits);
- a financial threshold may be used as a guide for which disposal route is most appropriate (see disposal routes);
- false identities or other personal details have been used;
- false or forged documents have been used;
- official documents have been altered or falsified;
- the person concerned occupied a position of trust;
- the person concerned assisted or encouraged others to commit offences;
- there is evidence of premeditation or organized fraud;

- the person concerned had previously been convicted or received a penalty for benefit fraud;
- the offer of an administrative penalty or caution is not accepted.[8]

9.7.3 HM Revenue & Customs (HMRC) Prosecution and Sanctions Options

HMRC have a broad range of criminal offences open to them through a range of bespoke legislation, or sections of legislation to deal with tax fraud/evasion, as well as tax credits.

Checklist—Legislation Available to HMRC

The primary legislation available to prosecute criminal cases by HMRC includes:

- common law, including cheating the public revenue;
- Customs and Excise Management Act 1979 (ss. 50, 170, 170B);
- Fraud Act 2006 (s. 1) (fraud by false representation);
- Taxes Management Act 1970 (s. 106A);
- Theft Act 1968 (s. 17) (false accounting);
- Value Added Tax Act 1994 (s. 72).

Other common tax offences include those of providing false documents to HMRC and evasion of duty (e.g. cigarettes) under the Customs and Excise Management Act 1979 (CEMA 1979), fraudulent evasion of tax under the Taxes Management Act 1970 (TMA 1970), and evasion of value-added tax (VAT) under VAT Act 1994.

The offence of failure to prevent the facilitation of tax evasion under the Criminal Finances Act 2017, Part 3, s. 45,[9] as this is a strict liability offence at the corporate level and criminal intent is not required to prove the offence.

Three steps exist for an offence to be prosecutable under this Act:

(1) criminal tax evasion by company or individual;
(2) criminal facilitation by 'an associated person' engaging in deliberate or dishonest behaviour;
(3) the entity fails to prevent the 'associate person' from committing the criminal act at stage 2.

---

[8] Ibid.

[9] Criminal Finances Act 2017, www.legislation.gov.uk/ukpga/2017/22/contents/enacted (accessed 18 April 2023).

The only defence in this case is for the company to show that it had effective prevention procedures in place to stop facilitation (Criminal Finances Act 2017, s. 47).

KEYPOINTS—GUIDANCE ABOUT PREVENTING FACILITATION OF TAX EVASION OFFENCES

The guidance is published by HMRC.[10] It describes the six guiding principles of prevention are described as:

- proportionality of risk-based prevention procedures;
- top-level commitment;
- risk assessment;
- due diligence;
- communication (including training);
- monitoring and review.

9.7.4 HMRC Litigation and Settlement Strategy

HMRC has a stated litigation and settlement strategy used in both individual and corporate cases where both parties are in dispute.[11] The case will usually have no clear resolution and the extent of liability owed (civil) to HMRC is in dispute.

Such cases can often be large and complex and if the dispute cannot be resolved will end up in a tribunal. Mediation, using a third party in cases where the working relationship has broken down, can be more effective and efficient by avoiding the need for tribunal, but HMRC will not settle a dispute just to avoid costs.

The aim is to ensure the party owing tax is clear on the ground rules HMRC must apply to reach a negotiated settlement and will not compromise on their view of the law. Further, HMRC will set out the grounds on why they think tax is owed including key data/evidence as well as any fines, interest, or other penalties that are applicable.

The negotiation will come to an agreed figure that is reflective of all the above and is an amount not less than HMRC would expect to secure if it did continue with litigation. In most cases, resolution by this route offers the most effective and efficient outcome.

Further Reading

- HMRC Litigation and Settlement Strategy, www.gov.uk/government/publications/litigation-and-settlement-strategy-lss(accessed 16 August 2023).

[10] HMRC, 'Tackling Tax Evasion: Government Guidance for the Corporate Offences of Failure to Prevent the Criminal Facilitation of Tax Evasion' (1 September 2017), https://assets.publishing.service.gov.uk/government/uploads/system/uploads/attachment_data/file/672231/Tackling-tax-evasion-corporate-offences.pdf (accessed 18 April 2023).

[11] www.gov.uk/hmrc-internal-manuals/alternative-dispute-resolution-guidance/adrg02600 (accessed 18 April 2023).

9.8 Restraint and Confiscation

9.8.1 Restraint Orders

Restraint orders are made under ss. 40 and 41 of the Proceeds of Crime Act 2002 (POCA 2002) and are made by a prosecutor supported by a statement made by the financial investigator. The applications are usually made *ex parte* and can take place once an investigation has commenced. The timing of any application should be carefully considered to ensure the action does not compromise the investigation. The intent of the order in effect is to freeze the suspect's property to prevent it from being dissipated before it can be realized to satisfy a future confiscation order. The CPS proceeds of crime guidance states:[12]

> Prosecutors should consider asset recovery in every case in which a defendant has benefited from criminal conduct and should instigate confiscation proceedings in appropriate cases.

KEY POINTS—RESTRAIN ORDER CONDITIONS

A judge may only grant a restraint order if any one of the five conditions set out in POCA 2002, s. 40 are satisfied.[13] The prosecutor must in all cases demonstrate there is a real risk that the assets may be dissipated and satisfy one of the following five conditions:

- Condition 1—the criminal investigation has been started in England and Wales about an offence and there are reasonable grounds to suspect that the alleged offender has benefited from his criminal conduct.
- Condition 2—that proceedings for an offence have been started in England and Wales and not concluded, and there is reasonable cause to believe that the defendant has benefited from his/her criminal conduct.
- Condition 3—if the prosecutor has applied (or is likely to apply) to the Crown Court
    - to reconsider making a confiscation order when no such order was made
    - to reconsider making a confiscation when no such order was made and there is new evidence that the defendant benefited from his or her criminal conduct
    - to make a confiscation order where a defendant absconds after conviction or committal); or
    - to make a confiscation order where a defendant absconded more than three months previously but was neither acquitted nor convicted in

[12] CPS, 'Proceeds of Crime' (19 December 2019), www.cps.gov.uk/legal-guidance/proceeds-crime (accessed 18 April 2023).

[13] Ibid.

commenced criminal proceedings); and there is reasonable cause to believe that the defendant has benefited from his criminal conduct.

- Condition 4—is satisfied if the prosecutor has applied (or is likely to apply) to the Crown Court to reconsider the benefit figure in a confiscation order and there is reasonable cause to believe that the court will decide that the amount found under the new benefit calculation of the defendant's benefit exceeds the relevant amount.
- Condition 5—is satisfied that the prosecutor has applied (or is likely to apply), to reconsider the amount available to satisfy a confiscation order and there is reasonable cause to believe that the court will decide that the amount found under the new calculation of the available amount exceeds the relevant amount.

9.8.2 **Confiscation Orders**

Confiscation orders are made by the Crown Court under POCA, s. 6, and two conditions are required to be met:

(1) The defendant is:
  a. convicted of an offence or offences in proceedings before the Crown Court; or
  b. Is committed to the Crown Court for sentence; or
  c. Is committed to the Crown Court with a view to a confiscation order being made (under s.70).

2. The prosecutor asks the court to proceed, or the court considers it appropriate to do so.

The court will then seek to establish three key points before making a confiscation order:

- Does the defendant have a criminal lifestyle?
- Value of the benefit of the criminal conduct?
- The available amount.

The process will then seek to establish what available assets the offender has, including any restrained assets and 'tainted gifts' (these are where the defendant has 'gifted' money or other assets to friend or family to dissipate them, and these were made entirely/in part as result of their criminal conduct).

The court will then order the confiscation of assets to the value of the established 'available amount' which may be the same or less than the benefit amount. The prosecution may seek inflationary increase on the value of loss if it was over an extended period. Time to pay will be agreed and this may be dependent on matters such as realizing assets in the form of property, any delay beyond the agreed time to pay will incur interest.

Case Study—POCA Confiscation Proceedings Including Detained Cash and Inflationary Loss Increase

In 2016, Azzam Mohammed was prosecuted for serious Housing Benefit fraud and ordered to repay £169,000 to Westminster City Council.

He had claimed Housing Benefit based on being employed part-time on minimum wage as a letting agent. However, evidence obtained in the case showed a luxury lifestyle including private education for his son. In addition, there was no evidence of him having any rent liability.

When he was arrested, and his property searched in a joint operation between Westminster City Council and police, the claimed part-time employee had more than £50,000 cash in his property. As no legitimate source for the money could be shown, it was subject to a cash detention order.

After his guilty plea to offences over four years resulted in a prison sentence of two years and he had to repay £169,000. This included inflation-proofing of the losses to Westminster Council. The confiscation order was payable to a compensation order in favour of the Council and to be paid within three months, including the use of the detained cash that was forfeited.

9.9 Civil Sanctions

9.9.1 Freezing Orders

Freezing orders are sought under s. 37 of the Senior Court Act 1981, which is a civil procedure. Such orders can be sought when there is a risk of assets being dissipated or disposed of before the conclusion of court proceedings, they are an interim injunction. They were previously referred to as *Mareva* injunctions. The process for the granting of these orders is detailed in the Civil Procedures Rules, Practice Direction 25a—Interim Injunctions.[14]

Freezing orders can be obtained to prevent suspected fraudsters from accessing their assets. Once the order is in place the assets remain frozen until conclusion of the investigation and if appropriate a recovery order made against the offender.

[14] MoJ, Practice Direction 25A—Interim Injunctions—CPR Part 25, www.justice.gov.uk/courts/procedure-rules/civil/rules/part25/pd_part25a#1.1 (accessed 2 May 2023).

Further Reading

- Injunctions—Senior Court Act 1981, s. 37, www.legislation.gov.uk/ukpga/1981/54/section/37/2014-04-22 (accessed 16 August 2023);
- Freezing Orders Court Procedure, www.justice.gov.uk/courts/procedure-rules/civil/rules/part25/pd_part25a#1.1 (accessed 16 August 2023);
- Fraud Advisory Panel Civil Fraud and asset recovery, www.fraudadvisorypanel.org/wp-content/uploads/2020/10/Civil-Fraud-and-Asset-Recovery-2nd-ed-Oct2020.pdf (accessed 16 August 2023).

In the civil space there are straightforward proceedings that seek 'redress' and are focused on recovering losses in areas such as landlord–tenant cases for rent arrears or repairs and compensating for any damages. Other areas of civil litigation include faulty goods and services, personal injury and employment issues relating to pay (separate but may run in parallel with employment tribunal cases dealing with matters of employment law).

In England and Wales, the above proceedings will start in the County Court and if successful will result in the issuing of a county court judgment (CCJ) and can be sought by anybody seeking redress. The rules for this are set down in the Civil Procedure Rules (CPR) and in the first instance complainants are encouraged to use mediation, or other means to seek resolution.

9.9.2 Company Director Disqualification

If an individual uses, or allows their company to be used for fraudulent purposes this can be considered a breach of company law and their duties as a director if they fail to:

- carry out their duties honestly and responsibly;
- make sure they or the company complies with the law and all relevant regulations;
- exercise adequate skill and care with proper regard to the interests of the company's creditors, customers, shareholders, employees, and, in some circumstances, the public.

A civil court can make a disqualification order against directors under the Company Directors Disqualification Act 1986 (CDDA 1986) and can be applied for up to fifteen years. However, most disqualifications are entered into on a voluntary basis known as a disqualification undertaking.

These are an administrative equivalent of a disqualification order agreed on a voluntary basis and do not require court proceedings. The offer though must be agreed by the Secretary of State for the Department for Business and Trade. These have identical restrictions to a court order, but once agreed can only be changed by an order of the court.

A director under investigation can make a voluntary offer to accept disqualification at any stage of an investigation but must meet a suitability test. If not met, the Secretary of State will refuse the offer. However, if acceptable and agreed before court proceedings commence the Insolvency Service will not seek recovery of costs. An offer can also be made once proceedings have commenced but costs may be sought at this point for the legal costs of the proceedings. This can be a significant incentive to consider offering an undertaking.

These undertakings have come into particular focus and public scrutiny because of the Covid-19 pandemic and fraud within the various government support offered to businesses.

Case Study—Covid-19 Bounce Back Loan Scheme

Bounce Back Loans were launched in May 2020, and designed to support small businesses through the Covid-19 pandemic allowing them to borrow up to 25 per cent of their turnover up to £50,000. Repayments did not commence until May 2021 and attracted low interest rates. The scheme has subsequently been found to have a range of fraud risks and lessons learned from these are being applied and have resulted in changes in how 'major' new spending initiatives have their fraud risk assessed.

An example of one of these risks is that some applicants exaggerated their declared turnover as this directly correlated to the value of the loan that could be awarded. Three company directors: Malcolm Forbes, Avin Habash, and Kamil Ozkan applied for Bounce Back Loans (BBLs) in respect of their individual take-away/food businesses.

Each director was found to have either inflated their declared turnover or not used the BBL for its intended purpose.

Malcolm Forbes the sole director of Nija Bite Limited in Hampshire, inflated his turnover by a factor of almost ten to £225,000. This secured him a loan of £50,000 rather than what he would have been eligible for of £6,000.

Avin Habash was the sole director of Hot Spot Liverpool Limited also secured a BBL of £50,000 declaring a turnover of £200,000. This was twice the reality so securing a loan also twice the £26,000 he was entitled to.

Kamil Ozkan, also the sole director of Papa Peterlee Limited in County Durham also secured a £50,000 BBL but transferred around £37,500 to his personal account and the BBL was not used to support his business.

In all three cases the Insolvency Service agreed to a disqualification of three years for each.

Observation for the Investigator/Disposal Decision-Maker:

Decision on case disposal should consider the range of facts outlined previously, considering aggravating and mitigating factors. This example shows the importance of considering what sanctions are available to your organization, having clear policies on these and applying the most appropriate that delivers the best outcome for the victim.

This case study shows the value of considering voluntary options that can avoid costs of court but can have the same practical result. As Mike Smith, Insolvency Service Chief Investigator observed in this case:

The three restaurateurs have now been removed from the corporate arena and creditors will be protected from any further harm. Their bans clearly demonstrate that we will not hesitate to take action against directors who have abused Covid-19 financial support like this.

9.10 Prosecution, Sanction, and Disposal Policies

The Government Functional Standard for Counter Fraud (GOVS 013) sets the expectations for the management of fraud, bribery, and corruption risk in government organizations. It states that organizations should have a policy and arrangements for managing fraud.

KEY POINTS—GOVERNMENT FUNCTIONAL STANDARD FOR COUNTER FRAUD (GOVS 013)

Key points relevant to case disposal include:

- How the organization responds to instances of fraud, bribery, and corruption.
- How the organization monitors the progress of investigations, and takes decisions on them.
- The roles and responsibilities of staff, teams, and individual functions in responding to instances of fraud, bribery, and corruption.
- How this information should be reported both within the organization, and to other relevant organizations (including law enforcement agencies).

Best practice for public sector bodies has been for them to have published prosecution/sanction policies that set out their approach to case disposal where fraud (criminal, civil, or both) has been established. This meets the expectation within the functional standard in respect of how it responds, how decisions are made, who is responsible for that decision, and how this is reported.

The key is that the organization has a clear policy that sets out fundamental principles that inform a decision, ensuring consistency of approach within the organization. It is vital that all cases and individuals are treated equally to ensure no bias or favour can manifest in disposal decisions. This is both morally and ethically essential but also reduces the risk of appeals, judicial reviews, and their associated costs.

Organizations should have an effective sanction, redress, and prosecution policy. Where these decisions are made internally via the investigating officer and decision-maker (who should be different people) there should be a formal sanction/prosecution/case disposal policy. This will detail what disposal options the organization has and the aggravating and mitigating factors that would be considered

Table 9.1 Common mitigating and aggravating factors

Mitigating factors	Aggravating factors
• vulnerability (e.g. learning difficulties); • not intentional from outset (e.g. failure to report a change); • poor long-term health/terminal illness; • disproportionate impact a conviction may have on an individual or linked individuals such as because they are someone's primary carer; • made voluntary recompense; • offence became known through voluntary disclosure[a]	• abuse of position of trust; • abuse of power; • planning of offence; • offence was group/organized/conspiracy; • conceal or dispose of evidence; • it is repeated relevant offending or previously received a caution, etc. for similar matter; • fraud committed against multiple organizations; • period of offending and multiple false declarations; • level of loss;[b] • used to finance a lavish lifestyle; • impacted third party (e.g. identity theft)

[a] Voluntary disclosure means unprompted confession to an offence such as writing to the organisation stating what they have done.

[b] Financial thresholds should be considered in context of the type of expenditure and never in isolation as a disposal decision mechanism.

and documented in the final decision. It should be updated on a regular basis, available to all staff, and where these can be applied to the public published in their internet sites.

Some organizations opt for a 'sanction panel' model also set out in the standard. This should be formed of experts from inside or outside the organization and determine the most appropriate case disposal for a case. This panel must have a clear terms of reference (ToR) covering what the disposal options are and any statutory sanction that can be applied by that organization.

Common mitigating and aggravating factors that should be considered in disposal decisions are set out in Table 9.1; this is not an exhaustive list but covers the most characteristic factors in fraud cases.

Further Reading

- Government Functional Standard GovS 013: Counter Fraud, www.gov.uk/government/publications/government-functional-standard-govs-013-counter-fraud (accessed 16 August 2023).

10

Countering Bribery and Corruption

Blackstone's Counter Fraud Professionals' Handbook. Michael J. Betts, Laura Eshelby, and David Whitehouse-Hayes, Oxford University Press.

DOI: 10.1093/9780191996955.003.0010

10.1 **Introduction**

In this chapter we take a deep dive into the world of bribery and corruption; we will examine its dynamics from the counter fraud professional's perspective detailing the essential underpinning knowledge to tackle this crime type. We will explore the motivations for offending, the profile of those typically involved and describe the key risks and controls that may be implemented to limit the offender's reach.

We look at the investigation of bribery from a professional's perspective with a review of the legislation and tools readily available. The provisions of the UK Bribery Act 2010 (UKBA 2010) are explained in practitioners' terms. The legislation relating to failing to prevent bribery by commercial organizations is explained. We have included relevant checklists and diagrams illustrating the key dynamics of corruption and bribery. A number of recent cases are explored and the lessons learned detailed; these will include the Airbus SE case.

The British government has worked to counter bribery and has introduced a raft of new initiatives to combat corruption, this has been driven by the UK anti-corruption strategy 2017–22.[1] These initiatives include the introduction of the Register of Overseas Entities operated by Companies House, the strengthening of Unexplained Wealth Orders (UWOs), and a tougher sanctions regime; how the counter fraud professional can maximize the use of these new powers is reviewed in this chapter.

The growth and impact of the Government Counter Fraud Profession (GCFP) and its Counter Bribery and Corruption (CBC) standard are detailed with a focus on its practical application.

10.1.1 **Transactional-Based Offending**

In essence, bribery is a transactional relationship-based offence, where one party offers or gives an advantage[2] to another inducing or rewarding them to do something that is improper.[3] This is often a secretive arrangement, shielded from the gaze of others, where witnesses and victims may suspect but don't know; this requires the investigator to utilize their investigative skills to first find the crime, link the offenders, and locate the relevant material. This is somewhat different to other crime types where usually the victim reports the crime, and the investigative challenge is to find the offenders; with bribery we have often suspected offenders but often the challenge is to find the crime.

[1] Home Office, 'UK Anti-Corruption Strategy 2017 to 2022' (11 December 2017), www.gov.uk/government/publications/uk-anti-corruption-strategy-2017-to-2022 (accessed 15 July 2023).

[2] The meaning of 'financial or other advantage' is left to be determined as a matter of common sense by the tribunal of fact. See Bribery Act 2010 Explanatory Notes, www.legislation.gov.uk/ukpga/2010/23/notes/division/5/1 (accessed 15 July 2023).

[3] Bribery Act 2010, www.legislation.gov.uk/ukpga/2010/23/section/4 (accessed 15 July 2023).

For those operating in the public sector, it is of note that the evolution of anti-corruption legislation has often been in direct response to specific bribery offending against the taxpayer and wider society, often with a focus on the prevention of this crime type; a theme that we will return to later in this chapter.

10.2 Defining Bribery and Corruption

Corruption is a word originating from the Latin word *corruptus* meaning to harm or damage. This word was used in the historic legislation as the focus was its prevention and the focus on the harm it wreaks on society. Much of what we may deem 'corrupt' is often a forerunner to bribery including activity like nepotism,[4] patronage,[5] and cronyism[6] fall into this category.

The Royal United Studies Institute (RUSI) occasional paper report entitled 'What's in a Name? Corruption and Fraud in the UK'[7] published in 2019, sought to assess the information available on corruption and fraud across four areas: the financial sector, construction, the National Health Service, and local government. Its objectives included the analysis of the 'dearth' of data on domestic corruption in the UK and to explore the meaning and understanding of the word's corruption and fraud. The report details that:

> Definitions of corruption that refer to abuse of entrusted power give some flavour of a broad range of conduct that can be considered corrupt. But they do not specify what exactly constitutes abuse of power. Opinions may differ, especially if different reference frameworks are used. For instance, some might only view abuse of power as involving conduct that runs counter to the law. Others might argue that some actions are unethical and corrupt even if they are legal, such as public officials being influenced by lobbying.[8]

Bribery is often stated to be a subset of corruption: it is clearly defined by the UKBA which clearly articulates the elements of the crime. The UKBA is focused on the offering, giving, asking for, or receiving an advantage in return for some improper performance of a relevant function. The UKBA is nuanced in several different ways which are explained later in this chapter.

---

[4] The practice among those with power or influence of favouring relatives, friends, or associates, especially by giving them jobs.

[5] The power to control appointments to office or the right to privileges.

[6] The appointment of friends and associates to positions of authority, without proper regard to their qualifications.

[7] Anton Moiseienko and Kayla Izenman, 'What's in a Name? Corruption and Fraud in the UK', RUSI Occasional Paper (June 2019), https://static.rusi.org/20190617_corruption_and_fraud_web.pdf (accessed 15 July 2023).

[8] Ibid.

Further Reading

- **United Nations Convention Against Corruption**[9]—a legally binding international anti-corruption multilateral treaty that came into force in 2005. Corruption is undefined, although it details a range of crimes that should be considered including bribery, embezzlement, and money laundering. See the UN Office on Drugs and Crime (UNDOC) website: www.unodc.org/unodc/en/treaties/CAC/ (accessed 15 July 2023).
- **Organisation for Economic Co-operation and Development (OECD) Convention on Combating Bribery of Foreign Public Officials in International Business Transactions**[10]—the 1997 Convention defines bribery as the offering, promising, or giving of something in order to influence a public official in the execution of his/her official duties, www.oecd.org/corruption/oecdantibriberyconvention.htm (accessed 15 July 2023).
- **Transparency International (TI)**—a non-governmental organization that works to end corruption. They define corruption as 'the abuse of entrusted power for private gain',[11] www.transparency.org/en (accessed 15 July 2023).

10.3 UK's Response to Corruption

The UK has been very proactive in addressing the issue of corruption. The UK Anti-Corruption Strategy 2017–22 was instrumental in driving a range of capacity and capability building supported by the introduction of important legislation. It articulated the framework to tackle corruption. Some of the highlights include:

- Economic Crime (Transparency and Enforcement) Act 2022—importantly introduced three key measures on beneficial ownership register of overseas entities owning UK property, UWOs, and sanctions;
- Companies House reform;
- growth in activity by the Office of Financial Sanctions Implementation (OFSI).

Further Reading

- UK Anti-Corruption Strategy 2017, www.gov.uk/government/publications/uk-anti-corruption-strategy-2017-to-2022 (accessed 15 July 2023);

[9] United Nations Convention Against Corruption, www.unodc.org/documents/brussels/UN_Convention_Against_Corruption.pdf (accessed 15 July 2023).

[10] Convention on Combating Bribery of Foreign Public Officials in International Business Transactions, www.oecd.org/daf/anti-bribery/ConvCombatBribery_ENG.pdf (accessed 15 July 2023).

[11] Transparency International, 'What Is corruption?', www.transparency.org/en/what-is-corruption (accessed 15 July 2023).

- Anti-Corruption Strategy: Year 3 Update, www.gov.uk/government/publications/anti-corruption-strategy-year-3-update/anti-corruption-strategy-year-3-update-accessible-version (accessed 15 July 2023);
- Economic Crime (Transparency and Enforcement) Act 2022, https://commonslibrary.parliament.uk/research-briefings/cbp-9486/ (accessed 15 July 2023);
- Office of Financial Sanctions Implementation, www.gov.uk/government/organisations/office-of-financial-sanctions-implementation (accessed 15 July 2023).

10.4 Evolution of Bribery Legislation

The origins of the UKBA can be seen in the Public Bodies Corrupt Practices Act 1889[12] and the subsequent corruption-related legislation, the background to which is rather interesting. In 1888 Lord Randolph Churchill, Winston Churchill's father, introduced a motion in the Houses of Commons demanding a royal commission be undertaken into the exploits of the Metropolitan Board of Works. The Board was responsible for public works across London, which following several scandals had become known as the 'Metropolitan Board of Perks' due to the perceived level of corruption. The Commission was headed by Lord Herschell and following two reports, the 1889 Act was introduced to counter corruption in local government. The penalties available make interesting reading today:

> Be liable to be imprisoned for any period not exceeding two years, with or without hard labour, or to pay a fine not exceeding five hundred pounds.[13]

The 1889 Act also introduced the concept of a restriction on prosecution with the consent required of the Attorney General (AG)[14] before proceedings could commence. The Bribery Act 2010 replaced the AG consent to the Director of Public Prosecutions (DPP) and others named in the Act.[15]

Following swiftly on from this legislation were issues in the supply chain to the British Army fighting the second Boer War (1899–1902) in South Africa. Interestingly Winston Churchill was present during the campaign, first as a journalist, and then for a short time in 1900, joined the South African Light Horse, a regiment of the British Army. It was alleged the supply chain was suffering from chronic corruption, including product substitution. A House of Commons Select Committee on War Office Contracts examined the issues of 'fraud and irregularity'[16] and on 1 August 1900 published its report. Among other findings it recommended that:

[12] Public Bodies Corrupt Practices Act 1889, www.legislation.gov.uk/ukpga/Vict/52-53/69/enacted (accessed 15 July 2023).

[13] Ibid.

[14] Ibid.

[15] Bribery Act 2010.

[16] Select Committee on War Office Contracts, *Report* (1900) held by British Library.

> Your committee further recommends that the criminal law should be strengthened by extending the Public Services Corrupt Practices Act, 1889 to the Government service, and that if adequate evidence can be procured prosecution should invariably follow.[17]

On 1 January 1907, the Prevention of Corruption Act 1906[18] was introduced, which extended the reach of the legislation across sectors including public and private; it was trailblazed as 'an Act for the better Prevention of Corruption'. Again, both parts of the transaction were covered in the legislation, namely those accepting or obtaining any gift or consideration and those corruptly giving, or agreeing to give, or offers of any gift or consideration, to any agent as an inducement or reward for doing some form of disfavour impacting on the principal's affairs. The legislation pivots around the relationship between an 'agent' and their responsibilities to their 'principal', often an employee–employer relationship.

Case Study—MoD Official Jailed for Taking Bribes from US Arms Dealer

On 16 April 2007, a civil servant, aged 58, employed by the Ministry of Defence pleaded guilty to nine counts of accepting bribes at Southwark Crown Court in London. The bribes were paid by Pacific Consolidated Industries (PCI), a US company located in California, between November 1999 and July 2003. The investigation was instigated when auditors noticed suspicious accounting in the records of PCI following a takeover.

The defendant was employed as a senior professional technology officer and team leader with responsibility for contracts relating to the supply of gas and containment equipment for the armed services. During a procurement exercise, he passed crucial confidential information to PCI after developing a 'friendship' with an employee of the company, which was subsequently awarded a multimillion-pound contract valued at £4.5 million.

In return, it was reported that PCI funded a lavish lifestyle, including a luxury villa in Spain, the use of exclusive hotels, travel to the USA, entertainment on a luxury yacht and nine separate payments totalling more than £217,000.

Interestingly the defendant initially denied the charges, claiming he had received the 'legitimate' payments in return for consultancy work, but later pleaded guilty to nine counts of corruption.

Sentencing the defendant, Judge Christopher Elwen said, 'as well as being a punishment to you, these sentences must also act as a deterrent to others in similar positions'.[19]

---

[17] Ibid.

[18] Prevention of Corruption Act 1906, www.legislation.gov.uk/ukpga/Edw7/6/34/enacted (accessed 15 July 2023).

[19] M. Taylor, 'MoD Official Jailed for Taking Bribes', *The Guardian* (17 April 2007), www.theguardian.com/uk/2007/apr/17/ukcrime.matthewtaylor (accessed 15 July 2023); 'Senior MoD Jailed for Taking Bribes from US Arms Dealer', *Mail Online* (16 April 2007), www.dailymail.co.uk/news/article-448968/Senior-MoD-jailed-taking-bribes-US-arms-dealer.html (accessed 15 July 2023.

In this case the defendant was the 'agent' of the Ministry of Defence who was the 'principal'.

Observations for the Investigator

In this case study the defendant held a position of trust and influence; he travelled to visit the organization and developed a trusted relationship with representatives of the company. The defendant received multiple benefits, ranging from hospitality to payments which is indicative of the process of grooming (a topic explored later in this chapter). The initial explanation that the payments were payments due to 'consultancy services' given is not uncommon in these cases and a defence the investigator should consider during the investigative process.

On 22 December 1916, emergency legislation, the Prevention of Corruption Act 1916 was enacted to amend the Prevention of Corruption Act 1906, this followed several difficult cases where it proved problematic to demonstrate the actual corrupt act the 'agent' had undertaken. Mr Justice Low, who presided over a case concerning allegations of corruption at the Royal Army Clothing Department, expressed frustration at the length of sentence available for corruption (then two years) and the difficulty in proving what the defendant had done in return for the bribe. At the conclusion of the case, he stated:

I should like to add this as a respectful suggestion to the legislature, that it is high time that a short measure should be passed giving power to the Courts, at all events during the continuance of the war, to inflict on persons convicted of bribery or attempting to bribe, Government employees, a long period of penal servitude, because the penalties are absolutely useless and inadequate to deal with matters of this sort.[20]

In essence the legislation introduced a presumption of corruption in certain cases, it stated:

Where in any proceedings against a person for an offence under the Prevention of Corruption Act, 1906, or the Public Bodies Corrupt Practices Act, 1889, it is proved that any money, gift, or other consideration has been paid or given to or received by a person in the employment of His Majesty or any Government Department or a public body by or from a person, or agent of a person, holding or seeking to obtain a contract from His Majesty or any Government Department or public body, the money, gift, or consideration shall be deemed to have been paid or given and received corruptly as such inducement or reward as is mentioned in such Act unless the contrary is proved.[21]

This was an important development in the legislation to address the threat of corruption and is a feature of the Bribery Act 2010, which we examine later in this chapter.

---

[20] *The Times* (18 September 1916) held by British Library.

[21] Prevention of Corruption Act 1916, www.legislation.gov.uk/ukpga/Geo5/6-7/64/enacted (accessed 15 July 2023).

The final development of the corruption related legislation prior to the introduction of the UKBA was the inclusion of ss. 108–110 in the Anti-terrorism, Crime and Security Act 2001. The inclusion of these paragraphs clarified that it was immaterial if the functions of the person who receives or is offered a reward, had no connection with the UK and were carried out in a country or territory outside the UK[22] linking to the three corruption Acts (1889, 1906, and 1916), though disregarded the 'presumption' provisions of the 1916 Act.

On 1 July 2011, the UK Bribery Act 2010 was introduced, and the previous legislation abolished. However, the evolution of corruption legislation is of significance to those involved in its response today. There are lessons to be learned from the drivers for the historic legislation which still have relevance in today's world of commerce, trade, and the public sector. History tells us bribes, bungs, and backhanders are repetitive in nature, as is the grooming process used to draw people into the spider's web of corruption. The development of the legislation has been inextricably linked to the growth of the public sector and the target it represents to those seeking the rewards from corruption.

10.5 **UK Bribery Act 2010 (UKBA)**

The Bribery Act 2010 received royal assent on 8 April 2010 and was one of the last pieces of legislation passed under the Labour government of Gordon Brown, who lost the election in May 2010, to be replaced by the coalition government of David Cameron (Conservative) and Nick Clegg (Liberal Democrat). It finally came into effect on 1 July 2011. This was after much debate around the guidance for the defence of the corporate offence of failing to prevent bribery (UKBA, s. 7) and the design of the Ministry of Justice's (MoJ) Adequate Procedures Guidance as required by s. 9 of the UKBA.

It is perhaps the greatest and most effective of all legislation to combat bribery, it brings clarity, is wonderfully articulate in defining the act of bribery between offenders, has special provisions for the bribery of overseas public officials, and introduces the powerful corporate offence for commercial organizations of failing to prevent bribery. It is an effective tool for those both wishing to prevent and investigate bribery. Between 2013 and 2020 the Crown Prosecution Service (CPS) secured over sixty UKBA convictions and the Serious Fraud Office (SFO) just four convictions.[23]

[22] Anti-terrorism, Crime and Security Act 2001, www.legislation.gov.uk/ukpga/2001/24/section/108/enacted (accessed 15 July 2023).

[23] SFO (2020) 2020-040—Bribery Act 2010—Serious Fraud Office, www.sfo.gov.uk/foi-request/2020-040-bribery-act-2010/ (accessed 15 July 2023).

We will now examine its various sections and identify the implications for the counter fraud professional.

10.5.1 UKBA 2010 General Bribery Offences

In this section we will explore the following sections:

- s. 1—Offences of bribing another person;
- s. 2—Offences relating to being bribed;
- s. 3—Function or activity to which bribe relates;
- s. 4—Improper performance to which bribe relates;
- s. 5—Expectation test;
- s. 6—Bribery of foreign public officials;
- s. 7—Failure of commercial organizations to prevent bribery;
- s. 9—Guidance on commercial organizations preventing bribery;
- s. 10—Consent to Prosecute;
- s. 11—Penalties;
- s. 12—Offences under the UKBA Territorial application;
- s. 13—Defence for certain bribery offences etc.;
- s. 14—Offences under ss. 1, 2, and 6 by bodies corporate etc.

10.5.2 Offences of Bribing Another Person (s. 1)

Section 1 details the offence of offering or giving an advantage to induce or reward improper performance of a relevant function.

10.5.3 Offences Relating to Being Bribed (s. 2)

Section 2 details the offence of asking for or receiving an advantage to do something that is improper. Several questions for the counter fraud professional need to be addressed relating to ss. 1 and 2:

- **Investigator question 1**—Is the function or activity held by the person being offered or receiving the advantage relevant for the purposes of the UKBA?
- **Investigator question 2**—Has the person suspected of improper performance breached one of the special conditions described in s. 3 of the UKBA?

10.5.4 Function or Activity to which Bribe Relates (s. 3)

Guidance can be taken from s. 3 of the UKBA, regarding relevant function or activity, this is described as including 'any function of a public nature, any activity connected with a business, any activity performed during a person's employment, or any activity performed by or on behalf of a body of persons (whether corporate or unincorporate)'.

Section 3 also adds that the activity of person concerned should meet one or more of three conditions, namely:

- Condition A is that a person performing the function or activity is expected to perform it in good faith;
- Condition B is that a person performing the function or activity is expected to perform it impartially;
- Condition C is that a person performing the function or activity is in a position of trust by virtue of performing it.

10.5.5 **Improper Performance to which Bribe Relates (s. 4)**

Section 4 describes the nature of 'improper performance' to which bribe relates as:

> is performed improperly if it is performed in breach of a relevant expectation, and
>
> is to be treated as being performed improperly if there is a failure to perform the function or activity and that failure is itself a breach of a relevant expectation.

(2) In subs. (1) 'relevant expectation'—

- in relation to a function or activity which meets condition A or B, means the expectation mentioned in the condition concerned, and
- in relation to a function or activity which meets condition C, means any expectation as to the manner in which, or the reasons for which, the function or activity will be performed that arises from the position of trust mentioned in that condition.

(3) Anything that a person does (or omits to do) arising from or in connection with that person's past performance of a relevant function or activity is to be treated for the purposes of this Act as being done (or omitted) by that person in the performance of that function or activity.[24]

10.5.6 **Expectation Test (s. 5)**

Section 5 of the UKBA details the 'expectation test' which is what a reasonable person would expect in relation to the performance of the type of function or activity concerned. In we look at the considerations that investigators should consider in relation to both ss. 1 and 2 of the UKBA.

[24] Bribery Act 2010, www.legislation.gov.uk/ukpga/2010/23/contents (accessed 15 July 2023).

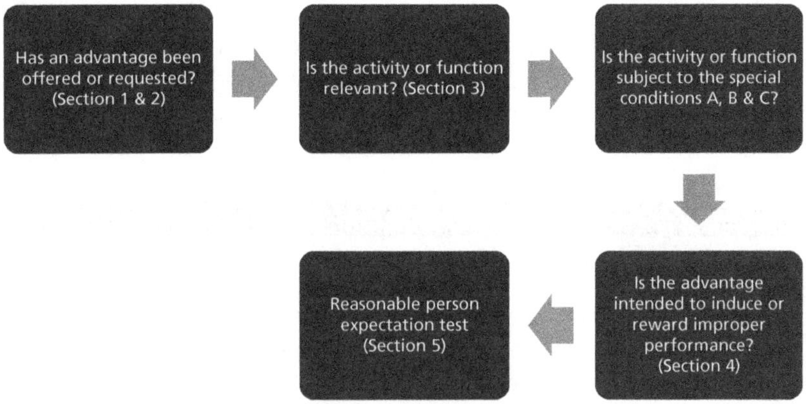

Figure 10.1 Investigator considerations UKBA (ss. 1–5)

10.5.7 Bribery of Foreign Public Officials (s. 6)

Section 6 of the UKBA details a specific offence of bribing a foreign public official. This section details who falls into the category of foreign public official which includes those holding a legislative, administrative, or judicial position of any kind, whether appointed or elected, of a country or territory outside the UK or a person who exercises a public function.

The person will be guilty if their intention is to influence the official in their capacity as a foreign public official. They must intend to obtain or retain a business advantage.

10.5.8 UKBA (ss. 7–9) (Failure of Commercial Organization to Prevent Bribery)

Sections 7–9 of the UKBA drove the change in the corporate responsibility with regard to bribery; it was a game changer.

10.5.9 Failure of Commercial Organizations to Prevent Bribery (s. 7)

Section 7 of the UKBA covers the failure of a commercial organization to prevent bribery. This section may be considered under the following conditions:

- the organization is a relevant commercial organization;
- the person associated with the organization bribes another to obtain or retain a business advantage, an associated person is in essence an employee, agent, or subsidiary (s. 8);
- s. 7 is triggered by ss. 1, 6, and 12;
- note that s. 2 of the Act *does not* trigger the s. 7 offence.

The s. 7 offence is one of strict liability: it does not matter if the senior management did not participate in or were not aware of the offer or passing of the bribe. If a person associated with the organization offered or paid a bribe, then the organization is 'guilty' unless it can demonstrate adequate procedures. In Monopoly terms it deploys its 'get out of jail free' card.

KEY POINTS—A RELEVANT COMMERCIAL ORGANIZATION

A 'relevant commercial organization' means—

a. a body which is incorporated under the law of any part of the UK, and which carries on a business (whether there or elsewhere),
b. any other body corporate (wherever incorporated) which carries on a business, or part of a business, in any part of the UK,
c. a partnership which is formed under the law of any part of the UK, and which carries on a business (whether there or elsewhere), or
d. any other partnership (wherever formed) which carries on a business, or part of a business, in any part of the UK,

and, for the purposes of this section, a trade or profession is a business.[25]

Importantly, there is a defence to the s. 7 offence, if the organization can show on the balance of probabilities it had in place adequate procedures designed to prevent persons associated with the organization from undertaking such conduct.

10.5.10 Guidance on Commercial Organizations Preventing Bribery (s. 9)

Section 9 of the UKBA states that the Secretary of State must publish guidance about procedures that relevant commercial organizations may put in place to prevent persons associated with them from bribing.

Under the s. 9 requirement, the MOJ has issued two documents: the first a quick start guide to the UKBA; second, the guidance on procedures which relevant commercial organizations can put into place, to prevent persons associated with them from bribing (Bribery Act 2010, s. 9). These must-read documents provide a detailed overview of the legislation and outline in detail the adequate procedures to be implemented. We explore the six adequate procedures later in this chapter.

[25] Ibid.

Further Reading

- MOJ, 'The Bribery Act 2010: Quick Start Guide', www.justice.gov.uk/downloads/legislation/bribery-act-2010-quick-start-guide.pdf (accessed 15 July 2023);
- MOJ, 'The Bribery Act 2010: Guidance about Procedures which Relevant Commercial Organizations Can Put into Place to Prevent Persons Associated with Them from Bribing', www.justice.gov.uk/downloads/legislation/bribery-act-2010-guidance.pdf (accessed 15 July 2023).

10.5.11 Consent to Prosecute (s. 10)

Section 10 of the UKBA deals with the consent to prosecution, as no proceedings for an offence under this Act may be instituted without the consent of:

- England and Wales by or with the consent of the DPP or the Director of the Serious Fraud Office.
- Northern Ireland by or with the consent of the DPP for Northern Ireland, or the Director of the Serious Fraud Office.
- There is no statutory requirement for the consent of the Lord Advocate to prosecutions of offences under the Bribery Act in the Scottish courts.[26]

Further Reading

The joint prosecution guidance of the Director of the SFO and the DPP sets out the approach to prosecutorial decision-making in respect of offences under the Act. Scotland and Northern Ireland are separate legal jurisdictions, so this guidance does not apply to decisions about prosecutions in those jurisdictions.

See www.cps.gov.uk/legal-guidance/bribery-act-2010-joint-prosecution-guidance-director-serious-fraud-office-and (accessed 15 July 2023)

10.5.12 Penalties (s. 11)

Section 11 of the UKBA details with the penalties an individual who is guilty of an offence under ss. 1, 2, or 6 is liable on summary conviction,[27] to imprisonment for a term not exceeding 12 months, or to a fine not exceeding the statutory maximum, or to both. On conviction on indictment, to imprisonment for a term not exceeding

[26] https://publications.parliament.uk/pa/ld201719/ldselect/ldbribact/303/30312.htm (accessed 15 July 2023).

[27] Summary offences are normally dealt with in the magistrates' court, www.cps.gov.uk/legal-guidance/summary-offences-and-crown-court (accessed 15 July 2023).

ten years, or to a fine, or to both. A 'person' guilty of an offence under s. 7 is liable on conviction on indictment to a fine.

The Sentencing Council's Fraud, Bribery and Money Laundering Offences guidelines provide granular detail on the structure, ranges, and starting points for sentencing; this guidance is web based.

This is in accordance with s. 120 of the Coroners and Justice Act 2009; the Sentencing Council issues this definitive guideline.[28]

KEY POINTS—SENTENCING COUNCIL'S FRAUD, BRIBERY AND MONEY LAUNDERING OFFENCES

- The Sentencing Council's Fraud, Bribery and Money Laundering Offences Definitive Guidelines apply to all individual offenders aged 18 and older and to organizations who are sentenced on or after 1 October 2014, regardless of the date of the offence.
- The guidelines apply to individual offenders aged 18 and older or organizations. The guidelines provide specified offence ranges—the range of sentences appropriate for each type of offence. For each offence, the Council has specified several categories which reflect varying degrees of seriousness. The offence range is split into category ranges—sentences appropriate for each level of seriousness. The Council has also identified a starting point for each category.
- See: www.sentencingcouncil.org.uk/outlines/ (accessed 15 July 2023).

10.5.13 Offences under the UKBA: Territorial Application (s. 12)

Section 12 of the UKBA concerns its territorial application. The Act applies to offences (act or omission) committed in England and Wales (E&W), Scotland, or Northern Ireland.

A person who has a close connection with the UK may commit an offence contrary to the UKBA even though no act takes place in the UK if the acts would form part of such an offence, if done in the UK.

KEY POINTS—CLOSE CONNECTION TO THE UNITED KINGDOM

A person has a close connection with the UK if, and only if, the person was one of the following at the time the acts or omissions concerned were done or made were:

a. a British citizen,
b. a British Overseas Territories citizen,

[28] www.sentencingcouncil.org.uk/wp-content/uploads/Fraud-Bribery-and-Money-Laundering-offences-definitive-guideline-Web.pdf (accessed 15 July 2023).

c. a British National (Overseas),
d. a British Overseas citizen,
e. a person who under the British Nationality Act 1981 was a British subject,
f. a British protected person within the meaning of that Act,
g. an individual ordinarily resident in the UK,
h. a body incorporated under the law of any part of the UK,
i. a Scottish partnership.

An offence is committed under s. 7 irrespective of whether the acts or omissions which form part of the offence take place in the UK or elsewhere.

10.5.14 Defence for Certain Bribery Offences etc. (s. 13)

Section 13 of the UKBA details the defence for certain bribery offences. It is a defence for a person charged with a relevant bribery offence to prove that the person's conduct was necessary for:

a. the proper exercise of any function of an intelligence service or
b. the proper exercise of any function of the armed forces when engaged on active service.

Each defence has a range of conditions that must be met prior to the defence being activated.

10.5.15 Offences under Sections 1, 2, and 6 by Bodies Corporate etc. (s. 14)

Section 14 of the UKBA details the offences under ss. 1, 2, and 6 when committed by a body corporate or a Scottish partnership. The offence is proved to have been committed with the consent or connivance of:

a. a senior officer of the body corporate or Scottish partnership, or
b. a person purporting to act in such a capacity.

The senior officer or person (as well as the body corporate or partnership) is guilty of the offence and liable to be proceeded against and punished accordingly.

10.5.16 Offences under Section 7 by Partnerships (s. 15)

Section 15 of the UKBA details offences under s. 7 by partnerships; proceedings for an offence under s.7 alleged to have been committed by a partnership must be brought in the name of the partnership (and not in that of any of the partners). The fine imposed on the partnership on its conviction for an offence under s. 7 is to be paid out of the partnership assets.

The remaining sections are mainly administrative in nature, but s. 16 makes it clear that the Act applies equally to individuals in the public service of the Crown as it applies to other individuals.

10.5.17 Understanding Adequate Procedures

The MoJ's UKBA guidance document details the six guiding principles that combined make up the 'adequate procedures'. It is important for all those concerned with counter bribery to understand these procedures. This guidance is not prescriptive and designed to be flexible in nature, depending on the risk profile of the organization. The 'adequacy' of the procedures will be a matter for the courts, where the facts of the case will be examined. It is stated that departures from this guidance will not in itself give rise to a presumption that the organizations do not have adequate procedures.

Case Study—*UKBA Adequate Procedures—R. v. Skansen Interiors Ltd*

In 2018, Skansen Interiors Ltd (SIL) was the first organization to contest an s. 7 charge of failing to have adequate procedures in place to prevent bribery.[29]

SIL was a small furniture business trading mainly in London. It employed in the region of thirty employees and was part of the larger Skansen Group. In 2013, SIL was successful in winning two tenders for office refurbishment from a company called DTZ, worth approximately £6 million. In 2014, the new chief executive officer (CEO) of SIL was informed that a bribe had been paid to an employee of DTZ for insider information and that a further payment was to be made on completion of the contract.

The CEO commenced an internal investigation and introduced an anti-bribery and corruption policy, having identified that none appeared to be in place.

SIL submitted a suspicious activity report to the National Crime Agency and reported the matter to the City of London Police. During the investigation, SIL cooperated with the police investigation.

At the conclusion of the investigation, employees of SIL and DTZ were charged with and pleaded guilty to offences under ss. 1 and 2 of the Act.

SIL itself was charged under s. 7, it pleaded not guilty on the grounds that it had in place adequate procedures to prevent bribery. Although its controls were limited, it argued that they were proportionate for a small company operating only in the UK. There were also clauses in the DTZ contracts prohibiting bribery and providing a termination right if bribery occurred.

However, the jury did not accept SIL's defence and returned a guilty verdict as these controls were deemed not adequate.

[29] House of Lords Select Committee, 'Bribery Act 2010: Post-Legislative Scrutiny' (14 March 2019), https://publications.parliament.uk/pa/ld201719/ldselect/ldbribact/303/303.pdf (accessed 15 July 2023).

The six principles forming the adequate procedures are:

(1) proportionate procedures;
(2) top-level commitment;
(3) risk assessment;
(4) due diligence;
(5) communication and training;
(6) monitor and review.

10.5.18 **Principle 1 Proportionate Procedures**

A commercial organization's procedures to prevent bribery by persons associated with it should be proportionate to the bribery risks it faces and to the nature, scale, and complexity of the commercial organization's activities. The procedures should be clear, practical, accessible, and effectively implemented and enforced.[30]

Checklist—Principle 1 Proportionate Procedures

Proportionate Approach

(1) Risk based on the size of the organization, nature, and complexity of its business.

(2) Risk should take account of the type and nature of the persons associated with it.

(3) A proportionate approach should provide the appropriate level of control.

Procedures and Policies

(1) Procedures should be proportionate.

(2) Procedures are supported by enabling policies.

(3) Policies should include the commitment to prevent bribery.

(4) Organizational approach to mitigate specific bribery risks.

(5) Strategy to implement the bribery prevention policies.

(6) Articulate the organization's top-level commitment.

(7) Organizational risk assessment activity.

[30] MoJ, Bribery Act 2010—Guidance (2011), www.justice.gov.uk/downloads/legislation/bribery-act-2010-guidance.pdf (accessed 15 July 2023).

(8) Methods deployed to undertake due diligence across the organization.

(9) Policies relating to gifts, hospitality, and promotional expenditure; charitable and political donations; or demands for facilitation payments.

(10) Embedded in HR policies and procedures.

(11) Detail the organizational governance.

(12) Embedded in accounting and financial controls.

(13) Detail the 'concerned employee' reporting procedures.[31]

(14) Policies detailing the communication and monitoring of the counter bribery management system.

10.5.19 **Principle 2 Top-Level Commitment**

This principle concerns the active engagement by those at the top of the organization to create a counter bribery culture that permeates throughout the organization. Those at the top set the tone promoting a zero tolerance to bribery.

Checklist—Top-Level Commitment

The following are examples of how an organization may demonstrate top-level commitment:

- be the voice of counter bribery within the organization;
- set a clear and consistent tone of zero tolerance;
- actively promote an ethical culture across the organization;
- support the reporting of suspicions and protect concerned employees;
- resource the counter bribery management system;
- be accountable for key decisions relating to the organizational counter bribery procedures and policies;
- be associated and promote organizational counter bribery material through the available communication channels;

[31] Public Interest Disclosure Act 1998, www.legislation.gov.uk/ukpga/1998/23/contents (accessed 15 July 2023).

- ensure all those associated with the organization hear the counter bribery message;
- frame the counter bribery messaging in a positive manner supporting the business objectives;
- ensure that failures in the counter bribery management system and reports of bribery are managed effectively.

10.5.20 **Principle 3 Risk Assessment**

This is fundamental to an organization demonstrating adequate procedures. Without a risk assessment it is incredibly difficult to introduce procedures that are proportionate to the risks. The guidance is not directive as to how a risk assessment should be undertaken, though of course any such activity needs to be 'adequate' or sufficient. The risk assessment may be part of a wider risk assessment exercise undertaken by the organization.

Checklist—Risk Assessment

The following should be taken into consideration when undertaking a bribery-related risk assessment.

(1) the nature, scale, transaction type, and geographical extent of its business;

(2) take account of all employees and those associated with the organization risk profile;

(3) the assessment should be recorded and retained for an appropriate length of time;

(4) the risk assessment will inform the range of controls required to minimize the risk of bribery to a tolerable level;

(5) the assessment should be undertaken by those with the appropriate range of skills and experience.

To inform the risk assessment there are a range of resources which include:

- Transparency International Public Sector Perception Index, www.transparency.org/en/cpi/2022 (accessed 15 July 2023);
- Transparency International Bribe Payers Index 2011, www.transparency.org/en/publications/bribe-payers-index-2011 (accessed 15 July 2023);

- TRACE International Bribery risk matrix, www.traceinternational.org/ (accessed 15 July 2023);
- HMG Guidance on Bribery and Corruption, www.gov.uk/guidance/bribery-and-corruption-in-trade-reducing-the-risk (accessed 15 July 2023);
- HMG Guidance on Bribery and Corruption, www.gov.uk/guidance/bribery-and-corruption-in-trade-reducing-the-risk (accessed 15 July 2023);
- UNODC Anti-Corruption Toolkit, www.unodc.org/documents/treaties/corruption/toolkit/toolkitv5_foreword.pdf (accessed 15 July 2023).

10.5.21 **Principle 4 Due Diligence**

Due diligence is a process of checking the background and reputation of those you are doing business with. It is good commercial practice and widely undertaken across sectors. It should be undertaken across the business to ensure the organization is aware of bribery risks with those it intends to engage with. It should be undertaken taking a risk-based approach. It includes the inner organizational context including staff vetting and the external context including suppliers.

Checklist—Due Diligence

The following should be taken into consideration when undertaking due diligence relating to the bribery context:

- undertake a proportionate response; some activities are higher risk such as the use of business associates require deeper levels of diligence;
- business associates are persons who perform or will perform services for or on behalf of the organization;
- the 'person' can be an individual or an incorporated or unincorporated body;
- business associates may include agents, intermediaries, and/or subsidiaries;
- due diligence procedures may include research and monitoring;
- record keeping is important to record the due diligence undertaken;
- this activity may form part of the wider corporate governance activity.

10.5.22 **Principle 5 Communication (Including Training)**

Communication and training are key aspects in the counter bribery management system. The purpose is to ensure the counter bribery message is spread both within the organization and to those who are associated with it. The policies and procedures will only be effective if they are understood and advocated for by employees and beyond. Corporate messaging shouldn't be static but regularly reinforced. The organization should embed the counter bribery message from induction through to the exit interview.

Checklist—Communication and Training

The following should be taken into consideration when undertaking communication and training:

- a risk-based, proportionate approach should be taken;
- learning packages should be tailored to the risk profile of those undertaking the training;
- learning should be designed and delivered by a competent person or platform;
- learning content may include examples of bribery, indicators, and how to report suspicions;
- learning should be mandated to all staff and repeated on a regular basis;
- records should be maintained of the learning delivered;
- communication of the counter bribery policies and procedures should be made widely available;
- messaging should be clear and accessible to all;
- content may include reference to higher risk areas such as hospitality and gifts, facilitation payments, and sponsorship.

10.5.23 Principle 6 Monitoring and Review

Once an effective counter bribery management system has been implemented, it is crucial to review, monitor and respond to deficiencies in the system in a timely manner.

Checklist—Monitor and Review

The following should be taken into consideration when considering monitor and review:

- ensure the ongoing effectiveness of the counter bribery management system;
- regularly review the controls and update accordingly;

- report on the effectiveness of the controls to the organization's top level;
- encourage feedback from the awareness training.

There is a range of commercially available certification to demonstrate adequate procedures are in place. However, certification relates to the time it took place and doesn't automatically provide the defence to the s. 7 offence.

The International Organization for Standardization[32] offers the ISO 37001, which is the Anti-Bribery Management System. Other certification is available from other international bodies.

Case Study—*Sweett Group plc*—First UKBA 2010, s. 7 Prosecution

On 19 February 2016, the construction and professional services company Sweett Group plc were sentenced by Judge Beddoe at Southwark Crown Court and ordered to pay £2.25 million; this followed a conviction arising from an SFO investigation into its activities in the United Arab Emirates.[33]

The SFO's investigation into Sweett Group plc, discovered that its subsidiary company, Cyril Sweett International Limited had made corrupt payments to Khaled Al Badie, the Vice Chairman of the Board and Chairman of the Real Estate and Investment Committee of AAAI (Al Ain Ahlia Insurance) to secure the award of a contract with AAAI for the building of the Rotana Hotel in Abu Dhabi.[34]

In 2015 the company had pleaded guilty to a charge of failing to prevent an act of bribery intended to secure and retain a contract with AAAI, the relevant conduct had occurred between 1 December 2012 and 1 December 2015, contrary to s. 7(1)(b) of the Bribery Act 2010 which states:

Failure of commercial organizations to prevent bribery

(1)A relevant commercial organisation ('C') is guilty of an offence under this section if a person ('A') associated with C bribes another person intending—

(a) to obtain or retain business for C, or
(b) to obtain or retain an advantage in the conduct of business for C.[35]

His Honour Judge Beddoe described the offence as a system failure and said that the offending was patently committed over a period of time.

[32] ISO, ISO 37001—Anti-bribery management systems, www.iso.org/iso-37001-anti-bribery-management.html (accessed 15 July 2023).

[33] SFO, 'Sweett Group PLC Sentenced and Ordered to Pay £2.25 Million after Bribery Act Conviction (19 February 2016), www.sfo.gov.uk/2016/02/19/sweett-group-plc-sentenced-and-ordered-to-pay-2-3-million-after-bribery-act-conviction/ (accessed 15 July 2023).

[34] Ibid.

[35] Bribery Act 2010.

Referring to s. 7 of the Bribery Act 2010 and to Sweett's ignorance of its subsidiary's actions, His Honour Beddoe said:

The whole point of section 7 is to impose a duty on those running such companies throughout the world properly to supervise them. Rogue elements can only operate in this way—and operate for so long—because of a failure properly to supervise what they are doing and the way they are doing it.

10.6 Understanding Bribery Offending Dynamics

To understand how to counter bribery from a prevention, detection, and investigation perspective, it is crucial to understand the dynamics of the offending. At the heart of any corruption is the relationship between two or more individuals. It is a relationship-based offence and relies to a degree on the trust between the parties to keep the arrangement secretive, as both parties are in peril if the bribery is revealed.

Figure 10.2 illustrates the simple dynamic at the centre of the bribery; one party being the influence holder, the other the seeker of influence. The seeker offers or gives the 'advantage' to the influence holder, inducing or rewarding improper performance of a relevant function.

The dynamic will be different depending on the style of the bribery; friendship corruption is seen often in the business setting where the offenders will develop a relationship, often starting as a business relationship, moving to a friendship, then a corrupt one. Foe bribery is often the domain of organized crime which seeks to corrupt those in authority, such as police and prison officers. Motivations for accepting bribes may be need or greed. The style of the bribery may be petty corruption,

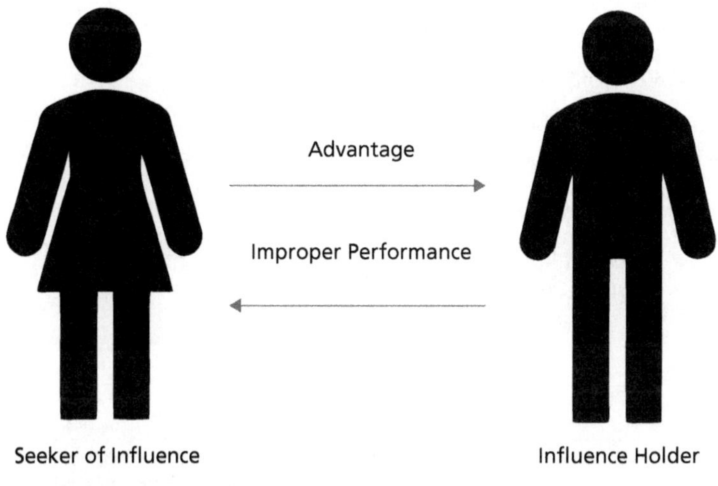

Figure 10.2 Simple bribery dynamics

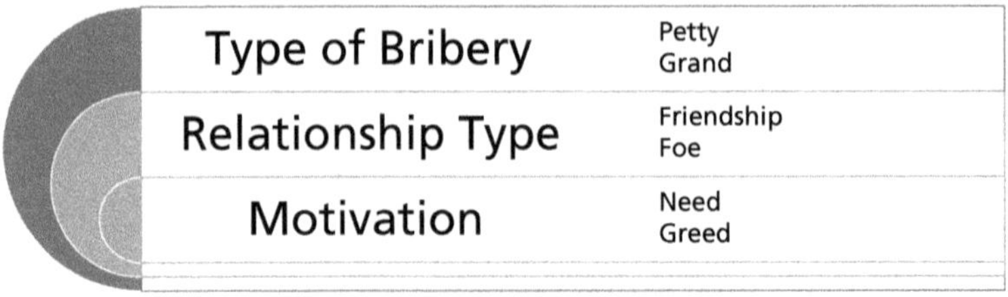

Figure 10.3 Bribery type, relationship, and motivation

frequent small value bribes usually paid to public sector officials or grand corruption large amounts paid to secure significant contracts. These dynamics are shown in Figure 10.3.

10.7 Bribery Offender Insights

Bribery offenders cut across society and can be those involved in petty corruption, low-ranking public officials, such as prison officers or indeed those engaged in grand corruption at board level. In 2019, an insightful research paper was published by Professor Mark Button and Mari Sognnaes Andresen, entitled 'The Profile and Detection of Bribery in Norway and England & Wales: A Comparative Study'.[36]

The paper contrasts offenders convicted of bribery in E&W and Norway; it examines seventy-five cases from E&W and forty-six from Norway over the period 2003–15. Its findings identified the following.

Characteristics of those convicted (E&W):

- male 91 per cent;
- female 9 per cent;
- average age on conviction 43.3 years;
- occupational status: higher grade professional or manager 33 per cent.

Financial advantage (E&W)

- average value of bribe £498,916;
- medium value of bribe £20,000.

Direction of bribe by sector (E&W):

- private to public 71 per cent;
- private to private 29 per cent.

[36] M. S. Andresen, and M. Button, 'The Profile and Detection of Bribery in Norway and England & Wales: A Comparative Study', *European Journal of Criminology* (2018) 16(1): 18–40, doi: https://doi.org/10.1177/1477370818764827 (accessed 15 July 2023).

Sector receiving bribe top three (E&W):

- public administration and defence 67 per cent;
- education 9 per cent;
- arts and entertainment 4 per cent.

Sector paying bribe top three (E&W):

- construction 12 per cent;
- manufacturing 7 per cent;
- real estate 5 per cent.

10.8 **Investigating Bribery**

Those investigating or responding to bribery require extensive knowledge of the legal and procedural frameworks, plus the requisite investigative skill to gather the relevant material from some of the most confidential and difficult to reach places that an investigator may encounter.

The key UKBA offences that have been described earlier in this chapter can signpost the lines of inquiry the investigator should consider. The main offences to consider are:

- s. 1 Offences of bribing another person;
- s. 2 Offences relating to being bribed;
- s. 6 Bribery of a foreign public official;
- s. 7 Failure of a commercial organization to prevent bribery;
- s. 14 Offences by bodies corporate.

The sequencing of the passing of the advantage (bribe) and the improper performance may occur in a differing order (i.e. the bribe may be passed before the improper performance takes place or vice versa).

To build a working hypothesis, the investigator should keep an open mind and take account of the fact that often the true scale of the corruption isn't normally established until all the relevant material has been recovered and examined.

10.8.1 **Case Initiation**

The investigator should analyse the material presented and develop a working hypothesis based on the known material. Each offence has a differing dynamic and each case needs to be considered on its own merit. That said, many cases have the same traits as the offending pivots around the advantage (bribe) and the resulting improper performance by the influence holder.

10.8.2 **Reactive or Proactive Approach**

The investigator will need to consider the approach to the investigation and whether they should take a reactive or proactive approach, or indeed a blend of both styles.

A reactive approach is where an investigator will investigate historic allegations of corruption and is focused on the recovery of historic material. A proactive approach often involves monitoring and surveillance of the suspect in a covert manner. It has the advantage of potentially monitoring the crime in action resulting in the recovery of compelling evidence. A third choice is to use the reactive approach to trigger a proactive response. Here one tactic, depending on the circumstances, is for example, to interview the suspect and then monitor their activity after that event to see where they go and who they contact.

The decision tree detailed in Figure 10.4 details the investigators considerations and linkage between s. 1 (offences of bribing another person) and s. 7 (failure of a commercial organization to prevent bribery) of the UKBA.

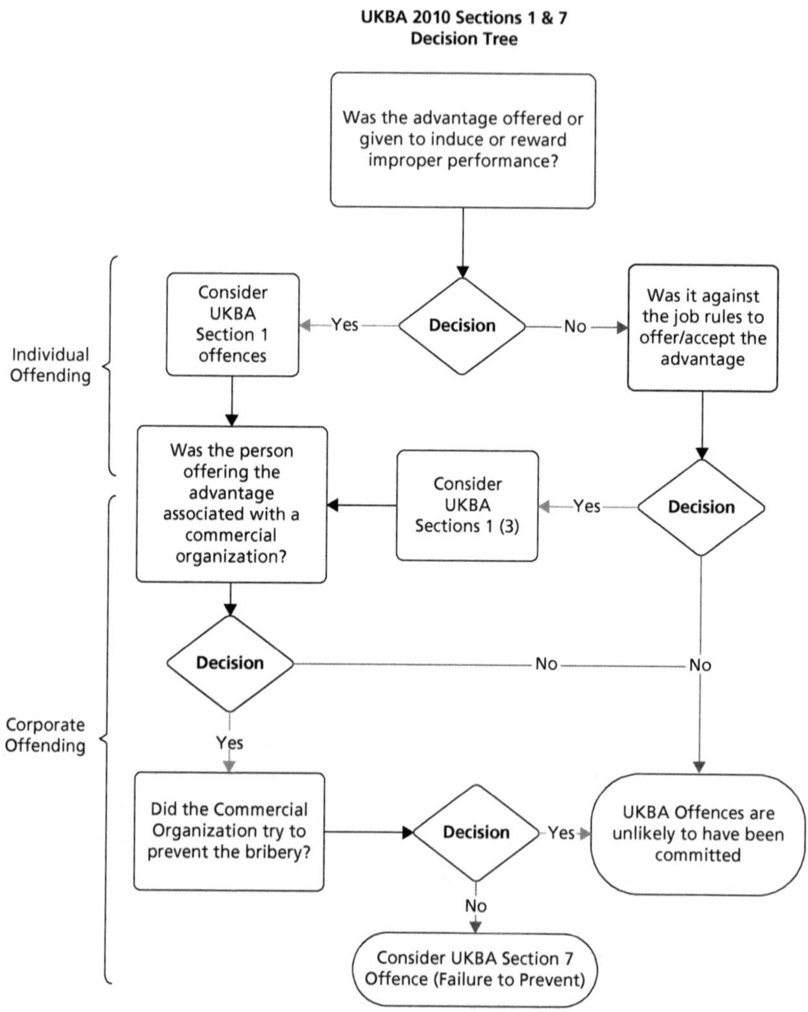

Figure 10.4 Decision tree: UKBA (ss. 1 and 7)

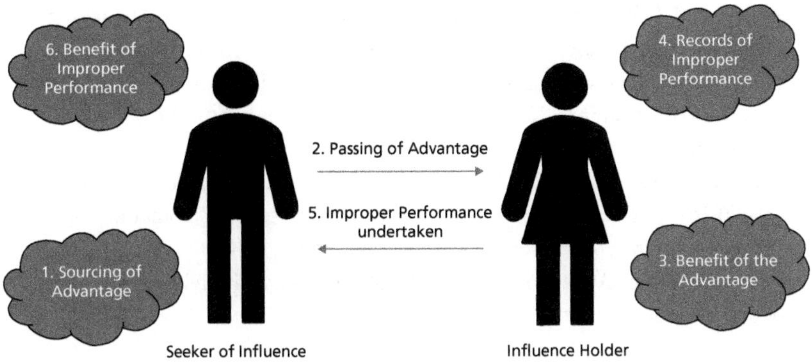

Figure 10.5 Visualization of lines of investigation

10.8.3 Establishing Lines of Inquiry

Figure 10.5 gives the investigative considerations and to some degree visualizes the offences under the UKBA. Each element should be considered; key decisions and the development of the investigative strategy may be informed by this visualization.

There are two principal lines of inquiry in bribery cases:

(1) identifying the advantage;
(2) identifying the improper performance.

10.8.4 Identifying the Advantage (the Bribe)

The word used to describe the bribe in the UKBA is 'advantage'. The word advantage isn't further defined in the UKBA. The Act's explanatory notes state:

> The meaning of 'financial or other advantage' is left to be determined as a matter of common sense by the tribunal of fact.[37]

We know that there is no minimum value for the advantage.

The investigator should seek to identify the advantage or range of advantages offered or passed to the influence holder. Consideration should be given to how these have been obtained by those seeking to bribe, how they were passed to the influence holder or those they are associated with. Finally, it is beneficial to identify where the advantage is now or how it was used or disposed of. Significantly this line of inquiry often requires the use of intrusive powers only available to those who can access these powers. The range of powers to gather the relevant material includes:

[37] MoJ, Bribery Act 2010—Explanatory Notes, www.legislation.gov.uk/ukpga/2010/23/notes/division/5/1 (accessed 15 July 2023).

- **Police and Criminal Evidence Act 1984**—this includes an extensive range of powers to gather material through the execution of search warrants for differing types of material including special procedure material.[38]
- **Proceeds of Crime Act 2002**—includes a range of powers for the investigation of money laundering, restraint, and confiscation.
- **Criminal Finances Act 2017**—introduced UWOs which enable law enforcement officials to make an application for a court order requiring someone to explain their interest in property and how they obtained it.
- **Criminal Justice Act 1987**—used by the SFO to compel individuals or companies to provide information.

Checklist—Typical Advantages (Bribes)

- hospitality and gifts including sporting and cultural events;
- provision of accommodation including hotels and longer-term accommodation;
- provision of vehicles for self and family members;
- 'money' in its various forms including loans and preferential rates;
- holidays in all forms including use of villas and discounted accommodation;
- provision of free or discounted travel;
- employment for self-and/or associates including family members;
- building works including properties off plan, conservatories, double glazing;
- surgery including plastic surgery and paid treatments;
- payment of private school fees.

A *third party* may benefit from the advantage, not the person who undertakes the improper performance, though there needs to be a link between the two entities.

UKBA, s. 1 (offences of bribing another person) states:

> In case 1 it does not matter whether the person to whom the advantage is offered, promised or given is the same person as the person who is to perform, or has performed, the function or activity concerned.[39]

[38] Material, other than items subject to legal privilege and excluded material, in possession of a person who: acquired or created it in the course of any trade, business, profession, or other occupation, or for the purpose of any paid or unpaid office.

[39] Bribery Act 2010.

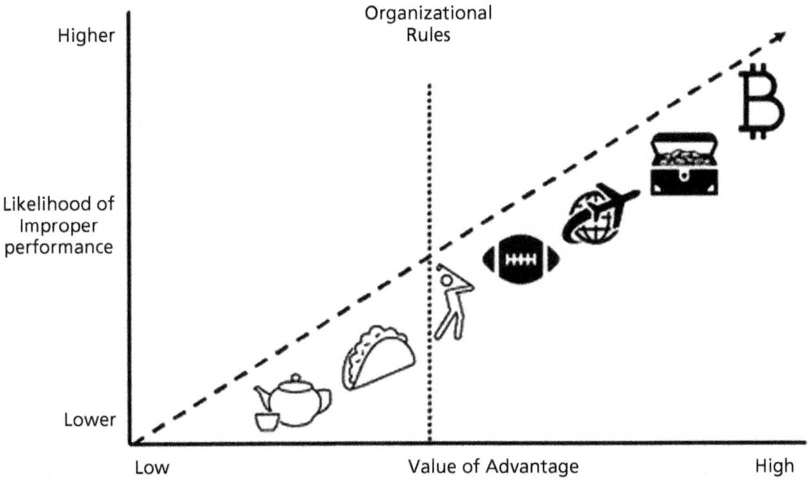

Figure 10.6 Grooming process

UKBA, s. 2 (offences relating to being bribed) states:

(1) A person ('R') is guilty of an offence if any of the following cases applies.

(3) Case 4 is where—

(b) whether the advantage is (or is to be) for the benefit of R or another person.

10.8.5 Grooming the Offender

It is not uncommon for those that have received the advantage to have been 'groomed'; starting with low-level advantages moving through to those of a higher value as detailed in Figure 10.6.

Often low-level gifting tests the water and tempts offenders into a relationship that it is difficult to extricate themselves from once they have moved from 'acceptable' gifts to those that are intended to corrupt. In a number of cases the passing of the bribe can be seen as almost the norm in that sector and accepted with little regard to the implications.

Case Study—The Sainsbury's Buyer

The case of Sainsbury's senior buyer is an excellent example of the range of gifts that may constitute the bribe, how they were funded, and the impact of the corruption on consumers. In essence this case concerned a series of bribes passed by the supplier to the buyer in return for contracts to supply potatoes to Sainsbury's; Greenvale, the company concerned, supplied approximately 45 per cent of all potatoes to Sainsbury's, and the contract value was worth in the region of £40 million.

The Sainsbury's senior buyer, who had been employed by Sainsbury's for twenty years, received bribes to the value of £4.9 million; Sainsbury's was reported to have been overcharged by £8.7 million. The bribes ranged from dining at expensive restaurants including Claridge's and the Dorchester and payments of £1.5 million into an account in Luxembourg. Of interest is the method the supplier used to fund the bribes which was via a fund created by the artificial inflation of the price to supply the potatoes.

The two directors engaged by Greenvale were convicted of corruption, one was jailed for three years, the finance director was jailed for thirty months. The Sainsbury's buyer was jailed for four years following a four-year police investigation.[40]

10.8.6 **Critical Touch Points**

The reality of bribery investigations is that this is a relationship-based offence, and the two or more offenders need to make contact in one way or another.

The identification of critical touch points can be helpful to gathering relevant material during the investigation. The term 'critical touch point' means in this context the points at which the offenders engage with one another. This is particularly apparent in friendship-style bribery cases. Often the business relationship becomes a friendship, which becomes corrupt. Of particular interest will be the contact between parties that takes place outside of the formal business setting. The closer the contact, the more opportunity for corrupt activity to take place.

Checklist—Establishing the Touch Points

- communication data;
- social media;
- digital media (photographs);
- financial records;
- travel related records;
- automatic number plate recognition (ANPR);
- business records (entertainment, gifts, and hospitality);
- gaming platforms;
- online game environments;
- digital platform apps;

[40] 'Three Jailed for £9m Sainsbury's Potato Scam', *The Guardian* (22 June 2012), www.theguardian.com/uk/2012/jun/22/three-jailed-sainsburys-potato-scam (accessed 15 July 2023).

- closed-circuit TV (CCTV);
- postal services;
- company records;
- memberships including clubs, cultural, sporting, and associations;
- witness accounts;
- open source searches.

10.8.7 Establishing the Improper Performance

The material relating to establishing the improper performance will often be held by the organization with whom the influence holder is associated. This material will need to be recovered and examined. Of importance is to establish what proper performance looks like; to establish this the investigation will need to use the services of an expert or those knowledgeable about the sector. Care should be taken when selecting an adviser of this nature, as you need to avoid someone who is conflicted either by association or role.

Examples of where an expert is required include:

- Planning related cases—someone who can independently describe the proper process and identify irregularities.
- Procurement related cases—someone who can advise on the proper tender process and be able to identify potential irregularities.

Checklist—Establishing Improper Performance

- establish proper performance;
- focus on the role of the offender;
- confirm their role is connected to a relevant function or activity;
- confirm their role includes one or more of; a position of trust, operates in good faith and/or requires impartiality;
- understand the role profile and/or job description of the offender;
- gather and review all relevant records including leave, disciplinary, and hospitality records;

- gather and review all relevant business records under the control of the offender;
- check to see if influence was directed through others;
- understand the organizational structure.

10.8.8 **Investigating Bribery: Summary**

In bribery investigations, power is knowledge and the tentacles of the corrupt spread far and wide. Those leading the investigation and team members must restrict access to case-specific information. Consideration given to team members signing a separate confidentiality agreement agreeing not to disclose information to non-authorized persons.

Checklist—Investigating Bribery: the Essentials

(1) Gather relevant material to establish the advantage (bribe).

(2) Gather relevant material to establish the improper performance, considering what 'proper' looks like.

(3) If it's a UKBA s. 1, 6, or 12 offence, establish if the organization failed to prevent the advantage/bribe being paid taking into account the UKBA s. 7 offence.

10.9 **Other Related Legislation**

There is a range of other legislation that may be considered in the investigation of bribery-related offending. Section 4 of the Fraud Act 2006 introduces an offence of fraud by abuse of position which may be considered for those abusing their relationship with a third party whose interest they should be safeguarding—particularly where there is a potential for financial gain or loss. Another powerful area of legislation is the common law offence of misconduct in a public office. This is relevant to those discharging a public function who misconduct themselves to such a degree that the matter should be heard in the court.

KEY POINTS—OTHER LEGAL REGIMES TO CONSIDER

- Fraud Act 2006, s. 4 (fraud by abuse of position);
- Misconduct in a Public Office;

- Criminal Justice and Courts Act 2015, s. 26 (corrupt or other improper exercise of police powers and privileges);
- Honours (Prevention of Abuses) Act 1925—Local Government and Housing Act 1989—every appointment to a paid office or employment under a local authority shall be made on merit;
- Localism Act 2011 (Part 1, ch. 7, s. 30);
- Representation of the People Act 1983.

Further Reading

- Bribery Act 2010, www.legislation.gov.uk/ukpga/2010/23/contents (accessed 15 July 2023);
- Bribery Act 2010 Explanatory Notes, www.legislation.gov.uk/ukpga/2010/23/notes/contents (accessed 15 July 2023);
- Public Bodies Corrupt Practices Act 1889, www.legislation.gov.uk/ukpga/Vict/52-53/69/enacted (accessed 15 July 2023);
- Prevention of Corruption Act 1906, www.legislation.gov.uk/ukpga/Edw7/6/34/enacted (accessed 15 July 2023);
- Prevention of Corruption Act 1916, www.legislation.gov.uk/ukpga/Geo5/6-7/64/enacted (accessed 15 July 2023);
- Anti-terrorism, Crime and Security Act 2001, www.legislation.gov.uk/ukpga/2001/24/section/108/enacted (accessed 15 July 2023);
- Anton Moiseienko and Kayla Izenman, 'What's in a Name? Corruption and Fraud in the UK', RUSI Occasional Paper (June 2019), https://static.rusi.org/20190617_corruption_and_fraud_web.pdf (accessed 15 July 2023).

10.10 Deferred Prosecution Agreements (DPAs)

The Crime and Courts Act 2013[41] introduced DPAs for organizations. It is a discretionary tool and may be used for fraud, bribery, and a very wide range of economic crime as listed in Schedule 17 Part 2 of the Act. A DPA may be applied to a body corporate, a partnership, or an unincorporated association, but not an individual.

A DPA is an efficient mechanism permitting, where an organization is charged with an offence, to have the prosecution deferred provided the criteria is met and agreed by the prosecutor. A DPA requires approval in the Crown Court, where the declaration is made. This declaration is under the supervision of a judge and should

[41] Crime and Courts Act 2013, www.legislation.gov.uk/ukpga/2013/22/schedule/17/enacted (accessed 15 July 2023).

state that the agreement is likely to be in the interests of justice, and that the proposed terms of the DPA are fair, reasonable, and proportionate.

The entity may be required to agree to a range of penalties including:

(1) to pay to the prosecutor a financial penalty;
(2) to compensate victims of the alleged offence;
(3) to donate money to a charity or other third party;
(4) to disgorge any profits made by the entity from the alleged offence;
(5) to implement a compliance programme or make changes to an existing compliance programme relating to the entities policies or to the training of entities' employees or both;
(6) to cooperate in any investigation related to the alleged offence; and/or
(7) to pay any reasonable costs of the prosecutor in relation to the alleged offence or the DPA.

There is a Deferred Prosecution Agreement's Code of Practice,[42] which is jointly published by the CPS and SFO, as required by paragraph 6(1) of Schedule 17 to the Act. This Code of Practice requires prosecutors to have 'regard' to the Code in the following circumstances:

(1) negotiating DPAs with an organization that the prosecutor is considering prosecuting for an offence specified in the Act;
(2) applying to the court for the approval of a DPA;
(3) overseeing DPAs after their approval by the court, in particular in relation to variation, breach, termination, and completion.[43]

The prosecutor is required to apply a two-stage test when considering a DPA, the first being the evidential stage, the second the public interest stage. The directors of both the CPS and SFO may decide to offer a DPA instead of pursuing the full prosecution. The Code lists the factors that may be considered when deciding whether to enter into a DPA, these include in summary:

(1) The existence of a proactive corporate compliance programme both at the time of offending and at the time of reporting but which failed to be effective in this instance.
(2) The offending represents isolated actions by individuals.
(3) The offending is not recent and the organization in its current form is effectively a different organization from that which committed the offences.
(4) A conviction is likely to have disproportionate consequences.
(5) A conviction is likely to have collateral effects on the public, employees, and shareholders and/or institutional pension holders.

[42] CPS, Deferred Prosecution Agreements—Code of Practice, www.cps.gov.uk/publication/deferred-prosecution-agreements-code-practice (accessed 15 July 2023).

[43] CPS, Deferred Prosecution Agreements Code of Practice Crime and Courts Act 2013, www.cps.gov.uk/sites/default/files/documents/publications/DPA-COP.pdf (accessed 15 July 2023).

A DPA requires the full cooperation of the organization and, if agreed, suspends the prosecution for a defined period. If there is a breach of the conditions of the DPA, the suspension of the prosecution can be revisited.

The SFO have used DPAs in a range of corporate offending, these cases include those shown in Table 10.1.

Table 10.1 SFO DPA cases

Year	Organization	Offence type	DPA penalty
2015	Standard Bank	Bribery Act 2010, s. 7	i. Ordered to pay financial penalty of US$25.2 million ii. Paid the Government of Tanzania US$7 million in compensation. iii. Paid SFO's costs of £330,000
2016	Sarclad Ltd	Corruption and failing to prevent bribery	i. Ordered to pay financial orders of £6,553,085, ii. Required to report all third-party intermediary transactions, and the completion and effectiveness of its existing anti-bribery and corruption controls, every twelve months for the duration of the DPA.
2017	Rolls-Royce	Offences of conspiracy to corrupt, false accounting, and failure to prevent bribery	i. DPA required Rolls-Royce to pay £497,252,645 ii. Rolls-Royce also reimbursed the SFO's costs in full reported to be in the region of £13 million
2017	Tesco Stores Limited	False accounting practices	i. Tesco agreed to pay a £129 million fine ii. To pay £3 million investigation costs iii. Tesco also undertook and implemented an ongoing compliance programme during the three-year term of the DPA
2019	Serco Geografix Ltd	Fraud and false accounting	i. Required to pay a financial penalty of £19.2 million ii. SFO's investigative costs (£3.7 million) iii. This was in addition to the £12.8 million compensation already paid by Serco to the MoJ as part of a £70 million civil settlement in 2013

(continued)

Table 10.1 Continued

Year	Organization	Offence type	DPA penalty
2019	Güralp Systems Ltd	Conspiracy to make corrupt payments and a failure to prevent bribery	i. Required to pay a total of £2,069,861 to the SFO for onward transmission to the Consolidated Fund ii. Güralp Systems Ltd required to cooperate fully and truthfully with the SFO and to review and maintain its existing internal controls, policies, and procedures regarding compliance with the Bribery Act 2010
2020	Airbus SE	Bribery	i. Required to pay €983.97 million ii. Pay the SFO's costs of €6.9 million iii. Agreed to full cooperation with the SFO and its law enforcement partners in any future investigations and prosecutions iv. Agreed to the disclosure of any subsequent wrongdoing by the company or its employees, subject to applicable laws
2020	G4S Care & Justice Services (UK) Ltd	Offences of fraud	i. G4S C&J required to pay a financial penalty of £38.5 million ii. Required to pay SFO's costs of £5.9 million iii. Compensation had already been paid to the MoJ as part of a £121.3 million civil settlement in 2014 iv. Bound G4S C&J to wide-ranging compliance obligations and improvements
2020	Airline Services Ltd	Failing to prevent bribery	i. Required to pay £2,979,685.76 ii. Including a contribution to the SFO's costs of £750,000 iii. Obliged to fully cooperate with the SFO and any other domestic or foreign law enforcement agency
2021	Amec Foster Wheeler Energy Ltd	Use of corrupt agents in the oil and gas sector	i. Required to pay a financial penalty and costs amounting to £103 million

Further Reading

- CPS/SFO DPA Code of Practice, www.cps.gov.uk/publication/deferred-prosecution-agreements-code-practice (accessed 15 July 2023);
- Crime and Courts Act 2013, www.legislation.gov.uk/ukpga/2013/22/contents/enacted (accessed 15 July 2023);
- SFO website, www.sfo.gov.uk (accessed 15 July 2023).

10.11 Investigation Insights: Airbus SE Case Study

On 31 January 2020, the Right Honourable Dame Victoria Sharpe, President of the Queen's Bench Division, made a landmark ruling at Southwark Crown Court in the case of the Director of the SFO and Airbus SE. She made an order for Airbus SE to pay a total financial sanction of €990,963,712. This was greater than the total of all sanctions previously ordered under all DPAs and represented double the total penalties from all fines paid regarding all criminal conduct across E&W in 2018. Not only were financial sanctions awarded by the Court, but action was also taken across other jurisdictions including France and the US.

Airbus SE was at the time one of the largest manufacturers of both civil and military aircraft in the world. It was registered as an organization in the Netherlands; however, as it carried on part of its business in the UK it was a 'relevant commercial organization' for the purposes of UKBA, s. 7.

Airbus SE Use of Business Partners (BPs)

A significant part of the case against Airbus SE related to the conduct of BPs who acted as third-party intermediaries and/or agents. They were, in essence, tasked to build the international presence, assist in generating sales, and were incentivized by the payment of a commission based on the value of the contract or in some cases on a fixed basis.

The use of BPs in this context can contribute to an environment where corruption can flourish, as shown in the bribery transparency, incentivization, and environment (TIE) triangle, as detailed in Figure 10.7.

(1) Lack of transparency: may relate to the use of BPs including intermediaries, agents, or other third parties associated with the organization but not necessarily a direct employee.
(2) Incentivization: includes factors such as the payment of commissions and other linked benefits.
(3) Environment factors: include the frequency of corruption within the jurisdiction, the lack of controls, or the enforcement of laws.

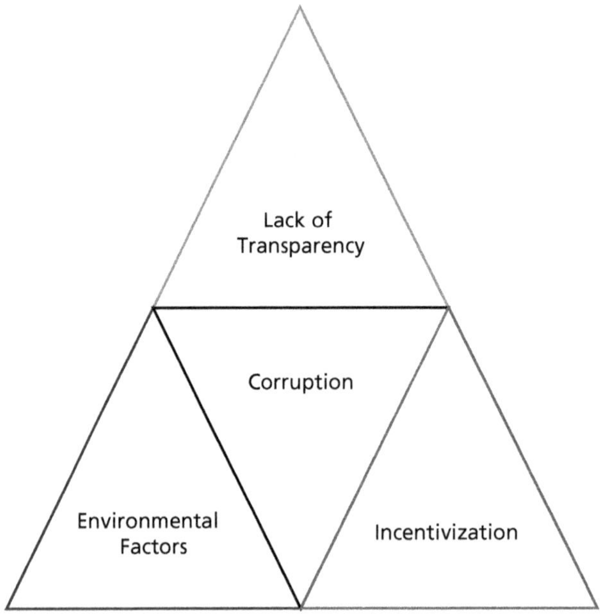

Figure 10.7 Bribery transparency, incentivization, and environment (TIE) triangle

10.11.1 **Events Timeline**

In this case Airbus SE self-reported and assisted the investigation into the alleged corrupt activities (the timeline of events is shown in Figure 10.8).

10.11.2 **Joint Investigation Team (JIT)**

In January 2017, the SFO entered into a JIT agreement with the Parquet National Financier (PNF) a French judicial institution with responsibilities for the investigation of serious economic and financial crime. The JIT was to investigate the allegations relating to Airbus SE and those associated with it.

A JIT is an agreement facilitating international cooperation between two or more competent authorities. The coordinating body for a JIT is the European Union Agency for Criminal Justice Cooperation.[44] The JIT usually comprises prosecutors and investigators and offers an effective mechanism for both the gathering and exchange of information.

The JIT in this case is reported to have been 'vast in scale and scope' and focused on approximately 110 BPs located around the globe.

[44] European Union Agency for Criminal Justice Cooperation, 'Joint Investigation Teams', www.eurojust.europa.eu/judicial-cooperation/instruments/joint-investigation-teams (accessed 15 July 2023).

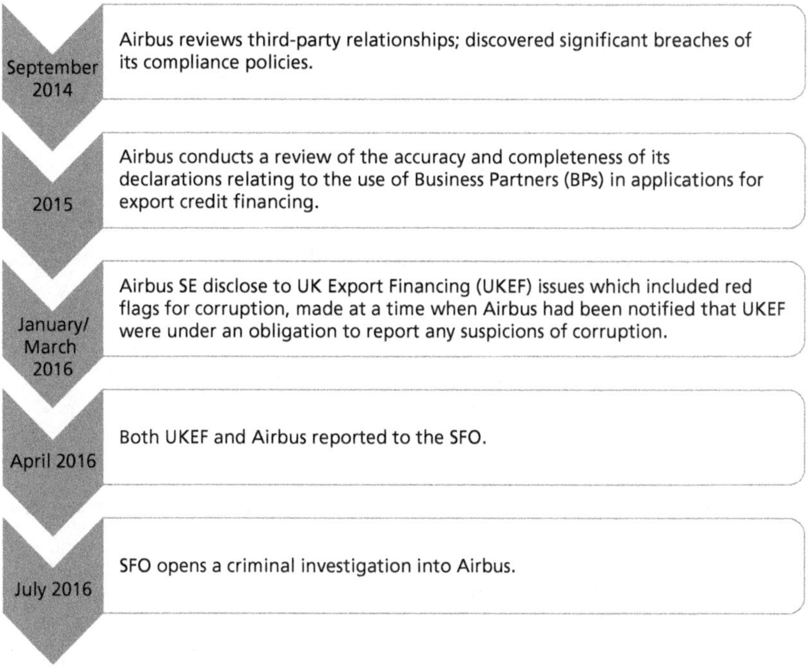

Figure 10.8 Airbus SE case timeline

10.11.3 **Airbus SE Cooperation**

During the investigation Airbus SE was cooperative, undertaking their own inquiry, and supporting the SFO investigation. The following were noted in the DPA:

a. Promptly providing the JIT with a significant amount of relevant information which may not have otherwise come to its attention
b. Providing extensive and detailed presentations with supporting documentation
c. In addition to providing information regarding prior UK Export Finance inaccuracies, Airbus also accepted that the UKBA had provided the SFO with extended extraterritorial powers and potential interest in the facts post 2011
d. Timely identification and provision of relevant material, including material from overseas (subject to applicable laws)
e. Using technology assisted review to prioritise and identify relevant material to expedite the investigation and detect previously unknown wrongdoing
f. Providing key information concerning bank accounts into which Airbus monies flowed at an early stage of the JIT investigation
g. Agreeing Airbus' approach to internal investigation interviews with the JIT and deferring interviews at the request of the JIT
h. Providing the first account of all relevant individuals
i. Disclosure of material including interview transcripts and memoranda to the JIT under a limited waiver of privilege for the purposes of the JIT investigation

j. Providing a schedule of contemporaneous documents withheld on the basis of privilege, including the reason for asserting privilege
k. Communicating with the JIT in respect of media reporting.[45]

10.11.4 Investigation Findings

Following the investigation, it was alleged that BPs and those associated with them representing Airbus SE were involved in a range of corrupt activity and that Airbus SE had failed to prevent bribery in the following cases:

(1) Malaysia concerning the purchase of aircraft by AirAsia and AirAsia X airlines.
(2) Sri Lanka concerning the purchase of aircraft by Sri Lankan Airlines.
(3) Taiwan concerning purchase of aircraft by TransAsia Airways.
(4) Indonesia concerning the purchase of aircraft by PT Garuda Indonesia and Citilink Indonesia.
(5) Ghana concerning the purchase of military transport aircraft by the government of Ghana.

The gross profit made in consequence of this wrongdoing was agreed at between €585,939,740 and €983,540,822.

KEY POINTS—AIRBUS INVESTIGATION LESSONS LEARNED

The following points are useful for the investigator to note in similar cases:

- Check that the organization and/or individuals are in scope of the UKBA.
- Apply the TIE triangle to assess the factors that impact on a reported scenario to establish lines of investigation.
- JITs proved to be an effective method of investigation across differing jurisdictions.
- Self-reporting and the cooperation with the JIT was of significant assistance to access a range of relevant material and to undertake a timely investigation.

Further Reading

- DPA Airbus, www.sfo.gov.uk/2020/01/31/sfo-enters-into-e991m-deferred-prosecution-agreement-with-airbus-as-part-of-a-e3-6bn-global-resolution/ (accessed 15 July 2023);
- *R.* v. *Airbus* (Approved Judgment) www.judiciary.uk/wp-content/uploads/2020/01/Director-of-the-Serious-Fraud-Office-v-Airbus-SE-1.pdf (accessed 15 July 2023).

[45] SFO, R v Airbus SE—Deferred Prosecution Agreement, www.sfo.gov.uk/download/airbus-se-deferred-prosecution-agreement-statement-of-facts/ (accessed 15 July 2023).

10.12 Government Counter Fraud Profession (GCFP) Counter Bribery and Corruption (CBC) Standard

The GCFP is a structure for counter fraud professionals across central government and beyond. It aims to bring the counter fraud community together under a common set of standards to develop that community as they protect public services and fight economic crime. The profession was formally launched in 2018 and at the time of writing had 7,000 members, it is now operated by the Public Sector Fraud Authority (PSFA).[46]

The GCFP has a standards framework which covers a wide range of core and subdisciplines which a public sector organization may use to counter the threat of fraud, bribery, and corruption. This framework has three levels:

(1) Organizational level: this is aimed at the organization. It is covered by the Counter Fraud Functional Standard[47] assured by the PSFA.
(2) Core disciplines: these include a functional leadership level (Leadership, Management, and Strategy) for those that are responsible for coordinating an organization's overall response to fraud and economic crime.
(3) Subdisciplines: these are areas of additional knowledge, skills, and experience that enhance capability across several core disciplines and include CBC.

10.12.1 GCFP CBC Standard

The CBC standard is focused on the skills, knowledge, and experience to counter the offence of bribery as defined by the UKBA. It is a really useful document which contains a significant amount of relevant information. The CBC standard details the agreed approach for CBC practitioners and provides a range of guidance for those working in the public sector to counter bribery. The CBC standard:

(1) describes the skills, knowledge, and experience needed for an individual to achieve practitioner level;
(2) provides guidance to those using the standards on the processes and products;
(3) details 'organizational guidance' that can also be used to consider what should be in place in an organization to be using this subdiscipline effectively.

[46] Public Sector Fraud Authority Mandate, www.gov.uk/government/publications/public-sector-fraud-authority-mandate (accessed 15 July 2023).

[47] Government Functional Standard GovS 013: Counter Fraud Management of counter fraud, bribery and corruption activity, https://assets.publishing.service.gov.uk/government/uploads/system/uploads/attachment_data/file/1014385/6.7628_CO_Govt-Functional-Std_GovS013-Counter-Fraud_v4.pdf (accessed 15 July 2023).

10.12.2 CBC Skills, Knowledge, and Experience

The requirements for the CBC professional are divided into eight separate components:

(1) **Organizational policy**—understand and apply specific bribery and corruption legislation and organizational policies to CBC.
(2) **Stakeholder engagement**—ability to identify and engage with a wide range of stakeholders both internal and external.
(3) **Prevention**—ability to develop, implement, and monitor the organizational bribery and corruption procedures and policy.
(4) **Intelligence**—ability to gather, assess, and disseminate intelligence in bribery and corruption inquiries.
(5) **Risk assessment**—knowledge and skills to carry out risk assessment including the identification of specific bribery and corruption risks and evaluation of organizational controls.
(6) **Typologies**—knowledge and understanding of differing types of bribery or corruption.
(7) **Investigation skills**—knowledge and experience to investigate bribery and corruption.
(8) **Sanctions and redress**—ability to utilize a range of civil, criminal, or parallel sanctions in response to bribery and corruption.

10.12.3 CBC Guidance on Processes

The guidance in the CBC standard details effective CBC processes: it suggests a four-point approach (detailed in Figure 10.9).

10.12.4 CBC Guidance on Products

The CBC standard document (May 2023) details a range of products that will assist in managing the CBC identification, risk, and response. These documents are aligned to the MoJ Adequate Procedures Guidance and include:

(1) CBC risk assessment;
(2) control improvement plan;
(3) gift, hospitality, and entertainment register;
(4) CBC strategy;
(5) CBC response plan.

10.12.5 Guidance for Organizations

The CBC standard follows the MoJ's Adequate Procedures Guidance. It states that such policy should be embedded across the organization and implemented in a

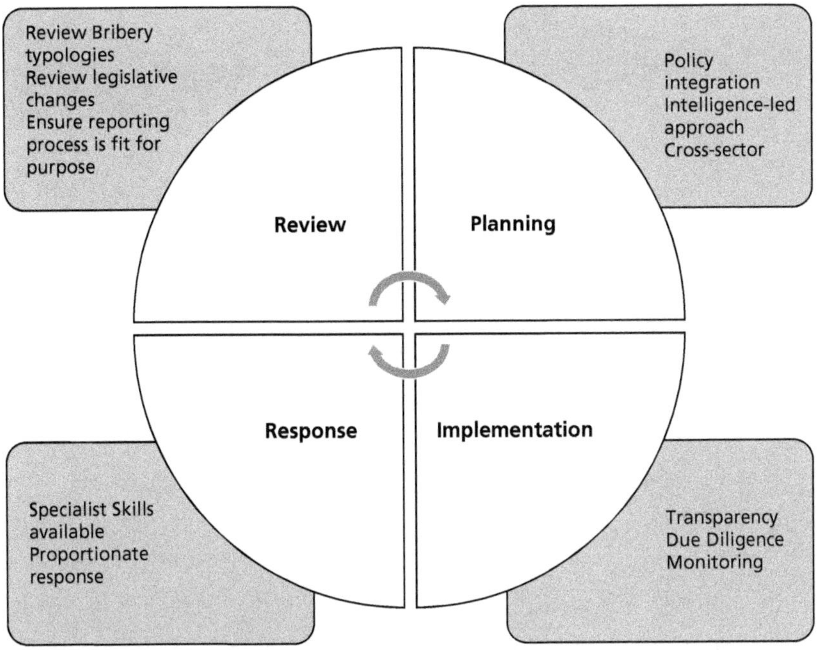

Figure 10.9 CBC standard four-point approach

proportionate way relevant to the risks identified in the organizational risk assessment. The organization should ensure its staff, and those who work on its behalf, are informed of the organizational policies and have access to them. Detailed guidance is given in relation to:

(1) top-level commitment;
(2) risk assessment;
(3) proportionate procedures;
(4) due diligence;
(5) communication and training;
(6) monitoring and review.

11

Counter Fraud Leadership

Blackstone's Counter Fraud Professionals' Handbook. Michael J. Betts, Laura Eshelby, and David Whitehouse-Hayes, Oxford University Press.

DOI: 10.1093/9780191996955.003.0011

11.1 **Introduction**

In this chapter we will explore what it takes to be an effective counter fraud leader. The principles, tools, and techniques we cover will have application across all sectors. We will explore the different approaches and techniques you can deploy to develop a high-performing team.

Leadership may be defined as:

> the action of leading a group of people or an organisation.[1]

You will often hear people debating the differences between leaders and managers. The role of the manager is to manage a group or group of individuals in order to achieve a specified objective, managers are often directive. The leader will seek to influence, motivate, and enable others to contribute to the organization's success and importantly lead them to effect change; this is often achieved through empowerment and support.

KEY POINTS—DIFFERENCES BETWEEN A LEADER AND A MANAGER

William Arruda describes five differences between the leader and manager:[2]

(1) leaders create a vision; managers execute the vision;
(2) leaders create change; managers react to change;
(3) leaders are people-focused; managers are structure-focused;
(4) leaders seek feedback; managers minimize weaknesses;
(5) leaders lead people; managers manage work.

In John Maxwell's *Laws of Leadership* (2007)[3] he describes the confusion of management and leadership as a myth. The main difference between leadership and management in his view is you influence people to follow you as a leader, while management is about maintaining systems and processes.

11.2 **Counter Fraud Knowledge**

When considering leadership in a counter fraud context it is important to understand what level of knowledge the leader has for the subject matter itself. To do so makes for a most effective leader, with expertise that will be highly regarded and persuasive to peers. This is comparable with other professional disciplines such as medicine, law, and finance where those leading have the requisite knowledge, often in advance of those they lead.

---

[1] *Oxford English Dictionary*, www.oed.com/?tl=true (accessed 24 July 2023).

[2] W. Arruda, '9 Differences between Being a Leader and a Manager' (15 November 2016), www.forbes.com/sites/williamarruda/2016/11/15/9-differences-between-being-a-leader-and-a-manager/ (accessed 25 July 2023).

[3] J. C. Maxwell, *The 21 Irrefutable Laws of Leadership* (Thomas Nelson, 2007) 13.

In the public sector and indeed broader often there is a single leader in post, who may have a broader remit than fraud alone, also requiring them to have knowledge of broader economic crime offences, including bribery and corruption.

KEY POINTS—LEADERSHIP COMPETENCY AND KNOWLEDGE REQUIREMENTS

The Government Counter Fraud Profession has identified the competency and knowledge requirements for leaders in the Leadership, Management and Strategy (LMS) standards, these are:

(1) Define fraud and demonstrate how this is applied in using both the civil and criminal evidential tests for the government. This element focuses on the need to be able to describe fraudulent activity and to understand the difference in evidence tests involved in progressing in a civil or criminal context.
(2) Demonstrate knowledge and apply the theories about the motivation of fraudsters and the elements of fraud such as the fraud triangle/diamond. This is vital, for leaders to fully understand why people may commit offences, including insiders and external parties; with the knowledge leaders can support control reviews and support the business in identifying vulnerabilities in systems that fraudsters may utilize.
(3) Demonstrate that there is a mechanism and/or communication strategy in place to keep the organization informed of new and emerging threats. As well as building knowledge of fraud types, and the risks associated with an organization, it is important that the leader regularly communicates to the wider business new and emerging threats.
(4) Demonstrate and apply knowledge of the difference between and importance of estimated, detected, recovered, prevented, and unknown fraud. Alongside understanding the types of fraud, and different motivators by those who commit it, leaders need to understand how to calculate and show the impact of work to counter fraud.
(5) Demonstrate and apply knowledge of a range of tools and techniques available to deter, prevent, detect, and investigate fraud and how technology has an increasing role in this area. This highlights the ability of a leader to compile business cases to secure relevant tools and resourcing to enable the organization to combat fraud.
(6) Demonstrate mature knowledge of how different organizations manage the risk of fraud and deter and prevent it; and the roles of distinct parts of the organization in doing this.
(7) Demonstrate knowledge and evaluate the interplay between tactical and strategic intelligence and fraud risk assessments (FRAs). There is an expectation that a leader will have the knowledge and ability to evaluate both tactical and strategic and have a well-developed knowledge of the external fraud landscape context.

(8) Demonstrate knowledge of what an effective investigation process should be. Is able to demonstrate prior experience of managing and/or leading investigations. Even with a modern fraud approach, which recognizes the need for a multidiscipline approach incorporating risk, measurement, and prevention it is still important fraud leaders are able to understand and lead as needed an investigation process.
(9) Demonstrate understanding and apply relevant legislation and policies that impact on the management of fraud risk.
(10) Has a full understanding of bribery and corruption and can explain their prevalence in relation to other areas of economic crime, including how to define business ethics and how it relates to bribery and corruption.

11.2.1 **Counter Fraud Knowledge: Summary**

The competencies outlined above are just some of the areas of counter fraud that leaders should be aware of and develop. In some organizations a counter fraud lead may be also leading in other functions such as finance and audit. In the public sector, if you are the designated functional lead for fraud, you cannot delegate accountability for this role. You may use third-party resources to bolster investigation and risk assessment skills, but you alone remain accountable for the effectiveness, performance, and outcomes of the fraud unit you lead.

This approach was taken to improve accountability and drive up the professionalism and credibility of leaders in counter fraud. This commences a journey/transformation to gain parity with other professions and give fraud leadership the recognition and respect deserved.

11.3 **Principles of Leadership**

There are a number of resources to draw upon for inspiration and one of the founding leaders in this space is Stephen Covey. He first developed key principles of approaching life, *7 Habits of Highly Effective People*, back in 1989,[4] and these have since been adopted by leaders across the globe. The 'habits' if deployed can lead to increased success as a leader, encouraging users to shift the paradigm in their thinking and approach.

The seven habits build on the fundamental concept of interdependence. Covey traces a personal development outline from:

- dependence in childhood, many people never grow out of a dependency culture

[4] F. Covey, 'The 7 Habits of Highly Effective People' (2022), https://www.franklincovey.com/the-7-habits/ (accessed 1 May 2024).

- independence in adolescence, moving to self-assurance, developing personality and a positive mental attitude
- interdependence: recognition that the optimum outcome results from everyone giving of their best, each aiming for the common goal with shared mission and vision but freedom to use their best judgement on how to go about achieving that common goal.

Checklist—Covey Seven Habits

(1) Be proactive—Focus and act on what you can control and influence instead of what you can't.

(2) Begin with the end in mind—define clear measures of success and a plan to achieve them.

(3) Put first things first—prioritize and achieve your most important goals instead of constantly reacting to seemingly urgent by not important tasks.

(4) Think win-win—collaborate more effectively by building high trust relationships.

(5) Seek first to understand—then to be understood—influence others by developing a deep understanding of their needs and perspective.

(6) Synergize—develop innovative solutions that leverage differences and satisfy all stakeholders.

(7) Sharpen the saw—increase motivation, energy, and work–life balance by being available for renewing activities.

John Maxwell[5] is another authority in this space and encourages the implementation of five key levels of leadership:

(1) Position: people follow you due to your position, because they have to.
(2) Permission: people follow you based on relationships, because they want to.
(3) Production: people follow you because you get things done.
(4) People development: this is summarized as reproduction, investing in others.
(5) Pinnacle: this is the highest level, recognizing your lifelong commitment to others.

There is an array of authoritative voices on leadership alongside Covey and Maxwell. Another, LeRoy Eims, author of *Be the Leader You Were Meant to Be*[6] stated, 'a leader is

[5] J. Maxwell, 'The 5 Levels of Leadership' (2016), https://www.johnmaxwell.com/blog/the-5-levels-of-leadership1/ (accessed 01 May 2024).

[6] L. Eims, *Be the Leader You Were Meant to Be: Growing into the Leader God Called You to Be* (Victor Books, 1996).

one who sees more than others see, who sees farther than others see and who sees before others do'.[7] The larger the organization, the more important it is that the leader can see ahead. A key part of leadership is setting an effective strategy, which is future focused and will take people on a journey over time. This principle of being able to set the vision and strategy is one we will come back to as we move forward.

11.4 Professional Approach to Leadership

The UK Government Counter Fraud Profession (GCFP) sets out twelve principles of leadership to be applied in a counter fraud environment.

KEY POINTS—PROFESSION SET OUT 12 ASPECTS OF BEHAVIOUR AND KNOWLEDGE

To be an established leader in a counter fraud environment, there are twelve aspects of behaviour and knowledge necessary:

(1) Demonstrate experience in leading and motivating a counter fraud function, team, or equivalent.
(2) Demonstrate that they consistently meet the leadership behaviours set out in the Civil Service (CS) Leadership Statement.
(3) Demonstrate and consistently apply the highest standards of independence, professionalism, objectivity, fairness, expertise, integrity, and vision (as aligned to the CS core values and Nolan Principles).[8]
(4) Be recognized as a role model for the organization's ethical approach, in line with the Counter Fraud Code of Ethics.
(5) Demonstrate transparency and accountability for decision-making; show good judgement and consider necessity, reasonableness, proportionality, and legality.
(6) Demonstrate a clear narrative on fraud and how it currently applies to the organization, linking it to the wider government approach to counter fraud.
(7) Demonstrate that they think progressively about counter fraud issues and push the boundaries of current practice across a range of the specialisms on the government counter fraud framework.
(8) Demonstrate that they communicate confidently and with impact and are able to use a variety of methods to suit the situation and/or stakeholder.
(9) Demonstrate that they interact with a range of staff and stakeholders; building a reputation as a recognized counter fraud professional with a strong presence and integrity; and where applicable may be a subject matter expert in one or more counter fraud specialisms.

[7] Lib Quotes, 'John C. Maxwell Quote' (n.d.), https://libquotes.com/john-c-maxwell/quote/lbh6w0v (accessed 24 May 2024).

[8] 'The Seven Principles of Public Life' (aka Nolan Principles) (31 May 1995), ww.gov.uk/government/publications/the-7-principles-of-public-life/the-7-principles-of-public-life--2 (accessed 24 July 2023).

(10) Demonstrate that a mature stakeholder network is in place across government and the counter fraud community; other sectors; law enforcement and where applicable regulators.
(11) Demonstrate that they collaborate with stakeholders from the network on shared areas of interest and risk and initiate conversation to explore pan government and cross-sector solutions.
(12) Demonstrate that they recognize and can manage uncertainty and change and can effectively undertake continuity planning.[9]

There is a real focus on being the visible leader, role model, and showing transparency and accountability for decision-making. Setting a strategy, a vision with a clear narrative on fraud and how it applies to the organization.

The GCFP encourages forward thinking, stipulates the requirements to be progressive, pushing the boundaries of current practice. There are some more general leadership qualities alongside, such as persuasive communication and stakeholder engagement skills, but these are bolstered by a need to be a subject matter expert in a range of counter fraud specialisms. The final two attributes are to focus on risk, considering this on a pan-government (or multi-organization) basis, and finally the ability to manage change and uncertainty.

The behaviours and knowledge requirements for leaders in counter fraud by the UK government here set a good foundation and example that could have equal applicability across sectors (see Figure 11.1).

The knowledge and behaviours set out as requirements by the GCFP include reference to their bespoke Code of Ethics, which their members follow. The Code of Ethics is aligned to the Civil Service Code of Conduct, as reflected in the four core principles:

- impartiality;
- integrity;
- objectivity;
- honesty.

11.5 Leading an Effective Team and Motivating Others

Traditionally leaders and managers have resorted to pay increases, bonuses, and sometimes flattery to encourage their employees to do more. Research shows that these kinds of interventions have a short-term impact.[10] To build effective teams and motivate members of staff the following should be considered:

[9] Kindly reproduced with the express permission of the Public Sector Fraud Authority.
[10] N. Nicholson, 'How to Motivate Your Problem People', *Harvard Business Review* (January 2003), https://hbr.org/2003/01/how-to-motivate-your-problem-people (accessed 24 July 2023).

Figure 11.1 Counter fraud leader's values

- **Step 1—Build an understanding of your employees**—their personal circumstances, their work-based goals; the two combined will give you insight into the environment they operate in. Showing an interest and building a rapport will also increase their motivation to perform.
- **Step 2—Make them feel valued**—people want to feel valued and love to receive praise and recognition for a job well done, especially in front of their peers. Praise can go a long way to make them feel like they are part of the team, achieving their goals.
- **Step 3—Clear frequent communication**—this is the key and will boost your team's success. Employees dislike being left in the dark on any issues, so communicate using a variety of tools.
- **Step 4—Encourage career progression**—create extra responsibilities for staff to expand their experience to put them in better stead for promotions. Provide training and development opportunities and as well as showing employees you have confidence in them.
- **Step 5—Create a positive working environment**—the office atmosphere can have a powerful impact on the way people work. Any conflict or negativity will certainly restrict workflow, so make sure you are providing appropriate platforms for employee feedback.
- **Step 6—Define their career paths**—as well as developing your staff for progression opportunities, it is important to show them where you think they are headed and help them get there. Regular appraisals and target-setting provide a good setting for this and are also a good opportunity to review and praise your employees' work.

- **Step 7—Employee surveys**—an effective way of finding out how employees really feel in their role is an anonymous employee survey. The findings of the survey may highlight issues you were not aware of and help you to identify changes you need to make. Keep staff informed by displaying the monthly results where they can be clearly seen.

11.5.1 Maslow Theory of Hierarchical Needs

One of the most important and famous approaches to motivating employees comes from the Maslow theory of hierarchical needs.

Abraham Maslow postulated that a person will be motivated when all his needs are fulfilled. People do not work for security or money, but they work to contribute and to use their skills.[11] He demonstrated this by creating a pyramid to show how people are motivated. The lowest-level needs in the pyramid are basic needs and unless these lower-level needs are satisfied people do not look at working towards satisfying the upper-level needs.

The hierarchy of needs:

- Physiological needs: are basic needs for survival such as air, sleep, food, water, clothing, sex, and shelter.
- Safety needs: protection from threats, deprivation, and other dangers (e.g. health, secure employment, and property).
- Social (belongingness and love) needs: the need for association, affiliation, friendship, and so on.
- Self-esteem needs: the need for respect and recognition.
- Self-actualization needs: the opportunity for personal development, learning, and fun/creative/challenging work. Self-actualization is the highest-level need to which a human being can aspire.

11.5.2 Herzberg's Motivator Hygiene Theory

Frederick Irving Herzberg[12] was an American psychologist who became one of the most influential names in business management. He is most famous for introducing job enrichment and the motivator-hygiene theory.

Hertzberg classified the needs into two broad categories: hygiene factors and motivating factors (see Table 11.1):

[11] Knowledge Hut, 'Motivation Theories—5 Famous Motivation Theories' (2019), www.knowledgehut.com/tutorials/project-management/motivation-theories (accessed 24 July 2023).

[12] 'Frederick Herzberg', *Wikipedia*, https://en.wikipedia.org/wiki/Frederick_Herzberg (accessed 24 July 2023).

Table 11.1 Herzberg 2 factor principles

Hertzberg 2 factor principles		
Influenced by *hygiene* factors (dis-satisfiers)	Improving motivator factors increases job satisfaction	Influenced by *motivator* factors(satisfiers)
• Working condition • Co-worker relations • Policies/rules • Supervisor quality	Improving the hygiene factors decreases job dissatisfaction	• Achievements • Recognition • Responsibility • Work itself • Personal growth

- poor hygiene factors may destroy motivation but improving them under most circumstances will not improve team motivation;
- hygiene factors only are not sufficient to motivate people, but motivator factors are also required.

11.5.3 Leading and Motivating Teams Summary

Motivation is the state of mind which pushes us all to perform to our highest potential, with good spirits and a positive attitude. The various motivation theories outlined help to understand what are the factors that drive motivation. It is a leader's job to ensure that every individual in the team and the organization is motivated and inspired to perform better than their best.

11.6 Developing High-Performing Teams

A high-performance team is a group of highly skilled people who focus on achieving a common business goal. The team is aligned with and committed to shared values and vision and work towards a common objective. A lot of the insight from how we motivate our team is relevant again here.

Checklist—The Benefits of High-Performing Teams

The benefits of high-performing teams include:

- a broad range of talents and skill sets;
- a group of innovative thinkers, each with their ideas and suggestions to bring to the table;

- little requirement for management input;
- improved morale;
- better productivity.

Individuals working within high-performing teams can be described as being:

- goal-oriented;
- committed to their colleagues and the overall team mission;
- experts in their field;
- collaborative, encouraging contribution from all team members;
- innovative;
- able to work to a high standard;
- willing to accept developmental feedback.

Professor Ina Toegel[13] suggests that high-performing teams should be formed of no more than eight people: 'too many people means challenges in coordination, increased tension, and reduced productivity'. She also advises considering the use of peer recruitment, enabling members of the existing team to play a part in the attraction and selection of their future peers.

11.6.1 How to Develop a High-Performing Team

Building a high-performing team is a vital part of any business success. The characteristics of a high-performing team can vary depending on the company's objectives, but one thing is certain—a high-performing team can help drive motivation, productivity, and profitability.

KEY POINTS—DEVELOPING A HIGH-PERFORMING TEAMS

There are seven key steps to focus on to develop a successful high-performing team:

(1) Prioritize communication—tailored to team preferences.
(2) Set SMART[14] objectives—with clear goals and include employees in setting objectives.
(3) Tackle conflict—acting as soon as an issue arises.
(4) Understand current and future dynamics—using these questions.
  (a) Do you know the strengths of the people working within your team?
  (b) Are you aware of any limitations which need to be improved upon?
  (c) What is the role of each person within the team?

[13] www.thomas.co/resources/type/blog/how-to-build-high-performance-teams (accessed 24 July 2024).
[14] Specific, Measurable, Achievable, Relevant and Time-bound (SMART).

(d) Why are they important?
(e) How does the team react to change?
(f) Are there any drivers for potential conflict within the team?

(5) Master emotional intelligence—understand and control your emotions to manage those of others.
(6) Establish trust—establishing trust between team members can help take the team from satisfactory performance levels to outstanding results.
(7) Feedback—is a gift and can show staff they are valued.

11.6.2 **Maintaining High Performance**

Once high-performance teams are formed, it is crucial to maintain their performance. A written team charter and agreed values can help to provide clarity on expectations, and it is important to ask for contributions from the team to empower them and gain buy-in.

Businesses should also be transparent about their efforts and get the whole team on board by making a collective commitment to individual and team improvements.

11.7 **Developing a Counter Fraud Strategy**

Integral to the development of an effective counter fraud strategy is knowledge and understanding of your fraud risks. Fraud risks are unique to an organization, to a payment stream, funding scheme or process, and so on. The first learning point for leaders, particularly those new to a role or new to an organization, is to complete an up-to-date FRA, before going forward to develop the counter fraud strategy. This will provide the functional lead with a clear understanding of the organization's fraud risks and the gaps and weaknesses in current controls. Once this is understood they can begin to consider what the strategic response should be to manage and reduce these fraud risks, in line with the agreed fraud risk appetite. It is recommended that the counter fraud strategy is risk based but it should also be proportionate and realistic in terms of its goals and timescales.

In the GCFP, they have established product guidance to assist with the steps needed to develop an effective strategy.

Step 1—Consider How FRAs Feed into the Strategy

A counter fraud leader should not rely on intelligence alone to inform them of their fraud risks as this will lead to a distorted picture where only known and reported fraud is prioritized; analyse the organization's FRAs and decide how they will feed into the development of their organizations counter fraud strategy. This may be done in conjunction with the fraud risk assessor and other stakeholders.

Step 2—Analyse and Define the Current Tactical and Strategic Challenges the Fraud Function Is Facing

An organization and function may face a high number of competing tactical and strategic fraud challenges at one time. These may be identified through its risk assessment, robust intelligence flows and loops, previous cases, audit reports, random sampling, policy evaluation, etc. In addition, there will be competing operational, structural, reputational, internal/external current and future challenges.

It is crucial that a lead is able to keep up to date with these challenges, as well as being able to make sense of what the priorities should be for the defined period in time that the counter fraud strategy will cover.

Leaders should define the current tactical and strategic challenges the organization and fraud function faces; ensure they have access to a diverse range of available information and intelligence and that it is continually reviewed not just at the time of setting the strategy but routinely; liaise with and seek guidance, input, and the support of specialists in the function and key stakeholders from their mature network; ensure that they consult with the accountable individual at board level to understand wider organizational needs; and consider forming and leading a counter fraud board for the organization. This can assist with providing diversity of ideas, strategic decision-making, agreed solutions, and a support structure.

Step 3—Horizon-Scan and Assess the Wider Environment (Threats/Risks)

A counter fraud strategy is more likely to be successful if it is developed by leads who understand the wider fraud landscape across sectors and in particular those where the organization typically engages. Strategic thinking tools such as PESTLE analysis[15] should be used to assist this process.

Leaders should link in with national threat assessments such as those completed by the National Crime Agency to ensure they are aware of emerging and current threats, and are set up to react to external fraud threats and the wider fraud landscape; network with other government fraud functions to share fraud challenges and strategies; locate and understand the organization's strategy and any business area strategies to ensure the counter fraud response ties into the wider organization approach and plans and analyse current knowledge and information from their own learning and progressive thinking and from mature networks across sectors.

Step 4—Business Operations, Financial and Strategic Challenges and Issues Evaluated and Prioritized

The counter fraud strategy should be a clear and accessible document, which sets out the prioritized activities that will be undertaken to manage and reduce fraud challenges in a defined period.

---

[15] Analysis model—Political, Economic, Social, Technological, Legal, and Environmental factors.

Leaders should work with key stakeholders and the accountable individual at board level to discuss the challenges they are facing and agree what a future aspirational state would look like; should set the high-level fraud risks and priorities for the forthcoming period considering wider organizational needs; may decide at this point to consider how the counter fraud response will be resourced. They should look at the fraud risks and decide what fraud skills and capability they need to deliver the counter fraud activity/response. Consideration will then need to be taken on whether these are best insourced or outsourced.

Step 5—Define/Redefine the Organization's Counter Fraud Maturity

When developing a counter fraud strategy time should be spent on analysing and defining the 'current state of the organization' in terms of its fraud provision, fraud response, and fraud approach. Leaders should then define or redefine the organization's counter fraud maturity and work with the accountable individual at board level to ensure that the board agrees the counter fraud maturity.

Step 6—Counter Fraud Strategy Development

The Strategy may also include bribery and corruption, money laundering, and wider business ethics. The counter fraud strategy should be updated yearly or when the business faces environmental change, for example when introducing a new service that is judged to have a high susceptibility to fraud.[16]

Step 7—Fraud Responsibilities Matrix Agreed (Organization to Determine Roles this Covers)

Leaders, in coordination with the accountable individual, should take responsibility for putting together a matrix, which sets out the key roles and responsibilities for those responsible for managing the organization's fraud risk. The matrix should be clear, accessible, and transparent.[17]

Step 8—Define How Progress against the Counter Fraud Strategy Will Be Monitored: Key Metrics for Success

The counter fraud strategy once developed and agreed is not the end of the process. It should be continually reinforced as a living document that is implemented, monitored to track progress, assessed and redefined, as necessary.

Leaders should work with the accountable individual at board level to agree what the key metrics for success are; outcome-based metrics may be different and unique

[16] For those working it in the public sector, the strategy should be shared to the Public Sector Fraud Authority for review and meet the standards as set out in the LMS for the GCF profession.

[17] Further guidance is available in the LMS Product standards via the GCF Profession.

to each fraud function; and work with key individuals from the counter fraud function to agree how progress against the strategy will be recorded, monitored, and reported upwards and how any variations to the counter fraud strategy can be achieved, based on the results and monitoring and reporting.

Step 9—Counter Fraud Strategy Continually Communicated and Progress Monitored

The counter fraud strategy needs to be visible, available, and understood. This can be achieved by utilizing communication methods that break down the strategy simply. Each department will have different communication rules, restrictions, and policies. The lead should decide how best this works for their function and department.

Leaders should decide how the counter fraud strategy is made available to all staff for example, staff intranet, hard copies, launch event; decide whether it's a publicly available document and then decide how this is achieved, for example gov.net, emailing copies to stakeholders; and ensure it forms part of the overall communication plan.

These nine steps provide a good overview of how to approach the development of the strategy for your counter fraud area. There is further information and guidance, drawn from the LMS standards agreed for the public sector but with wider utilization across sectors to help you put the steps into practice and develop your own strategy.

Checklist—Developing a Counter Fraud Strategy

A counter fraud strategy should:

(1) Clearly define its scope (i.e. what parts of the organization and its supply chain are/are not covered by the strategy).

(2) Define the current tactical challenges that the organization and fraud function are facing. These may include fraud challenges, as well as business operations, structural, reputational, and internal/external challenges;

(3) Define the future strategic challenges that the business and fraud function may face. These may include fraud challenges as well as business operations, structural, reputational, and internal/external challenges.

(4) Use tools, such as PESTLE analysis, to understand the wider environment of the organization, the sector, associated sectors, administrations, and fraud risk in these contexts.

(5) Demonstrate how the organization's FRA feeds into the strategy.

(6) Demonstrate an understanding of the key strengths and weaknesses of the current counter fraud provision and fraud approach.

(7) Simply present a clear picture of what the aspirational future state is. This should deal with some of the challenges identified.

(8) Define the time period that the strategy will cover, a minimum of three years is suggested.

(9) Define key activities that will be undertaken to move to the aspirational future state and/or aspects of it in the timescale defined.

(10) Define who the key stakeholders are; this may not be in the strategy itself, it may be in a complementary document.

(11) Simply and compellingly, in language appropriate to the organization, categorize the actions into areas that aid the communication of the strategy.

(12) Define how progress against the strategy will be monitored, what the key metrics for success are, and how the organization will know it is being successful.

(13) State where the delivery plan for the strategy is held. This is likely to be the annual action plan.

11.7.1 Tools to Help Develop a Strategy

11.7.1.1 PESTLE Analysis

A PESTLE analysis studies the key external factors that influence an organization. It can be used in a range of different scenarios, and can guide leaders in strategic decision-making:

- Political
- Economic
- Sociological
- Technological
- Legal
- Environmental

11.7.1.2 SWOT Analysis

You will often find that alongside PESTLE it is helpful to use a SWOT analysis to support the targeting of your findings. SWOT stands for:

- Strengths
- Weaknesses
- Opportunities
- Threats

A SWOT analysis is a technique for assessing these four aspects of your fraud function. SWOT analysis is a tool that can help you to analyse what you do best now, and to devise a successful strategy for the future.

11.8 Fraud Control Strategies

A counter fraud strategy is a mid- to long-term plan of action considering current and future strengths, weaknesses, opportunities, and threats, and looks to build towards a defined future state. A fraud control strategy is an operational product that allows an organization to prioritize their response against identified fraud threats and risks in a defined period (usually twelve months). Depending on how broad ranging the fraud control strategy is, it may be that the annual action plan and the fraud risk management action Plan form part of it, as detailed in Table 11.2.

KEY POINTS—FRAUD CONTROL STRATEGY

The key aspects of a fraud control strategy:

(1) Set out the operational priorities for the counter fraud function (i.e. what threat and risk areas will be focused on).
(2) Detail the rationale for the prioritization process.
(3) Allocate an owner to each priority.
(4) Describe what activities will be undertaken for each of the prioritized threats and risks; this may include both treatment and response.
(5) Set out how resources are to be deployed.
(6) Explain how activity is to be tasked.

Table 11.2 Annual action and the fraud risk management action plans

Annual action plan	Fraud risk management action plan
The annual action plan includes all activity to develop the fraud response and capability.	The fraud risk management action plan includes the change to controls to reduce the risk of fraud.
The annual action plan sets out clearly what activity on counter fraud over and above business-as-usual activity will happen in that year; it will take the organization towards the strategy and help deliver it.	The fraud risk management action plan should set out clearly the organizations risk appetite, the key risks the business is taking action to mitigate (i.e. over and above business-as-usual/operational activity).

Note: Any significant control changes detailed in the fraud risk management action plan may be referred to in the annual action plan (e.g. if an organization deploys a new system to reduce fraud risk this would be referenced).

(7) Set out where intelligence gathering is focused, linking to the strategic.
(8) Intelligence assessment.
(9) Set out what stakeholder activity will look like.
(10) Consider including detail on the controls that will be implemented to reduce the risks and what other activities can be undertaken in the business to increase capability in the fraud response.
(11) Be continually reviewed and updated at least every 12 months.

11.9 The Importance of Ethics and Integrity

Leaders who ignore ethics also run the risk of personal and corporate liability in today's legal environment, particularly with the emergence of the failure to prevent offences being introduced by the Corporate Transparency Act 2023, by the UK government: 'Under the new offence, an organisation will be liable where a specified fraud offence is committed by an employee or agent, for the organisation's benefit, and the organisation did not have reasonable fraud prevention procedures in place.'[18]

It is important that leaders keep up to date with business ethics best practices, across their relevant sector and apply these to their organization, developing a business ethics approach reflecting the importance of the prevention of financial crime, and other related crimes including modern slavery, misconduct, and unethical behaviour (i.e. discrimination).[19] To support the development of best practice, leaders are encouraged to network across the organization and other sectors, to broaden their understanding of approaches and insight.

Using the information gathered from networking and research, leaders can then use an organization specific approach to a code of ethics—as outlined earlier in the chapter using the example of the GCFP.

Once developed a code of ethics should be promoted and accessible across an organization. Leaders also have a responsibility to role-model the code, to help embed the code of ethics within the organization's culture. This in turn will be the catalyst for how they influence and collaborate with the senior leadership/executive team members of that organization, to set the tone from the top that appropriate ethical behaviour, both at corporate and individual level, should be integral to doing business. They should also take practical steps to work with the relevant board, or equivalent, to help them take ownership and regularly review the organization's corporate ethics.

[18] Economic Crime and Corporate Transparency Bill 2022: Factsheets, www.gov.uk/government/publications/economic-crime-and-corporate-transparency-bill-2022-factsheets (accessed 24 July 2023).
[19] GCFP LSM standards 2018.

Once a code of ethics has been developed, fraud leaders should also take steps to demonstrate that they can test that understanding of the code permeates all levels of staff and the supply chain. It is equally important third parties and agents acting on behalf of the organization also abide by the code as set.

Working with third parties can be more challenging, but to truly embed a positive culture the fraud leader and the wider organization leadership must stand up to commercial partners and challenges where necessary. This will involve regular engagement with those involved in procurement, contractors, and subcontractors to uphold business ethics and integrity; as well as managing the supply chain through risk rating and audit.

It will be essential to be effective that the organization has a clear policy for dealing with the supply chain and the limits of the organization's responsibilities, which is transparent and available to all stakeholders.

11.10 Seeking Investment at an Organizational Level

Operating in a counter fraud or wider economic crime environment can sometimes be a challenging place to be able to demonstrate return on investment and build a persuasive business case for more investment. However, by understanding the outcomes and impact your organization is having in relation to counter fraud, you can be successful in this pursuit.

As a leader in an organization, it is important to monitor and if metrics do not exist, to introduce metrics to benchmark against performance. This can be tracked and used alongside other relevant information (FRAs, detection, prevention, and recovery rates) to build a profile of the current performance, the gaps, and the steps that can be taken to increase performance and impact. The bringing of this information all together is the foundation of a business case that can be taken to increase the capacity, capability, and access to the tools you may need to improve your performance.

The most persuasive way to develop a successful business case is to develop options based on what resources are available currently, and what required through further investment to effectively deal with the organization's defined fraud problem.

A second consideration when seeking investment is to identify what and when specific technical skills need to be brought in, for a particular assignment, or sub-assignment. This could be for example for thematic work, data analytics exploration, or further FRA required. The key is to articulate the value for money of a counter fraud function and when and how to negotiate for resources or investment for both business-as-usual and innovative/proactive counter fraud activity.[20] It is also helpful to be clear when returns are likely to come and if these translate to cashable or non-cashable for the business. Some areas like building capability or

[20] Ibid.

investing in new analytical tools may have a longer-term financial impact and return on investment, therefore.

11.11 Measuring Performance and Impact

Underpinning any successful business case is the ability to demonstrate prior success or build confidence that the investment will lead to future success. Therefore, it is essential to introduce measures to measure performance, and have metrics that monitor performance regularly, are SMART. Failure to do so may be detrimental to seeking more investment and delay the ability to do so.

11.12 Commissioning and Managing Fraud Services

Fraud leaders may operate in a variety of different organizations, in terms of scale and capability. It may be that you are not necessarily leading a team operationally within the organization and may have recourse to outsource some or all of the function.[21]

To be most effective a leader must build knowledge of the difference between counter fraud services, internal and external audit services, forensic services, risk services, and the part they play in the three lines of defence against fraud. This knowledge alongside established knowledge in counter fraud will help to influence and shape how counter fraud management contributes to, and interacts with, corporate governance.

11.13 Challenge and Holding Staff to Account

One other key role a leader has is to put in measures and procedures to ensure that counter fraud activity, and especially investigations, are not subject to inappropriate influence from senior managers or other staff. To achieve this a process of regular case review and quality assurance will be required, as well as clear, transparent routes for staff to raise concerns. This includes those involving allegations relating to senior officials, to mitigate the risks of any undue influence or bias in case outcomes.

[21] Government standards for leadership advocate that if you outsource services the organization remains accountable and responsible for the fraud outcome. This is the approach in the public sector.

Checklist—Key Fraud Management Skills

Key skills that will support effective fraud management and secure investment include the ability to demonstrate how to:

(1) plan, secure and manage a budget effectively;

(2) undertake effective resource planning;

(3) develop options (i.e. based on what resources are available and what may be required through further investment to effectively deal with the organization's defined fraud problem);

(4) prioritize the acquisition of skills and capability and be able to identify when specific technical skills need to be bought in, for a particular assignment, or sub-assignment;

(5) outsource fraud specialisms externally and how to monitor, evaluate, and quality-assure them, to get the best possible value out of the services;

(6) articulate value for money of a counter fraud function and when and how to negotiate for resource or investment for both businesses as usual and innovative/proactive counter fraud activity;

(7) produce and oversee the production of robust and persuasive business cases to support investment in counter fraud activities that may or may not have an immediate or measurable financial return.

11.14 Conclusion

The role of a functional leader is multifaceted and involves building and maintaining a range of knowledge and skills, including but not limited to understanding risk, how to influence upwards, across, and downwards in an organization to effect change, instil collective responsibility for fraud management, and inspire a strong anti-fraud culture.

The role of a leader is also not to follow or accept the status quo, and understand the theories, approaches, and tools available to increase performance and outcomes, which can be done in collaboration with the wider organization and by intrinsically understanding the specific fraud problem, via the FRA, of their organization. Fraud leaders should have integrity, be inspiring but also, where needed, by challenging—given the context they operate within.

Index

For the benefit of digital users, indexed terms that span two pages (e.g., 52–53) may, on occasion, appear on only one of those pages.

Tables and figures are indicated by an italic *t* and *f* following the page number.